Simone de Beauvoir's Philosophy of Individuation

Simone de Beauvoir's Philosophy of Individuation

The Problem of The Second Sex

LAURA HENGEHOLD

EDINBURGH
University Press

Edinburgh University Press is one of the leading university presses in the UK. We publish academic books and journals in our selected subject areas across the humanities and social sciences, combining cutting-edge scholarship with high editorial and production values to produce academic works of lasting importance. For more information visit our website: edinburghuniversitypress.com

© Laura Hengehold, 2017

Edinburgh University Press Ltd
The Tun – Holyrood Road, 12(2f) Jackson's Entry, Edinburgh EH8 8PJ

Typeset in 11/13 Adobe Sabon by
IDSUK (DataConnection) Ltd

A CIP record for this book is available from the British Library

ISBN 978 1 4744 1887 4 (hardback)
ISBN 978 1 4744 4412 5 (pbk.)
ISBN 978 1 4744 1888 1 (webready PDF)
ISBN 978 1 4744 1889 8 (epub)

The right of Laura Hengehold to be identified as the author of this work has been asserted in accordance with the Copyright, Designs and Patents Act 1988, and the Copyright and Related Rights Regulations 2003 (SI No. 2498).

Contents

Acknowledgements		vii
List of Abbreviations		ix
1	Introduction: Blocked Singularities	1
	Phenomenology	4
	Sense and the Event	6
	Historicity of the Problem	11
2	The Problem of Sexist Sense	25
	Representation and the Creation of Concepts	26
	Transcendence – Components of the Concept	34
	Conceptual Personae and the Pre-philosophical Plane	42
3	Lived Experience	58
	Consciousness and Habit	59
	Varieties of Immanence	66
	Maternity	72
	Work	77
	Narcissism, Love and Mysticism	82
4	The Freedom of Others	95
	'Pyrrhus and Cineas'	98
	The Ethics of Ambiguity	103
	Recognition and Communication	108
	Transindividuality	112
	Back to *Mitsein*	117
5	Territories and Assemblages	129
	Philosophical and Literary Problems	130
	Ambiguities of Sex	135
	Universal or Just Common?	149

6	Virtual Conflicts	162
	Ethics and Politics from the *milieu*	163
	Equal how?	172
	Whose History? Which Event?	181
	What can Institutions do?	189
7	Conclusion	199
	Works Cited	216
	Index	237

Acknowledgements

Maybe every book is a silent conversation that picks up where voices leave off. A book's singularity evolves according to multiple temporalities and I am sure many of my interlocutors did not know they were responding to one another by way of a problem that only appeared after many years, any more than they knew how much they sustained me in the act of writing. This book emerged between Cleveland and Paris and thus, between my networks in both cities. It works in part because of its gaps and failures, which are also the author's responsibility after friends have done everything possible to enhance its powers.

First, I want to recognise Case Western Reserve University for making possible the sabbatical year during which this book was written. I also want to thank Maggie Kaminski, John Orlock, and Peter Knox of the Baker-Nord Center for the Humanities at CWRU for enabling me to present portions of this manuscript at several international Deleuze Studies conferences and for a research grant to finalise the manuscript. Anne Van Leeuwen's thoughtful and imaginative approach to phenomenology gave me faith that this project had a future. She and Cheryl Toman enabled my sabbatical in countless practical ways; as did Shannon French, who gave her extraordinary administrative gifts to run our department in my absence. I am lucky to have such enthusiastic and supportive colleagues. Last but not least, Megan Weber offered moral support and outstanding editorial assistance.

My students were essential stimuli to thinking, particularly Tony Yanick, whose passion for Deleuze made it possible for me to justify over half a year working through *Difference and Repetition*; Jason Walsh, thanks to his determination to understand Spinoza and materialist philosophy of history; and k.c. Layton, for numerous thoughtful conversations testing both of our investments (or lack thereof) in the molar concept of 'woman'. Brent Adkins and Andrew Cutrofello know how deeply I am indebted to them, not only for carefully reading all or most of this manuscript and others, but also for patiently and cheerfully enduring, via email, the near-daily roller coaster of my affects. In addition, Ryan Johnson, Audrey Wasser, Joe Hughes, and especially Jeff Bell were generous with their reading time and expertise on Deleuze, while I thank Ewa Ziarek and two anonymous readers at Edinburgh University Press for encouragement and specific improvements regarding the Introduction. I also benefited from the conversations, questions and ambiance at the Deleuze Studies conferences, even if I cannot remember or name everyone who contributed a few molecules.

To Seloua Luste Boulbina, Brahim Tissini and Sylvain Tessier for friendship and provocation in Paris, mille fois merci. To Kyoo Lee, who like the incorporeal event moves in all directions at once but is rarely actualised in a geographical state of affairs, there are not enough languages to express my appreciation for your experimental spirit. And likewise to colleagues and friends in Cleveland: particularly Kenny Fountain, Renee Holland-Golphin, Matt Bakaitis, Andrew Dessecker and Joe Cairnes. Whether or not they know it, my family is an imperceptible part of this project, so I do not want to overlook whatever support we have been and may yet be for one other. Finally, for her optimism, her sincerity, and her extraordinary professionalism, I am deeply grateful to have worked with Carol Macdonald at Edinburgh University Press, as well as with James Dale and Christine Barton, who brought this text to material fruition.

Excerpt(s) from *The Second Sex* by Simone de Beauvoir and translated by Constance Borde and Sheila Malovany-Chevallier, translation copyright © 2009 by Constance Borde and Sheila Malovany-Chevallier. Used by permission of Alfred A. Knopf, an imprint of the Knopf Doubleday Publishing Group, a division of Penguin Random House LLC. All rights reserved.

From *The Second Sex* by Simone de Beauvoir, translated by Borde/Malovany-Chevallier.
Published by Jonathan Cape.
Reprinted by permission of The Random House Group Limited.

Abbreviations

References are to English texts and translations. In some cases, corresponding pages to the original French edition are given after a / (slash) and publication data may be found in Works Cited.

AO   Deleuze and Guattari, *Anti-Oedipus* (*L'Anti-Œdipe*)
BN   Sartre, *Being and Nothingness*
DR   Deleuze, *Difference and Repetition* (*Différence et répétition*)
EA   Beauvoir, *The Ethics of Ambiguity* ('Pour une morale de l'ambiguïté')
FC   Beauvoir, *Force of Circumstance*
FM   Nzegwu, *Family Matters*
IC   Nancy, *The Inoperative Community*
IPC   Simondon, *L'Individuation Psychique et Collective*
LS   Deleuze, *The Logic of Sense* (*Logique du sens*)
MDD   Beauvoir, *Memoirs of a Dutiful Daughter*
PC   Beauvoir, 'Pyrrhus and Cineas' ('Pyrrhus et Cineás')
PL   Beauvoir, *Prime of Life* (*La force de l'âge*)
SS   Beauvoir, *The Second Sex* (*Le deuxième sexe*, 2 vols)
TE   Sartre, *Transcendence of the Ego*
TFW   Bergson, *Time and Free Will*
TP   Deleuze and Guattari, *A Thousand Plateaus* (*Mille plateaux*)
WIP   Deleuze and Guattari, *What is Philosophy?* (*Qu'est-ce que la philosophie?*)

Chapter 1

Introduction: Blocked Singularities

'One is not born, but rather becomes, woman' (SS 283/2:13). 'On ne naît pas femme, on le devient.' Simone de Beauvoir's statement puts becoming at the heart of her ontology. However, we tend to focus on what becoming a *woman* might mean, taking the meaning of *becoming* as self-evident. We are not born philosophers either, and just as womanhood may be something we never actually achieve, becoming a philosopher is not something that happens once and for all. A focus on becoming unsettles even our confidence as to what 'being born' might mean.

Concepts are points of passage for becoming. Concepts may name discrete entities such as pianos or musical notes. But pianos are occasions for notes to repeat themselves from one concert or chord to the next, while the memory and desire for music encourage the continual movement of people and instruments around the globe. Pianos also take time to be built and to be tuned so that they are more than mute pieces of furniture, and they break down if left unused or untended. Those becoming philosophers are the people who can't help but notice that just as notes blend into one another and objects gradually shift from one category to another, acting back on the other things they encounter, concepts themselves change colour and meaning depending on the light and on their environment. But unlike a piano, or even the concept of piano, which might belong to a particular technological era and vanish with it, philosophical concepts have an intemporal capacity to enter and slip out of any historical milieu.

Along with discrete bodies, buildings, words, or emotions, we grapple with the continual change, modulation, or interruption of environments and media, even the media of our own physiology and language. Whether or not humankind is the measure of all things, one's choice of a measure is shaped by the *quality* of one's encounter with the given. Measures are selected from the flow of ongoing experiences and events, but the clock and the scale are so familiar that they make change seem as standardised and infrequent as the beings who undergo change. My body, always adding and losing cells, is a way station in the becoming of water or nutrients that might also irrigate a field or be frozen in a glacier. My kitchen is filled with plastic boxes that were once petroleum and could yet become part of a landfill on which housing is built. The molecules that make up plastic are currently organised to store portions of food; but, entering into combination with other dishes, their contents may unlock the movement of verbal significance over a meal.

Every noticeable phase of a thing's existence lasts for a certain duration and is conceptually 'cut' from a longer transformation, even if it is a very, very slow one.[1] And every experience holds its quality only for so long, whether or not we reflect on our state of mind or remain focused on the (more or less) stable phenomena around us. Words, gestures, feelings appear and evolve; so do the stacks of paper in my apartment, overlapping, criss-crossed, clipped, for which I am apparently a means of reproduction. The shifts between becomings and the *beings* with which they are identified in language and intention are fraught with indeterminacy. As Toril Moi has pointed out, none of us is ever a *woman* to the exclusion of other social or natural identities, capacities and aspirations;[2] none of us is ever just a philosopher, either.

Simone de Beauvoir is increasingly taken seriously as a philosopher. This is, in part, because her training in philosophy and her references to the history of philosophy were recognised by members of the profession in numerous countries. She could be situated with respect to similar thinkers at a certain historical moment. But one also wonders what kind of philosopher Beauvoir could have become *for us* if we had thought about the history of philosophy – including its contemporary practice – in a non-linear fashion whereby biography and works do not accompany one another chronologically, and influences do not always precede their effects. If history is a way of delimiting and connecting becomings, then it is hard to say exactly when concepts are born in the flow of significance and from whom. Maybe this is why Socrates identified himself merely as a midwife.

Debra Bergoffen, Eleanore Holveck, Sara Heinämaa and Anne Van Leeuwen read Beauvoir as a phenomenologist because this is the tradition from which she draws her named sources, the tradition in which her friends wrote philosophy, and the tradition of ideas to which her own contributions seem most similar.[3] Other scholars, such as Eva Lundgren-Gothlin, Jo-Ann Pilardi, and Nancy Bauer, read Beauvoir's phenomenology as peculiarly Hegelian, because of the nineteenth-century philosopher's presence in *The Second Sex* [1949], and because Beauvoir engaged in a more extensive dialogue with Hegel than did her colleagues.[4] But Toril Moi reads Beauvoir as an ordinary language philosopher, in accordance with an English philosophical tradition with which Beauvoir would have had no direct acquaintance. *The Second Sex*, according to Moi, clarifies meanings and exposes the irrational assumptions behind our use of everyday terms like 'woman' just as Gilbert Ryle or Ludwig Wittgenstein might have called for.[5]

One need not draw on a common philosophical heritage or library of names to explicate the concepts of a philosopher or philosophical school. This book reads Beauvoir's concepts according to the definition of philosophy laid down by Gilles Deleuze, even though he did not become famous until her career was almost finished.[6] Reading Beauvoir with Deleuze gives more weight to the ontology of 'becoming' announced in *The Second Sex*. It allows us to bring her text into relation with more events that cannot easily be traced to linear cause-effect relations, events that emerge only in retrospect, including events in the international history of feminist movements.[7] Moreover, this reading reveals another philosophical side to Beauvoir's corpus, one Margaret Simons identified with Bergson and Leibniz in Beauvoir's student writings, although I argue that it extends to texts, including novels, late in her career. Even as a text of existential phenomenology, *The Second Sex* simply makes more sense, relates to the rest of her work, and is able to do more when we understand philosophy the way Deleuze did, rather than the way Beauvoir's precursors or contemporaries did.

Approaching *The Second Sex* as an exercise in the creation of concepts also allows us to resolve some problems in Beauvoir's reception. Like versions of the phenomenological reading that focus on literature, this approach renders Beauvoir's reluctance to call herself a philosopher less controversial or mysterious. It lets us see a reciprocal experimental process at work in Beauvoir's thinking and the course of her unconventional personal relationships:

her bisexuality, her principled non-monogamy, and the support and acknowledgement she gave to other philosophers in her life. It elaborates the stakes involved in resisting historicism among philosophers, including feminist philosophers from different geographical regions whose historical relations of influence have not and may never settle into a single story. By focusing on *concepts* rather than on universals, finally, it allows us to tackle the critiques of Beauvoir's supposed universalism and the manifest universalism of some movements she influenced, critiques that have emerged internationally over the last thirty years, particularly from women in the African diaspora.

While some feminists have investigated Deleuze's notion of becoming-woman, this reading of Beauvoir helps us to think more clearly about future events in which women's thinking, like the thinking of others, *becomes philosophical*. My goal in this text is not to make Beauvoir a Deleuzian but, above all, to trace a problem or process of becoming that implicates both thinkers. Such a project subtly transforms Deleuze by forcing his concepts to respond to the exigencies of at least one woman's quest for creativity. In *Anti-Oedipus* [1972], Deleuze and Guattari discuss Nietzsche's identification with 'every name in history' insofar as he was a bundle of becomings rather than a given being (AO 21/28). What I want to understand is the process through which Beauvoir's own life and concepts were generated, differentiated from others, and participate in the *differentiating* and *becoming of concepts* that Deleuze identifies with philosophy 'itself', apart from any individual thinker.

Phenomenology

But first, what does it mean to read *The Second Sex* as a work of phenomenology? Phenomenology is a philosophical project developed by Edmund Husserl toward the end of the nineteenth century. Husserl aspired to a rigorous description of the conditions linking humans to their world and thereby making knowledge and action possible. The *meaning* or *significance* of any phenomenon, he argued, could only be accounted for in terms of a consciousness that was 'intentional', oriented *towards* or *about* something, and in terms of its relationship to a world whose givenness facilitated and resisted these intentions. Phenomenology focuses on the quality of experience as the result of typical, habitual encounters between conscious beings and their perceptions, hopes, memories, objects of knowledge and everyday practices. The structure of experience, he believed, was the basis for eventual knowledge claims. As he reformulated the project over the course of his career, Husserl moved from describing this structure to justifying his conclusions compared to the claims of existing disciplines. Thus phenomenology, especially after its first phase, was also a struggle against the tendency towards naïve empiricism and unacknowledged intellectual prejudices in logic, mathematics, psychology and the human sciences.

Eleanore Holveck persuasively describes *The Second Sex* as a phenomenological text whose two volumes correspond respectively to the two *reductions* or shifts of intellectual perspective recommended by Husserl.[8] *Reduction* is the reflective act by which we set aside our everyday, inherited beliefs about the nature of the mind and the world, beliefs that often incorporate bits of metaphysical, scientific, and folk terminology and assumptions (which he calls the 'natural attitude'), and thereby attend more closely to the nature of the encounter *between* living experience and its objects or meanings.[9] Husserl's phenomenology requires us to render experience manageable by 'reducing' it to the relationship between consciousness and its world (this, he called the *phenomenological* and later the *transcendental* reduction). Until late in his career, he also believed we must further reduce the elements of that relationship to their most typical or ideal forms (a process called the *eidetic* reduction).

Like many of Husserl's works, *The Second Sex* begins by bracketing the natural sciences' understanding of some 'object' – in this case, 'woman' – and by challenging the natural attitude that leads both scientists and ordinary readers to accept the reality of entities as they are described by science.[10] For example, *The Second Sex* examines discourses like biology, psychology (psychoanalysis), and economics (historical materialism) that claim knowledge about women and claim to explain women's social inferiority. In *Volume One: Facts and Myths* (*Les Faits et les Myths*), Beauvoir shows that these disciplines are not rooted in the basic structure of human experiences of sensation, imagination and reason. Rather, these disciplines reflect the experiences in which *men* engage with their world, as well as some of men's unjustified biases. In other words, the tacit notion of masculinity is part of the 'natural attitude' prejudicing the sciences. Thus Holveck writes:

One of the most important contributions of *The Second Sex* for feminists today is that it argues for all time that no scientific theory, in Husserl's broad sense of *Wissenschaft*, about what males and females 'are', can be used to justify treating men and women unequally. A scientific theory presupposes that rational, reflective human beings are trying to achieve universal knowledge.[11]

The phenomenological reduction focuses our attention on the relationship between consciousness and its world, rather than on preconceived metaphysical or empiricist beliefs about the contents of that world, much less everyday cultural or psychological prejudices. In doing so, it reveals that women's appearance as an empirical social and scientific phenomenon is strongly conditioned by the *meaning* or *sense* [*sens*, *Sinn*] of womanhood and sexual difference in Western societies. In Hegelian terms, this meaning posits woman as 'Other' to the very model of subjectivity considered foundational for human experience and knowledge. Beauvoir also discovered that such disciplines ignored the evidence of women's *own* experience and their *own* reflection on the structure, values, ideas and activities comprising that experience. This is what Beauvoir proceeds to describe in *Volume Two: Lived Experience* (*L'Expérience Vécue*). Beauvoir's hope, according to Holveck, is to re-ground the sciences in a structure of consciousness that is genuinely universal, rather than biased towards the masculine. This means including effects of sexual difference *among* the aspects of intersubjectivity that are necessary conditions for human experience and knowledge.

Sense and the event

Given Beauvoir's frequent philosophical exchanges with Sartre and Merleau-Ponty, this is a remarkably persuasive account of *The Second Sex*, and one that Holveck further reinforces by looking at specific aspects of Beauvoir's novels that could be interpreted as phenomenological thought experiments. I do not wish to discount the phenomenological approach to Beauvoir's thought. Indeed, I draw on phenomenological readings of Deleuze such as those by Joe Hughes and Len Lawlor that allow both historically linear and non-linear encounters with Beauvoir to be identified.[12] *Sense* and *repetition* enable Beauvoir's phenomenology to become something other than the description of lived experience or the pursuit of a more impartial universal science. We might be able to experiment with alternatives if we could analyse the *meaning* of this absolute Other and the spans of time or the repetitive encounters and acts in which women seem to be frozen as the Other.

For Husserl, sense was the target of intentional consciousness in its relationship to the world. Husserl wanted to replace the classic opposition between subject and object with a bipolar relationship, stretched between ego and world or between the activity of *noesis* (intentionality) and its *noetic correlate* (the meaning at which intentionality aims; i.e. the tree or the tune being remembered). In works by Deleuze such as *Difference and Repetition* [1968] and *The Logic of Sense* [1969], sense is less an *individual meaning* than what makes it *possible* for a proposition to refer to speakers ('manifestation'), states of affairs ('denotation'), or other propositions ('signification') and for these propositions to then be true or false (LS 12–18/22–8).[13] Put differently, sense is what a proposition *expresses* (as a whole) rather than what it refers to. Sense allows us to understand *why* a speaker would mention something in the first place. In *Difference and Repetition*, sense *results* from the repetition of pre-personal habits that structure the experience of time, as well as from the breakdown of such structures. *The Logic of Sense* explores the conditions under which sense collapses, such as schizophrenia, and the logical paradoxes that sustain sense, such as those found in the fiction of Lewis Carroll.

Deleuze's notion of habit owes much to the 'genetic' phenomenology with which Husserl replaced his earlier, 'static' focus on the objects of conscious intentional acts; a perspective that trickled into published works only towards the end of Husserl's life.[14] Genetic phenomenology responds to the question: how did a consciousness capable of sense emerge in the first place? Husserl realised this was an increasingly important question as he tackled the problems of *justifying* knowledge and explaining the *temporality* of consciousness itself, as well as fleeting objects of consciousness. He could not explain sense without the *passive synthesis* of the capacity to hold them in mind.[15]

But Deleuze also traces the study of sense to the ancient Stoics. Husserl links sense to *horizons*, which implies some kind of external limit (the back of the house which is hidden from us). But this spatial connotation is misleading, although for Deleuze, too, sense is a dimension of being. However, it is more like an invisible *surface* in the world of intentionality, with one side turned toward things and one side touching language. Following the Stoics, Deleuze describes sense as an 'event': 'on the condition', he says, 'that the event is not confused with its spatio-temporal realization in a state of affairs' (LS 21–2/33–5).[16] Sense is an existentially orienting network of relations linking linguistic meaning (which Deleuze calls the level of effects) and states of affairs involving bodies (which he calls the level of causes). So while a proposition may describe an event in which physical causes lead to physical effects, the physical world also 'causes' events in language and language, in turn, allows us to separate the physical world into bodies that affect one another.

In *A Thousand Plateaus* [1980], Deleuze and Guattari describe the organisation of becomings into a world of stability and change as a process of *stratification*, and point to the flows of inorganic matter, living matter and signs as some of the most important flows from which phenomena emerge.[17] Only certain minerals form rock or metal ores under certain temperature conditions; only some texts are adopted into the canon of philosophy after having been the object of sufficient responses or commentaries; and citizens must pass through various anatomical, cultural and psychological filters to pass as 'women' among their peers. These stable tendencies are selected by a form of sense that is not just 'intentional' for consciousness but also produced 'unintentionally'. From a Deleuzian standpoint, the meaning of gender and the bodies, attitudes and behaviour necessary to identify gender in a given historical situation are *events*, and the event of their actualisation ties together innumerable bodily moments as an effect crowns its causes.[18] While Husserlian phenomenology begins with deliberate reflection, the act of a professional philosopher *setting aside* his professional and everyday habits (the *epoché*), Deleuzian philosophy begins with habit itself and with disorienting experiences of nonsense or shocks in which those habits prove unrecognisable.[19]

We can read *The Second Sex* as the result of deliberate curiosity about the biased conditions of current 'knowledge' about women or the masculinism of the social and natural sciences. But we can also read it as Beauvoir's response to the repeated failure to recognise *herself* and the freedom of her singularity in the habitual, historical imago men believe they encounter in women. 'If I want to define myself', Beauvoir writes, 'I first have to say, "I am a woman"; all other assertions will arise from this basic truth. A man never begins by positing himself as an individual of a certain sex . . .' (SS 5/1:13–14).

In other words, women's lives and thinking have no becoming apart from their sex, while men's are assumed to evolve 'in the middle' of multiple becomings. 'An autonomous freedom' like all others, women must struggle against being 'frozen' as objects for a consciousness other than their own and must struggle to 'transcend' and intend' only by identifying with an alien consciousness (SS 17/1:31).

The Second Sex, therefore, effects a 'destratification' from woman and from the plane on which she is defined as Other – for in its pages, Beauvoir finds herself floating between ontological tendencies, becoming apparently incompatible things at one time, but nonetheless swimming 'upstream' against the current that would assign her a certain fixed place. Beauvoir uses the non-sense running through these ontological strata to heat or shake up their remaining sediment and to disturb the seeming self-evidence of sexual and social categories. As Bauer puts it, she reveals 'the extent to which being a woman poses a *philosophical* problem – which is to say, a problem for and of philosophy'.[20]

According to *The Second Sex*, the inhibition and self-consciousness imposed on women's public activities and personal enjoyment through informal phenomena like street harassment; advertising reminders to reduce weight, enjoy motherhood more, or to buy better and better cleaning supplies; or, in some societies, formal surveillance by morality police are instances of provocative *nonsense* that arise again and again in apparently rational interactions with others who are proud to be 'modern'. In 1949, moreover, such disparities were far more entrenched in Western European and North American societies than they are today.

Men's efforts to control women's fertility even when they have no interest in supporting or caring for children, men's and women's disproportionate scepticism regarding the value of claims or proposals uttered in a female voice, and the deliberate imposition of archaic mores on women in societies fuelled by innovation and exchange constitute a kind of 'sexist sense'. This sense connects women's intentionality to possible objects and conditions the way women's speech and statements about them are judged true or false. The social and individual habits responsible for generating and reproducing womanhood as social 'Other' impose a representational screen, separating women from the singularity of their own freedom and generally putting it at the service of male becoming – even if women are affected to different degrees and not all men can take equal advantage of its effects. These representations make it seem as if women's way of being is eternal and unchangeable, an irreversible product of *history* if not of *nature*. For many women, such experiences involve physical violence, but the impact of nonsense on the woman thinker is also violent, in the same way that, according to Fanon, 'for a man whose only weapon is reason there is nothing more neurotic than contact with unreason'.[21]

In fact, Anne Van Leeuwen brings the phenomenological reading of Simone de Beauvoir very close to Deleuze when she interprets *The Second Sex* in terms of the concept of 'ambiguity'.[22] Ambiguity refers to the indeterminacy or undecidability of a given phenomenon or action's meaning. In many contexts, this means ambiguity is a matter of uncertainty as to what phenomenon or action one is dealing with at all.

Like Holveck, Van Leeuwen reads *The Second Sex* as an inquiry into the 'sense' that determines men's relations to women. But she points out that Husserlian sense is always something doubly ambiguous, first because the world of *which it is the sense* is ambiguous (never given a priori), and second because that world is never 'fixed' or 'accomplished' – sense changes as humans engage with the world and with each other, and thereby the world also changes.[23] In Deleuzian terms, ambiguity means that a given encounter or situation is unique, as well as intrinsically multiple and caught in multiple processes of stratification. Not only is the scientific view of women 'true' only within the horizons of a sexist historical situation, Van Leeuwen suggests, but it can also be contested and revised as new situations emerge, providing new evidence and altering the identity and interests of the intentional subject.

The early Husserl would have understood this sense as the (static) object of an intentional act, perhaps one absorbed unthinkingly by men and women into their 'natural attitude'.[24] Later Husserl would have regarded it as a dynamic, changing world of a dynamic, evolving consciousness. For Deleuze, however, sense is required to form a 'world' in the first place. Indeed, sense itself involves a reciprocal process of problematisation (the first form of ambiguity) and dramatisation (the second form of ambiguity), the undoing of old strata and the congealing of new ones, virtuality and actuality. These two levels would be an ambiguity *within* sense, although too much focus on their unity, Deleuze would argue, might dangerously collapse the dynamic process of sense-creation into a static transcendental, which is why he relentlessly asserts the *multiplicity* of all becomings and assemblages.

Historicity of the problem

It may seem anachronistic to read Beauvoir in light of Deleuze unless we are on the lookout for *anachronic* as opposed to *chronological* events; that is, events that challenge our notion of what counts as a meaningful or interesting chronology.[25] However, since both Beauvoir and Deleuze consciously responded to Husserl, one can also draw bridges between their becomings using ordinary narrative history.

Having read his *Logical Investigations* [1900–1] and other early writings focused on consciousness and its categories of intentional experience, Sartre went to Berlin in 1933/4 to study Husserl more carefully at the French Institute (PL 112). Several years later, after encountering phenomenology independently from Sartre, Merleau-Ponty visited the Husserl archives in Louvain and was granted posthumous access to some of the unpublished manuscripts in which Husserl had been reworking his earlier presentation of phenomenology to explain how such categories emerged historically and in the life of individual consciousness.[26]

Sartre's *Transcendence of the Ego* [1937] criticised aspects of Husserl's turn to transcendental philosophy found in the text *Ideas I* [1913].[27] Husserl, Sartre believed, had been wrong to 'double' the spontaneity of impersonal consciousness with a 'transcendental ego' when the only ego to be found in consciousness was, like everything else, an object *for* consciousness. But at the time Sartre visited Berlin, Husserl had already begun investigating the *genetic* processes through which such categories and structures entered the circuit between consciousness and its world, although little of this material appeared in published texts during his life. These investigations included analyses of phenomena such as temporality, embodiment and intersubjectivity. Consulting these unpublished manuscripts shortly after Husserl's death made it possible for Merleau-Ponty to consider his *Phenomenology of Perception* [1945] a work with essentially Husserlian commitments although it differed significantly from published Husserl texts, as well as from Sartre's reading of Husserl.[28]

Beauvoir followed Sartre's studies at a distance and read Husserl's *On the Phenomenology of the Consciousness of Internal Time* [1928], as well as the *Cartesian Meditations* [1929], which Husserl recommended as an introduction to phenomenology, despite potential conflicts with his unpublished views on intersubjectivity.[29] She also consulted the relevant secondary scholarship by Emmanuel Lévinas and Eugen Fink. All her philosophical texts, particularly *The Ethics of Ambiguity* [1947] and *The Second Sex*, contain distinctive terminology associated with phenomenology. Beauvoir's positive review of *The Phenomenology of Perception* shows that she was exposed to the intersubjective, bodily and historical phenomenology Merleau-Ponty attributed in that text to Husserl's *Ideas II* and the *Crisis of European Sciences*.[30] Sara Heinämaa argues that whether her knowledge was first or second hand, Beauvoir's understanding of embodiment owes a great deal to ideas found in Husserl manuscripts that were, in part because of the intervening war, only published several decades later.

On the other hand, it is not necessary for us to draw a detailed causal connection between Deleuze and Beauvoir via Husserl, Merleau-Ponty or Sartre. For even before she encountered any of these phenomenological thinkers, Beauvoir was fascinated as a student with two other philosophers of paramount interest to Deleuze: Bergson and Leibniz.[31] In *Memoirs of a Dutiful Daughter* [1958], she reports enthusiastically 'recognize[ing] her own experience' in 'Bergson's theories about "the social ego and the personal ego"' (MDD 207).[32] In her diaries, as Margaret Simons discovered, Beauvoir associates Bergson and Leibniz with the problem of the Other, the problem that seems to have served as a leitmotif through her many years of literary and philosophical work.

In their biographical origin, Beauvoir's questions about Otherness are related to the relative value of qualitative experience, which she seems to associate with literature, and to the problem of 'indiscernibles' – namely, how two items identified by the same concept can be distinguished.[33] This latter problem derives from Leibniz, for whom every existing entity, if it is truly numerically distinct, ultimately has a slightly different, distinctive concept known only by God.[34] Kant, on the other hand, argued that *space* as general form of outer human intuition allowed items to be numerically distinct while thought under the same 'universal' concept. Kant allowed God to be removed from the picture; he also relieved epistemology of any need to consider 'inner differences' that elude our spatial perception and existing concepts.[35] Beauvoir wanted to preserve that singularity, which Bergson associated with *becoming* rather than being.[36]

As her work matured, Beauvoir clearly became more aware of the myriad ways in which institutions treat people as 'indiscernible' beings under this or that 'universal' rather than singular becomings. Representation 'blocks' becoming by opposing beings to one another in a perceptual or conceptual matrix. People themselves often collude with their erasure and that of others. The notion of *oppression* from *The Ethics of Ambiguity*, for example, describes such a situation (EA 81–96/117–39). The denial of singularity is Beauvoir's reason for objecting to the utilitarianism of economic liberalism as well as Marxist-Leninism (EA 99–114/143–66). Towards the end of her life, Beauvoir studied the effacement of older people's singularity by social institutions and by their distance from an increasingly young population.[37] *The Second Sex* emerges from a similar concern, for the becoming of half of the human race seems subjugated to a system of representation that does violence to both sexes' capacity for sense and meaning.

Now, one might easily object that Beauvoir does not discuss Husserl, Leibniz or Bergson in *The Second Sex* (and rarely in her other published writings). In fact, when discussing the Other she often refers to G. W. F. Hegel, whom Deleuze accuses of taking representation as an image of thought to its most pernicious extreme.[38] Hegel does focus on movement and becoming, rather than on being, but he focuses only on the becomings of those beings that can be conceptually opposed to one another, which (Deleuze might argue) leaves much of reality outside the picture. For Hegel, what is most real is the particular insofar as it contains universal moments – in other words, the particular musical tone or train carriage, not just isolated, but in relation to every other musical tone, musical instrument and means of transport that could be envisioned, as well as the social and historical institutions that resulted in pianos, concert halls, train stations and containerisation.

But Beauvoir also read Hegel in combination and often in tension with Kierkegaard.[39] For Kierkegaard, what is most real is the deliberate effort to identify and appreciate whatever distinguishes this instant or encounter from every other, and to hold onto that singularity in faith despite the fact that, he believed, it can never be identified in concepts. For Deleuze, like Kierkegaard, the 'things' that stand out as most real are these *ways of repeating*.[40] Becomings are ways of repeating that gradually reveal singularity. Only as becomings, Beauvoir commented, could women be compared with men (SS 45–6/1:72). She is committed to Kierkegaard's ethical task of individuating, or discovering and creating distinction from others who might seem to fall under a common universal.

The published texts Beauvoir would have been able to read by Husserl in the 1930s downplayed intersubjectivity, when they did not give a downright solipsistic portrait of the phenomenological enterprise. Although Husserl did consider intersubjectivity a background condition for individual experience, as Merleau-Ponty discovered in Louvain, and some of Husserl's unpublished texts did grapple with the problem of human uniqueness, they are ambiguous and less well known even today.[41] Sartre seems not to have engaged with them at all. Since Beauvoir consistently rejected Hegel's pursuit of a timeless universal standpoint, it appears that what she took from Hegel was his robust discussion of intersubjective and historical aspects of human becoming and obstacles to becoming, including affects of desire and aggression that threaten to overturn the boundaries of selves in opposition. Thus I believe that Beauvoir recruited Hegel to pursue an interest in intersubjectivity that originated with Bergson and Leibniz and was whetted, but probably not solved, by her own engagement with Husserl's ideas.[42]

The next chapter rereads the Introduction to *The Second Sex* closely to assess the plausibility of considering Beauvoir's philosophy as an act of critique in Deleuze's sense. By this I mean it does not just analyse a phenomenon such as 'sexist sense' but explains its emergence.[43] In doing so, philosophy also emerges along its own 'line of flight' to pose problems and to create concepts. Deleuze understands philosophical concepts as forming and extending a plane of relations among themselves (an absolute plane of immanence, rather than immanence to consciousness) (WIP 35–6/38–9). This chapter examines Beauvoir's concepts, such as 'transcendence', in light of Deleuze's criteria for philosophical invention, including the reterritorialisation of ideas by other thinkers such as Bergson, Leibniz and Sartre and the construction of conceptual personae. The plane formed by such concepts, which Beauvoir loosely terms 'existentialist morality', might enable women to escape the system of representation that poses them as the social Other; the state of immanence within which they struggle to transcend.

The third chapter reads Volume 2 of *The Second Sex* as a description of the passive syntheses and habits that build up a truly problematic experience of the world for women. Nevertheless, the community in which women participate both willingly and inadvertently requires this sense of them. When Beauvoir tries to understand why women have not formed a revolutionary class against men as a group, her answer involves the claim that 'their opposition took shape within an original *Mitsein*'; a term from Heidegger that means literally 'being-with' (SS 9/1:19). For Beauvoir, the critique of representation would involve a critique of the *Mitsein* in coupled heterosexual life and in society at large. *Mitsein* would be an example of stratification in which select forms of human coexistence appear as unchanging natural forms. What could this *Mitsein* do if it were rethought as an assemblage along Deleuzian lines? Could its habits be recomposed around the value of reciprocity? This chapter also touches on the difficulty of identifying habits that are complicit with or resistant towards 'sexist sense' in the midst of a qualitative multiplicity fusing an indefinite number of social practices.

The fourth chapter situates Beauvoir's demand for freedom on behalf of women in *The Second Sex* with respect to the ethics of the 'appeal' from 'Pyrrhus and Cineas' [1944] and her formulation (in 'Pyrrhus and Cineas' and *The Ethics of Ambiguity*) of freedom as dependent in some ways on the freedom of all others. In this chapter, I want to understand how the plane of immanence defining Beauvoir's thought as singular seems to pass through and be defined through the free becoming of others. I ask how *The Second Sex* lets us critique or understand the genesis of *Mitsein* with an eye to creating new assemblages, particularly those involving reciprocity. This is not an idea one finds anywhere in Deleuze. However, we may find something similar in Bergson's last writings and in the concept of 'transindividuality' proposed by philosopher of technology Gilbert Simondon, who had an unmistakeable influence on Deleuze and Guattari.

If philosophy involves the formulation of problems in response to a shocking, compelling or nonsensical experience, even the experience of witnessing others' suffering, this does not mean that everyone, even everyone who suffers, will formulate the same problems. The fifth chapter suggests that there need be no *one* form of sexist sense, oppressing women everywhere on the globe, for it to be worthwhile to problematise *one* or *some* of those forms in a way that suggests how others might understand the singular problems confronting *them*. Deleuze and Guattari explicitly stated that they did not expect becoming-woman would have anything to do with feminism, for feminism is a movement on behalf of 'molar' women – fully constituted beings rather than 'molecular' multiplicities in the process of composition or decomposition (TP 275–6/337–9). Was a 'molar' women's movement the only way that Beauvoir's Idea could have been actualised? To what extent does the Idea involve becomings for which 'becoming-woman' would not even be the first or most important name?

Any new system of representations produced as solutions to a philosophical problem has its own incongruities that may lead to the formulation of other problems. The sixth chapter will consider side effects and difficulties that this way of reading Beauvoir might force us to anticipate. For example, according to Deleuze, no becoming or thought can be conceived apart from a hierarchy of forces and interpretations. Such hierarchies are necessary for beings and their transformations or interactions to be noticeable in the first place. Is there a place for this fundamental *inequality* in Beauvoir's egalitarianism and her expectation that 'authentic' individuals and institutions, those fostering the freedom of all, will also be egalitarian? What becomes of the notion of *justice* in the thought of both Beauvoir and Deleuze? Finally, how does Beauvoir herself understand 'events', including the repetitions and processes leading to sexism, feminist social movement, or women's equality?

We usually think of events as neutral moments or changes in a series, which can only be recognised against a backdrop of continuity. As mentioned above, Deleuze suggests that the meaningful relationship between speakers, states of affairs, and other statements is also an *event* (LS 19/30–1). In fact, he then reverses the equation and asks whether the only real events might not be relationships of sense! Thus Deleuze identifies two series of time – the time of mute bodies and states of affairs, and the time of the events in which they are linked and become available for reflection and communication to others. The first time series (*Chronos*) is a kind of perpetual, thick present, a *duration*; while the second series (*Aion*) is the changing or becoming itself, facing both past and future. Both are perspectives on the *same* time: one with respect to irreversibility and the other with respect to reversibility; one with respect to the beings in an encounter and the other with respect to the encounter itself, in which elements dissolve.

According to the Stoics, we have no control over bodies and their states of affairs; we do not even have adequate knowledge of them – what we can control, however, is the *events* through which we connect them. And since events often affect our bodies unpleasantly, the best we can do is to conceive of a second event in which we would be the *cause* of that unhappy event, changing it from one we suffer passively to one we actively embrace and bring about. The body wills now not exactly what occurs, but something *in* that which occurs, something yet to come which would be consistent with what occurs, in accordance with the laws of an obscure, humorous conformity: the Event. It is in this sense that the *Amor fati* is one with the struggle of free men. (LS 149/175)

Deleuze calls this will 'counter-actualisation' (*contre-effectuation*). It does not just resignify that 'first' unpleasant event but re-enacts it, repeats it (in French, the word *répétition* also means 'rehearsal') so as to alter its sense, and 'retrospectively' brings about a better event, better because free. Causes of an identified event do not necessarily exhaust themselves in their effects but coexist with those effects, as parents coexist with and continue to affect the children whom they have shaped, sometimes in ways they find problematic and deeply moving. At this point, the effect becomes a cause, or parents and children become both causes *and* effects in cumulative ways. They rewrite their own narratives, at the same time that they are affected by their larger social environment and act back on it. For in fact there *is* no event except insofar as multiple, differing repetitions have built up a context in which actors, meanings and states of affairs relate to each other.

In *Prime of Life*, Beauvoir claims that during World War II, 'history burst over me' or collapsed and tore her away from the comforting comprehensiveness of studying Hegel; 'I dissolved into fragments' (L'Histoire fondit sur moi, j'éclatai') (PL 295/381). We can also choose to think of lives, no less than history, as non-linear, marked by normal stretches and significant turning points (DR 188–9/244–5). A philosophy cannot be read entirely apart from a life – or an author's other acts of creativity – not to find which comes first, or to reduce later events to earlier ones, but to see later events as co-contributors to earlier ones, which only 'come into their own' from a standpoint that might even be impersonal, outside that life.

Of what event is *The Second Sex* a part, if not a history of progress in the actualisation of freedom? In other words, in what process or 'becoming' do the concepts of this book mark a distinctive turn, differentiation or deviation? To what trauma might it correspond as a counter-actualisation?[24] *The Second Sex* has generally been read as a moment in the history of feminism – an enduring moment, to be sure, one that only burst over women's heads some ten to twenty years after its publication, a moment that constantly changes, moreover, due to repeated re-evaluations and reinterpretations. Some feminist scholars have reclaimed *The Second Sex* as a moment in the history of phenomenological philosophy, perhaps the emergence of a thread in the qualitative multiplicity of that movement allowing sexual difference to become an enduring source of questions and claims. But Beauvoir's text also marks a turn in the history of liberal theories and institutions, a transformation in the meaning of equality and liberty as essential elements of 'modern' attitudes towards government and power, in which Hegel himself plays a significant but perhaps not eternal role. And what other histories have we not even noticed emerging or bursting over us?

According to Beauvoir, 'There is no other justification for present existence than its expansion toward an indefinitely open future' (SS 16/1:31). Thinking about history neither as a tale of modern progress nor as a repetition of the (same) past makes it conceivable to participate in an open history of philosophy, and to participate in history on the side of philosophy's becoming, without having to take a break from either feminism, as Janet Halley suggests, or philosophy, as Gayle Salamon mused more recently.[45] At the same time, it acknowledges that the risks of such breaks are inevitable. Deleuze's reading of Nietzsche suggests that there would be an 'active' and a 'reactive' way to take such breaks, which would mean that abandoning the morality of a particular discursive practice might not require us to abandon ethics, preference, or selectivity altogether. We need not be 'women' or even, perhaps, self-consciously feminist to pursue planes populated with concepts that liberate women, nor need we identify with the 'West' to defend the frightening creativity associated with differentiations of sex and desire.

My reading of Beauvoir is motivated by the stubbornness of singularity. My gamble that Beauvoir's ideas can be freer through Deleuze responds to her own stubborn advocacy for the singularity of others, insofar as they, too, resist being easily representable and recognisable. For these reasons, I have tried to select only those ideas from the vast phylum of Deleuze's writings, alone and with Guattari, that enable me to push Beauvoir in this direction, or release her, as the case may be, while freeing the reader from the task of absorbing a vast terminology. Beauvoir, on the other hand, wrote at the crossroads of many ambiguous ideas, texts and schools of phenomenological thought whose respective legacies are still being worked out today. I have tried to give a coherent portrait of the phenomenology to which she and Deleuze responded, and identify sites for further research as well as point readers towards the criticism of those with more expertise on specific debates. Finally, I have only engaged in a limited way with Deleuzean feminists, although I would not be unhappy if this book made Deleuze more user-friendly to new feminist readers. If Deleuze and Guattari are correct that desiring-machines only work by breaking down, including the desiring-machines of philosophical thought, I hope someone can find positivity in my omissions.

One dies, one thinks, but the Deleuzian Other is the one for whom the possibilities I can only imagine are a part of reality. The conclusion, accordingly, asks how Beauvoir's concept of the Other, no less than Deleuze's, changes our notion of the future imagined by feminists.

Notes

1. See Lorraine, *Deleuze and Guattari's Immanent Ethics*, 33–8.
2. Moi, *What is a Woman?*, 204–6. A shortened version of Moi's book with the same pagination has been published under the title *Sex, Gender, and the Body*.
3. Bergoffen, *The Philosophy of Simone de Beauvoir: Gendered Phenomenologies, Erotic Generosities*; Holveck, *Simone de Beauvoir's Philosophy of Lived Experience*; Heinämaa, *Toward a Phenomenology of Sexual Difference*; Van Leeuwen, 'Beauvoir, Irigaray, and the Possibility of Feminist Phenomenology'.
4. Beauvoir, *The Second Sex* (SS)/*Le deuxième sexe*; Lundgren-Gothlin, *Sex and Existence*; Pilardi, *Simone de Beauvoir Writing the Self*; and Bauer, *Simone de Beauvoir, Philosophy, and Feminism*, as well as chapter 3 of Hutchings, *Hegel and Feminist Philosophy*. Beauvoir read Hegel while Sartre was a prisoner of war and her diary and letters contain reading reports. See Beauvoir, *Wartime Diary*, 304–14, 319–25.
5. While Bauer reads Beauvoir primarily in light of Hegel, her own commitments to the ordinary language tradition are evident in *Simone de Beauvoir, Philosophy, and Feminism*.
6. This possibility is raised by Michèle Le Dœuff in *Hipparchia's Choice* when she points to the understanding of cross-disciplinary fertilisation found in Bergson and Deleuze as a model for philosophical work (168–9). Linnell Secomb experiments with a similar reading in 'Beauvoir's Minoritarian Philosophy', but does not focus on specific Beauvoirian texts.
7. Here I follow Spinoza's principle in *Ethics* Book 4, Proposition 38: 'that which so disposes the human body that it can be affected in

more ways, or which renders it capable of affecting external bodies in more ways, is advantageous to man, and proportionately more advantageous as the body is thereby rendered more capable of being affected in more ways and of affecting other bodies in more ways' (Spinoza, *Ethics*, 177).
8. Holveck, *Philosophy of Lived Experience*, 21–3, 111–23.
9. For example, on the reduction, see Husserl, *Ideas I*, §31–2 and *Cartesian Meditations*, 19–21; on the natural attitude, see Husserl, *Ideas I*, §27. For a general discussion, see Welton, *The Other Husserl*, 87–93.
10. Holveck, *Philosophy of Lived Experience*, 112–14.
11. Holveck, *Philosophy of Lived Experience*, 115.
12. Hughes, *Difference and Repetition: A Reader's Guide*; Lawlor, *Thinking Through French Philosophy*.
13. Welton, *The Other Husserl*, 22, 86, 89–90. In Husserl's early work, and most of what was published during his lifetime (such as *Ideas I*), the constitution of sense is the work of the 'consciousness' pole of the field relating consciousness, world and others. In work published later, including *Ideas II*, the constitution of sense is a reciprocal process involving multiple poles, even if Husserl believed it could only be *analysed* from the standpoint of reflective consciousness. See Zahavi, 'Merleau-Ponty on Husserl', 13–15; Husserl, *Ideas I*, §55; *Cartesian Meditations*, 44–6. Len Lawlor, drawing connections between Husserl and Deleuze via Merleau-Ponty, points out that sense is always *singular* even when it is the sense of an essence or a universal expressing many particulars (Lawlor, 'The End of Phenomenology', 19–20).
14. See Hughes, *Deleuze's Difference and Repetition*, 6–10. Husserl's transition from static to genetic phenomenology occurred between 1913 (*Ideas I*) and 1921 ('On Static and Genetic Phenomenological Method'). *Logical Investigations* and *Ideas I* are 'static' in the sense that they describe the constitution of relatively unchanging rather than open-ended and evolving structures or meanings. The distinction is mentioned in *Cartesian Meditations*, 135–6. See Zahavi, *Husserl's Phenomenology*, 94; Welton, *The Other Husserl*, 93. Merleau-Ponty mentions 'genetic phenomenology' on the first page of *Phenomenology of Perception* in connection with Eugen Fink's writings on Husserl's *Cartesian Meditations*, and states that phenomenology can be a phenomenology of origins, not just 'true and immutable natures' (Merleau-Ponty, *Phenomenology of Perception*, vii, xviii). Husserl's perspectives on intersubjectivity, individuation and the role of embodiment in establishing intersubjectivity evolved between 1907 (*Thing and Space*), the *Cartesian Meditations* (1929), the lectures on intersubjectivity which were developed over more than a decade starting in the 1920s, and *Ideas II* (last revised in 1928, but not published until many years after his death).

15. In its simplest form, passive synthesis involves the 'association' of ideas or perceptions – at a more complex level, the cumulative effect of perception and experience on further perception and experience. The relationship between genesis and both types of synthesis is discussed in Husserl, *Cartesian Meditations*, 75–81. See Welton, *The Other Husserl*, 202–4; Zahavi, 'Merleau-Ponty on Husserl', 21–3.
16. The event in which an incorporeal sense shapes our vision is perhaps exemplified by an ambiguous 'gestalt' such as the duck/rabbit figure (particularly in a context that lends itself to one interpretation rather than another). If the figure moves – hops or waddles – and disrupts the sense of our perception, that too is an event. 'Performatives' like 'I do' or 'I swear!' or official actions like government devaluation of currency may function as incorporeals inasmuch as they change the material combinations into which the affected bodies can enter (Adkins, *Deleuze and Guattari's A Thousand Plateaus*, 77–8).
17. See chapter 3 of *A Thousand Plateaus*, '10,000 B.C.: The Geology of Morals', for a detailed exploration of stratification. Along with the concept of phylum, discussed in chapter 12, '1227: Treatise on Nomadology' (esp. 406–11/506–12), *stratification* enables Deleuze and Guattari to focus their ontology on becoming and on the *process* by which stable entities appear rather than on *substances* defined by 'form' and 'matter'. Strata, they write, 'consist of giving form to matters, of imprisoning intensities or locking singularities into systems of resonance and redundancy, of producing upon the body of the earth molecules large and small and organizing them into molar aggregates' (TP 40/54). Here, 'molecules' are relatively ephemeral encounters or events of combination, while 'molar' aggregates tend to have the longevity and consistency of 'being'.
18. Merleau-Ponty, for whom the intentional act *constitutes* its object by pulling together awareness, perception and bits of the environment or ongoing discourse along a line of tension or fold so that bodies can reveal and distinguish themselves in the first place, might also understand sense as an event. See Merleau-Ponty, *Phenomenology of Perception*, 77–9.
19. This is why *nonsense* is both phenomenally and methodologically crucial; as Lawlor explains, it has both generative and dissociative effects. Lawlor, 'The End of Phenomenology', 20–1; Husserl, *Cartesian Meditations*, 84.
20. Bauer, *Simone de Beauvoir, Philosophy, and Feminism*, 1.
21. Fanon, *Black Skin White Masks*, 118.
22. Van Leeuwen, 'Possibility of Feminist Phenomenology'.
23. Van Leeuwen, 'Possibility of Feminist Phenomenology', 478. Drawing parallels with Merleau-Ponty, Gail Weiss notes that Gestalt psychology also focuses on the ambiguity of perceptual objects and

optical illusions. Several scholars including Weiss see 'ambiguity' informing Beauvoir's discussion of the body and sexuality in *The Second Sex*, but for Van Leeuwen ambiguity is found at the level of forms of knowledge (Weiss, 'Beauvoir and Merleau-Ponty', and Bergoffen, *Gendered Phenomenologies*).
24. Zahavi, *Husserl's Phenomenology*, 94.
25. See Lundy, *History and Becoming*; Browne, *Feminism, Time, and Nonlinear History*.
26. Heinämaa, *Phenomenology of Sexual Difference*, 36–7; Zahavi, 'Merleau-Ponty on Husserl', Van Breda, 'Merleau-Ponty and the Husserl Archives'.
27. His critique aims primarily at section 57 of *Ideas I*: 'There is no I on the unreflected level', and therefore one need not and should not assume the existence of any such thing as a 'transcendental' ego. Sartre, *Transcendence of the Ego* (TE), 48.
28. Zahavi, 'Merleau-Ponty on Husserl'.
29. Beauvoir, *Prime of Life*, 162; Heinämaa, 'Body as Instrument', 72; Heinämaa, *Phenomenology of Sexual Difference*, 53–6. Sartre learned about phenomenology in 1932, from Raymond Aron and Lévinas's book on *Ideas I*, but Simons thinks that Beauvoir may have learned about Husserl from Jean Baruzi even before 1926 (Simons, 'Beauvoir's Early Philosophy', 198–200). However, Beauvoir's understanding of phenomenology, and probably Husserl, was influenced by discussions with Merleau-Ponty, who seems to have rejected the 'Kantian', 'Cartesian', or otherwise 'egological' reading of transcendental phenomenology to which Sartre subscribed and many contemporary readers of Husserl still subscribe. See Heinämaa, *Phenomenology of Sexual Difference*, xx n. 10; Zahavi, 'Merleau-Ponty on Husserl', 4–7.
30. Beauvoir, 'Review of *The Phenomenology of Perception*'. Husserl's *Ideas II* and *Crisis of the European Sciences* were not published until after his death.
31. Deleuze's dialogue with Bergson and Leibniz lasts through his entire career. Many of the ideas from *Difference and Repetition* appear in 'Bergson's Conception of Difference' (first published in 1956); *Bergsonism* [1966] revisits the subject, and *The Fold: Leibniz* [1988] represents a lifetime of reflection on Leibniz's philosophy in the context of the history of forms of art.
32. See also Beauvoir, *Diary of a Philosophy Student*, 58–61; Simons, 'Beauvoir's Early Philosophy', 195–6; Simons, 'Bergson's Influence on Beauvoir's Philosophical Methodology'; and Simons, 'Beauvoir and Bergson'; as well as Meryl Altman's introduction to 'Notes for a Novel', 338–41. Beauvoir's retrospective comments can be found in *Prime of Life* (PL 86) and in Simons, Benjamin and Beauvoir, 'Simone de Beauvoir: An Interview'.

33. Beauvoir, *Diary of a Philosophy Student*, 279.
34. Leibniz, *Discourse on Metaphysics*, 13–14.
35. Kant, *Critique of Pure Reason*, B327–30; Leibniz, *Monadology*, §8–16 (252–4).
36. Although they are often opposed, Husserl and Bergson were both interested in the irreducibly qualitative nature of temporal experience and particularly the temporality of bodily experience, which provisionally 'measures' other phenomena and allows them to be arranged in memory. See Winkler, 'Husserl and Bergson'; and Björk, 'Simone de Beauvoir and Life'.
37. Beauvoir, *The Coming of Age* [*La Vieillesse*, 1970]; published in the UK as *Old Age*.
38. Deleuze, *Nietzsche and Philosophy* [1962], 8–10, 156–9; *Difference and Repetition*, 133–6/174–8.
39. After an indifferent encounter in 1930, Beauvoir read Kierkegaard seriously ten years later, around the same time that she first read Hegel in earnest (PL 44, 364–73). In her 'Introduction' to *Wartime Diary*, Margaret Simons also cross-references Beauvoir's letters to Sartre from 20–1 March 1940 when Beauvoir began reading *Fear and Trembling* and her letters from 9 January 1941, which discuss both Hegel and Kierkegaard. See Beauvoir, *Wartime Diary*, 28, 270, 304–14, 319–25; Beauvoir, *Letters to Sartre*, 366–7; Heinämaa, 'The Background of Simone de Beauvoir's Metaphysical Novel'; and Green and Green, 'A Founding Feminist's Appreciation of Kierkegaard'.
40. Kierkegaard's theory of repetition is a source for *Difference and Repetition* and, according to Beauvoir's *Force of Circumstance*, an inspiration for *The Mandarins* (FC 270). Beauvoir, who had not yet read Kierkegaard in 1927, wrote in her diary: 'we must try to determine which one [choice] repeats our changing self the most often'; but '"most often" is not always' (*Diary of a Philosophy Student*, 246).
41. In the *Cartesian Meditations*, Husserl writes: 'A priori, my ego, given to me apodictically . . . can be a world-experiencing ego only by being in communion with others like himself . . . Conversely, I cannot conceive a plurality of monads otherwise than as explicitly or implicitly in communion' (139). He also explicitly disavows the charge of solipsism. But because this follows his reduction of consciousness to a 'sphere of ownness' and because, like Descartes, he presented the reduction as bracketing the *existence* of others (as elements of the phenomenal world known in the natural attitude), it is difficult for the reader to reinsert the conclusions of that reduction in the Fifth Meditation's broader discussion of embodied transindividuality. See Husserl, *Cartesian Meditations*, 120–4, 139. On the complex ambiguity of *Cartesian Meditations*, which can scarcely be explored here but which is decisive for many readings of his whole

philosophy, see Welton, *The Other Husserl*, 111–13; Zahavi, *Husserl's Phenomenology*, 122.
42. In *Cartesian Meditations*, as in the earlier essay 'On Static and Genetic Phenomenological Method' (1921), Husserl himself presents the problem of intersubjectivity and knowledge of the Other as a person in Leibnizian terms, speaking of them as 'monads'.
43. On critique as involving an account of genesis, see Deleuze, *Nietzsche and Philosophy*, 86–94, and Hughes, *Deleuze's Difference and Repetition*, 1–3. Here the object of Beauvoir's critique is what I am calling 'sexist sense'; however, 'the problem of woman has always been a problem of men' (SS 148/1:216), so the critique of man's problem is also a first step toward the resolution of a problem by and for women.
44. See Lorraine, *Deleuze and Guattari's Immanent Ethics*, particularly chapter 5.
45. Halley, *Split Decisions*; Salamon, 'Musings'; also, Butler, *Undoing Gender*, particularly chapter 11, 'Can the Other of Philosophy Speak?'

Chapter 2

The Problem of Sexist Sense

'To what are we dedicated if not to those problems which demand the very transformation of our body and our language?'
(DR 192/248)

In *What is a Woman?*, Toril Moi interprets *The Second Sex*, particularly its Introduction, as sharing assumptions about the relationship between philosophy, voice and the everyday with ordinary language philosophers.[1] 'What is a woman?' in other words, what does this word really refer to, and why does it seem to bring so much more baggage with it than simple reference to a human being with female anatomy? Moi hoped to show that Simone de Beauvoir was arguing against a very specific notion of femininity as somehow 'pervasive' in every aspect of such a human being's life, such that nothing women did could remain untouched by sexual or reproductive concerns.[2] She also wanted to show how Beauvoir's style negotiated the pitfalls of her implication in 'false' philosophical problems such as the supposed partiality obstructing her legitimacy as a philosopher.[3] In doing so, finally, Moi wished to detach Beauvoir from contemporary claims about the 'social construction' of gender, no less than from 'essentialism', and indeed from any notion of a distinction between sex and gender.[4]

Both Moi and Nancy Bauer contend that the term 'woman' can be useful to feminists without entailing metaphysical commitments.[5] Indeed, Bauer believes that *The Second Sex* and other feminist writings provide evidence for why philosophy ought to reconceive itself apart from metaphysics.[6]

Without wishing to deny the validity of many of Moi's points, and in keeping with her interest in the way a philosophical *oeuvre* balances personal and impersonal elements, I want to read the same text as an account of the formation of a *problem* and its associated concepts. *The Second Sex* is a work of critique in Deleuze's sense – a work that not only delimits and detaches from its object in thought, but also explains how that object came to be.[7] In this sense, it is the critique of a certain metaphysics, even if it obviously does not evade metaphysics altogether.

Difference and Repetition, for example, is a critique of representation as an image for what it means to think – and much of that book is occupied with explaining where representation comes from, so that we might be able to experiment with alternate models of thought. Thinking, for Deleuze, is never detached from bodies – rather, it is an event organising bodies and thereby influencing what they can do. As critique, Beauvoir's thinking alters the mixture of identifiable processes and entities that generated it, the subject of knowledge as well as those that are imperceptible, indiscernible and impersonal.

Representation and the creation of concepts

In *Difference and Repetition* and, later, *What is Philosophy?* Deleuze (and Guattari) define philosophy as the creation of concepts (DR xx/3; WIP 2/8).[8] The concepts created by philosophy are not empirical concepts (such as the concept of piano or train). The Idea whose object is a *problem* for us is a singularity, not a generality.[9] Nor is the problem a *question*, especially the kind of question 'What is X?' that expects a generality for its answer (DR 188–91/243–7). But identifying a true *problem* is not an easy or frequent event.[10]

Who formulates a problem, Idea, or concept? *What is Philosophy?* states that it is accessible only to those who join in philosophical activity. *Difference and Repetition* describes the formation, through degrees of repetition, of a subject whose habitual tendency is to rest content with *recognising* the objects in its environment and to think in generalities. This subject conforms to what Deleuze polemically calls the 'dogmatic image of thought' (DR 131–2/172) – assuming, with most of the history of Western philosophy, that humans naturally desire the truth, that the best form of thought combines good sense (a hierarchy of values) and common sense (a shared set of values), that it consists in recognising the truth rather than in stumbling with disorientation or misrecognition, etc.

(DR 148–65/192–214). It takes a shock for this subject to notice that matters are not as self-evident as they seem, and effort to get past the generalities, representations and objects of recognition among which we ordinarily move (DR 139/181–2). In later works on art, Deleuze refers to these as clichés.

Deleuze gets from Husserl the notion that such a subject is built up and comes to have objects of thought (dogmatic or otherwise) through passive synthesis (DR 71–85/97–115).[11] Where Deleuze parts from Husserl is in insisting that the true objects of thought – as well as experience – are singularities rather than typifying structures.[12] Husserl believes that we only encounter singularities in experience; but insofar as it is reflective, truly philosophical/phenomenological thought is different from experience inasmuch as it pursues generalities. According to Deleuze, thinking begins when the self – built up through passive synthesis, beating with a rhythm that makes temporal order and memory possible – ultimately fails to recognise itself in habitual intellectual reactions to an unfamiliar or imperceptible stimulus. This is a *dynamic genesis*.

'It is though the *I* were fractured from one end to the other', Deleuze writes, 'fractured by the pure and empty form of time . . . Time signifies a fault or a fracture in the *I* and a passivity in the self' (DR 86/117). The formulation of a 'problem' allows the self to survive this stressful moment of incongruity, its failure to catch up with its own reaction to the new stimulus. A problem protects as well as probes; it keeps incongruity itself at sufficient distance that *Ideas* can emerge in the crack where the 'I' once believed it was capable of grasping the world as a whole (DR 87–9, 144–5/117–21, 187–9). Such Ideas or solutions, like Kant's Ideas, organise subsequent entities and judgments in a process Deleuze calls actualisation, dramatisation, or *static genesis* (DR 183–4/237–8). They project a new vision of the subject and a new spread of entities or strata with which it can combine. Ultimately, these interactions are manifest in new habits.

Kant took this fracture and this passive self to be two sides of a single transcendental structure of experience. In *Time and Free Will*, Bergson describes a similar incommensurability between the 'crust' of sociable self-understanding and the 'true self', but neither of these selves will be 'true' for Deleuze, for what matters fundamentally is the *productive* difference or inequality between them. For Beauvoir, the false self or the incongruous 'I' is the self that emerges from habits imposed on women in a sexist society, the self women see because it is what men also imagine or hope to see.[13] Beauvoir shows that neither good sense (which associates habits and traits with sexual difference) nor common sense (which gathers the traits associated with masculinity on the side of the subject and consigns those associated with femininity to the object or Other) are compatible with her existence as a thinker, and she repeatedly expresses frustration that far too many people of either sex are content with this stupidity.

In the Introduction to *The Second Sex*, Beauvoir proceeds, through a series of questions, to draw the reader into acknowledging this problem. At this point in her inquiry, the Idea answering to Beauvoir's problem is still undetermined. Moreover, if she succeeds in articulating it, the standpoint from which she poses the problem may cease to exist. The problem is this:

> Every individual concerned with justifying his existence experiences his existence as an indefinite need to transcend himself. But what singularly defines the situation of woman is that being, like all humans, an autonomous freedom, she discovers and chooses herself in a world where men force her to assume herself as Other: an attempt is made to freeze her as an object and doom her to immanence, since her transcendence will be forever transcended by another essential and sovereign consciousness. (SS 16–17/1:31)

Did this problem arise in the way Deleuze describes? Let us briefly examine the structure of the Introduction:[14]

> First, 'Is there a problem? And what is it? Are there even women?' (SS 3/1:11)

In response to this question, as Deleuze warns is usual in Western philosophy, Beauvoir considers searching for a definition, asking: 'What is a woman?' (SS 5/1:13).[15] Specifically, what are the women whose essence is asserted by Platonism and denied by nominalism? But quickly Beauvoir focuses on the situation that provokes this question in the first place. This is a situation in which Beauvoir, unlike men, must consider her sex identity when defining herself: 'woman is the negative, to such a point that any determination is imputed to her as a limitation, without reciprocity' (SS 5/1:14).[16] This reveals that 'to be' a woman is a *situation* mixed with innumerable other people and bodies, organised by sense.

Beauvoir then proposes that this situation should be analysed in terms of the categories of Same and Other, a move she justifies in terms of both Hegel and Lévi-Strauss (SS 6–7/1:16–17).[17]

How, she asks, does the situation of women with respect to men differ from other instances of Same and Other which resulted in reciprocity or at least revolution? (SS 7–8/1:17–18). This question *How does it differ?* resembles the questions like 'Which one?' or 'How much?' that Deleuze finds far more fruitful than the classic 'What is X?'[18] It is also, we might note, a question challenging good sense, inasmuch as it refuses to find analogies between all forms of subordination; and common sense, inasmuch as it overturns the subject position for which such subordination is either natural or historical, but not ambiguously both.

Consulting Kojève's reading of Hegel, Beauvoir distinguishes between those hierarchical situations that had a historical origin (such as colonial domination or slavery) and that are therefore historically reversible, and those which seem to be 'natural' because they do not result from an identifiable event or process.[19] 'As far back as history can be traced, [women] have always been subordinate to men; their dependence is not the consequence of an event or a becoming, it did not *happen*' ('Elle n'est pas arrivée') (SS 8/1:18).

Michel Kail has focused on this curious notion of an event that did not happen historically.[20] Kail suggests that this means Beauvoir refuses a historiography in which signs of womanhood are given as 'natural data'. But she also refuses a historiography in which signs of womanhood *symbolise* and *stabilise* the relationship we expect to find between 'natural' and 'historical' data.[21] For Kail, the notion of 'natural history' is useful because it draws our attention to the way nature is used in historical explanations or narratives to make certain *ways* of writing history seem 'natural'. But reference to nature also leads us to regard the 'historical' dimension as overly ephemeral, when the distinction itself is faulty and both are unthinkable without each other. A 'history-icon' like femininity seems to mark off certain elements of history as impervious to change because they either are too 'natural' or too 'ephemeral' – casting power relations in stone *ahistorically* and discouraging their transformation.[22]

But when Beauvoir protests that women's 'dependence is not the consequence of an event or a becoming', perhaps this means that women's dependence is not something that arose sequentially, but seems to be co-substantial with the kind of *sense* that makes it possible for our society (and perhaps others?) to position itself in time and to make true or false claims about past, present and future. Sense is the way meaning relates to a 'form of life', in

Wittgenstein's use of the phrase. It isolates the slowest and stablest becomings and presents them as beings whose transformation is unusual or impossible. One cannot speak meaningfully of a sequence of events unless sense has already made it possible to distinguish and order them (DR 188–9/244). As an 'event', sense is what links the sequential or chronologically historical with the intemporal or non-sequential. With reference to Lewis Carroll, Deleuze writes: 'When I say "Alice becomes larger", I mean that she becomes larger than she was. By the same token, however, she becomes smaller than she is now' (LS 1/9).

It seems that the reason women are *absolutely* rather than only relatively 'other' is that they were designated as such in a *Mitsein* that has never begun and therefore seems impossible to end (SS 9/1:19) without overturning sense itself in a terrifying delirium. *Mitsein* – or 'being-with' – is a concept from Heidegger's *Being and Time*, pointing to the irreducibly social nature of human ontology, its spatiality, situatedness and historicity.[23] It refers to what Husserl called the 'lifeworld' of shared objects and practices, an aspect of being-in-the-world more generally. In a humanistic reading of phenomenology, such relationships are 'essential' to human nature, stabler even than the processes generating sandstone in a rock formation.[24] Moreover, most men and women, particularly elite women, have no desire to end the reign of this *Mitsein* (SS 663, 755/2:454, 562).

Nevertheless, Beauvoir insists 'How did this story begin?' Now, what are we to make of this odd question, which substitutes a story for an event that 'did not happen'? What is the relationship between event and story? A story has a direction, for one thing, whereas the event of sense goes in every direction at once. How can an event 'begin' or actualise itself with respect to a population, except perhaps by intersecting with another event or process? 'Beginning' can happen when an event or repetition is situated with respect to another process – either one that seems slower and stabler, or one whose rapidity punctuates and cuts up an apparent continuity. Either women's subordination must be posed against the long backdrop of biological evolution, or it must be situated with respect to revolutions, upheavals and surprising new meanings.

Later in the section on 'History' Beauvoir will attempt an answer (SS 88–9/1:131–2), and in the section on 'Myth' she will try to explain why, once begun, the situation seems to endure through time rather than 'outside' of time. For the moment, she notes that all accounts are suspicious because they have been provided by men – and would, therefore, depend on the same sexist 'sense' that Beauvoir herself finds problematic (SS 10–12/1:22–5). Nor does Beauvoir trust 'feminist' accounts because they are, to borrow a Nietzschean concept, 'reactive'; 'very often their attempt to polemicize robs them of all value' (SS 15/1:28). In Deleuze's terms, these narratives, like all stories, are masks at play in a struggle for domination (DR 110/145–6). They present the being 'woman' as more stable than a geological formation, regardless of her capacities for mutation and transformative combination. And herein lies the relation of event to story: Whether put forward by conservative or liberal interests, these masks/stories are responsible for women's having 'become' inferior rather than merely *being* such.

> The scope of the verb *to be* must be understood; bad faith means giving it a substantive value, when in fact it has the sense of the Hegelian dynamic: *to be* is to have become, to have been made as one manifests oneself. Yes, women in general *are* today inferior to men; that is, their situation provides them with fewer possibilities: the question is whether this state of affairs must be perpetuated. (SS 12–13/1:25)

These several pages set up the structure of Beauvoir's two volumes. This event that 'did not happen' appears between the statements and bodies organised by biology, psychology and political economy like a paradoxical element, which Beauvoir glimpses because of the profoundly disregulating effects that it has on women's ability to function in the world.[25] As Eugene Holland might put it, paraphrasing Althusser, this event seems to have 'become-necessary' through a perfect storm of economic and cultural factors although it could never have been predicted.[26] This event is perhaps even more obviously shaped by myths about woman and by literary depictions of female lives and motives, with which the rest of Volume 1 is occupied, than by any overt acts of discrimination.

Volume 2 explains the passive syntheses through which this form of sense is built up in women's *own* lives, at each period in their lives, through contradictory social demands that almost all of them fail to reconcile. They are forced to think or drown. But the goal of this text is to 'counter-actualise' the event which causes such distress – to act out the drama it prescribes in such a way that its meaning changes (LS 149/174–5).[27] This means identifying it *as* a becoming, putting it into a story that reveals all the larger processes from which the elements of 'woman' were selected. To truly counter-actualise the event would require a series of habitual syntheses comparable to those that produce contemporary psychological and cultural 'femininity' and institutions that support 'non-sexist sense' even when individual men and women are adrift.[28] Since such institutions are lacking, Beauvoir uses herself as an example, and, through the rest of the book, experiences from historical writing and literary writing about and by women.[29]

In fact, the account I have given of Deleuze's concept-formation focuses on the constitution of the individual thinker's consciousness. However, the three syntheses of habit in *Difference and Repetition* are also complemented by an account in terms of impersonal faculties that show themselves *through* the passive syntheses and their 'activation' by the unfamiliar stimulus. If the habits from which phenomenological 'selves' or 'consciousnesses' are formed do change, we still need some way to talk about events of thought, desire and perception – about 'lived experiences' that need not be the experience of a conscious subject – and the language of faculties makes this possible. Moreover, in *What is Philosophy?* Deleuze contends that the formulation of concepts is *internal* to philosophy itself and can only be connected with other philosophical events, not situated with respect to them in a causal or linear way (WIP 27–8, 32/31–2, 36).[30]

Thinking, or stumbling into a problem, is a special (singular) kind of event differing from the (ordinary) events that count as solutions to that problem (DR 188–9/244), or, as in *The Logic of Sense*, from the states of affairs and bodies they organise. Thus a true event in thought is not the same as a biographical incident, even an incident in the life of a philosopher. It is an event on a plane of immanence that links singularities, not an event in the immanence tying an individual intentional consciousness to its world. This event *selects* a certain number of becomings in which it finds a certain resonance, while blocking out or minimising all the rest, which loom on the horizon of thought as chaos (WIP 42–3/44–5).

This brings us to Beauvoir's last question in the Introduction: how can *we* (who have been shaped by this event into living female bodies) ask this question, and 'who are we to ask it?' (SS 15/1:29). At this point, Beauvoir invokes the standpoint of 'existentialist morality' (*morale existentialiste*), a doctrine that sounds Sartrean but that most scholars agree did not really exist apart from her own invention; for example, in 'Pyrrhus and Cineas' and *The Ethics of Ambiguity*.[31] I take 'existentialist morality' as Beauvoir's shorthand for the plane of immanence whose emergence from her own pre-personal singularities (and those of others) she has begun to recognise. For the moment, the 'Who are we?' has no simple answer because its object is undergoing decomposition and recomposition.

In *What is Philosophy?* Deleuze and Guattari define the concept as a multiplicity involving philosophical components, conceptual personae and a pre-philosophical plane (WIP 15–18/21–4). The philosophical components, despite their respective histories, have a kind of internal consistency (WIP 19/24–5), mobility and tension.[32] As Deleuze explains further in *Pure Immanence*, the concept also maintains relations of consistency with other non-philosophical fields of knowledge and social life.[33]

Indeed, Beauvoir's concepts come with their own histories and components, such as Sartrean transcendence, Heidegger's *Mitsein*, the 'Other' of Lévi-Strauss and Hegel, and elsewhere in the book, Merleau-Ponty's notion of the body as ambiguous and both biological and historical. But it is a mistake to think that these concepts can play the same role in Beauvoir's philosophy as they played in their 'original' settings. Rather, if Deleuze is right, these concepts have been deterritorialised and 'remixed' for consistency on a new plane. 'The history of philosophy means that we evaluate not only the historical novelty of the concepts created by a philosopher but also the power of their becoming when they pass into one another' (WIP 32/36).

Deutscher contends that some 'clusters' of concepts in *The Second Sex* lead to dead ends and others to open-ended discussions, which we might interpret as their becoming.[34] Instead of saying 'deterritorialising', however, she prefers the term 'converting': 'Changing the substance in addition to the context and sense of concepts – of the resources of German and French philosophers such that the "presence" of their phenomenology is powerfully transformed into the *absence* of Beauvoir's problematic.'[35] Beauvoir's 'conversion' suggests non-dialectical work on the self (EA 12–13/16–18). Indeed, one might think of 'conversion' as a kind of Kierkegaardian repetition. However, while Deleuze would applaud the resistance to dialectics, deterritorialisation is not an interiorising act; indeed it may disrupt the boundaries of the self.

Other philosophers can be present in a work as names for *combinations of concepts* – but may also play the role of *conceptual personae* dramatising the important assumptions, desires and gestures of the concept (WIP 64–7/62–5). This way of being present in someone's thought should not be confused with acting as an *influence;* for it also projects a vision of who one *might be* or *might have been*, the zone of indiscernibility between the author and his or her imaginative doubles.[36]

> The conceptual persona is not the philosopher's representative but, rather, the reverse: the philosopher is only the envelope of his principal conceptual persona and of all the other personae who are the intercessors [*intercesseurs*], the real subjects of his philosophy ... The destiny of the philosopher is to become his conceptual persona or personae, at the same time that these personae become something other than what they are historically, mythologically, or commonly ... (WIP 64/62)

For example, although Beauvoir's thought (and her conception of existentialist morality) certainly owes something to Kierkegaard, in most of *The Second Sex* Kierkegaard is, or is *also*, a conceptual persona dramatising a particular attitude toward women and marriage (SS 203, 269/1:295–6, 387). Sartre also plays multiple functions: he is an element in Beauvoir's *life* from which she sometimes had trouble distinguishing herself; some of his concepts like 'lack-of-being' or 'detotalised totality' are adapted into her own philosophical flight; but Sartre is also a conceptual persona, often disguised, dramatising a point of view, or offering a foil against which her work bounces and launches itself.[37]

Last but not least, the concept refers to a non-philosophical 'plane' that supports this consistency (WIP 40–1/42–4) – what we might call the 'point of view' from which the concept's functioning and relationships make sense.

Transcendence – components of the concept

Let us consider one important example. In her summary of 'existentialist morality', Beauvoir opposes the standpoint of the 'general good' and describes human beings as transcendences (SS 16–17/1:31). Transcendence is one way of translating the complex Hegelian term 'Aufhebung', which means both to cancel out and to preserve something on a higher level. The concept of transcendence has also been responsible for the worst misunderstandings of Beauvoir's philosophy.

In Husserlian phenomenology, transcendence means 'surpassing' to the extent that our intentional orientation toward a given object (say a glass on the table, or the meaning of democracy) is limited by our situational perspective and can always be fulfilled or improved by the addition of more perspectives that correspond to other perceivers or thinkers situated on the other side of the table or the other side of the political spectrum. Moreover, the Other who might actually be sitting across from me is not transparent; I cannot see her back when she faces me, nor can I grasp the whole complex history that makes up her sensibility and her motivation. Each act of reorientation to see (or imagine) my intentional objects in greater detail is a transcendence of what was already given, imagined or synthesised.

While the glass might be an example of a typical universal (barware in general), and the other person might also be grasped that way (bar patron), the Other is obviously also *singular* in a way that ordinary objects are rarely if ever singular. Like me, the Other is so unique that her acts seem to merit description as 'free'. The Other and her glass are both objects of 'transcendence' within the immanence of conscious intentionality, but the Other's inaccessibility seems to blur the horizon of my intentionality altogether.

Transcendence has this phenomenological meaning of *intentionality* in Sartre's *Being and Nothingness* [1943]. Consciousness exists only as consciousness *of something*, a content that may or may not be concrete (as it could also be imaginary). Conversely, it makes no sense to speak of those contents, especially the 'self', *apart from* consciousness. But here consciousness is an ontological kind – being *pour-soi* (for-itself). Consciousness transcends by contrasting the world to Nothingness; thereby it also establishes a difference between being for-itself and being *en-soi* or in-itself (the object of consciousness). Consciousness organises contents of its world and its own self-reflection in relation to the reality and possibility of nothingness, in temporal terms, and consciousness is driven back and forth by anxiety over being identified with these contents and with its own capacity to negate or reinterpret them. But although consciousness is limited by the *facticity* of prior experiences – including awareness of the perception of others – all reflection on selfhood is 'immanent' to consciousness in the sense that motives, habits or values depend upon it for reality. Moreover, all contents of phenomenal experience are immanent to the for-itself's initial differentiation between Being and Nothingness (BN 71, 83).

What it means for Sartrean intentionality to be an originary form of freedom is that it refuses to identify with a self or 'essence' in-itself as if it were an object that could be turned around, grasped from all sides, and summed up in a general concept. Indeed, Sartrean intentionality is *incapable* of doing so except through wilful self-deception (BN 76). In *Being and Nothingness*, Sartre gives as an example of 'bad faith' the gay man who, despite being aware of his desires and acts, would deny he is homosexual in order to avoid voluntarily identifying with this term's meaning for those who are prejudiced (BN 107–9). The man clearly recognises that this label will restrict his ability to see himself as free – as capable of practical and intentional acts that are *new* and go beyond anyone's anticipations. Sexist sense acts in the same way to restrict men's expectations about women's freedom and women's expectations for their own freedom.

Beauvoir argued in *The Ethics of Ambiguity*, however, that the spontaneity of intentionality could be morally valuable insofar, and only insofar, as it is both *chosen* and upheld through the mutual affirmation of others' freedom – their singularity or comparable intentionality (EA 12, 23–4, 67/16, 32–3, 97).[38] From her earliest reported conversations with Sartre, she objected that the spontaneous freedom of consciousness was shaped by the conditions under which people became aware of themselves as individual agents.[39] Thus Beauvoir believes that women, like the gay man described by Sartre, are not so much *guilty* of denying their situation as prevented from transcending it in practical terms or even knowing that there might be an alternative to heterosexism as a system of sense.

Accordingly, Beauvoir defines transcendence by *opposition* to immanence, where Sartre speaks of intentionality as transcendent *within* immanence.[40] An immanent consciousness, for Beauvoir, may engage in spontaneous acts of reflexivity, but does so without grasping these acts or desiring to grasp them as acts of a self separated from others or supporting their freedom. In *Being and Nothingness*, such acts would be considered morally neutral limitations on the *scope* of a freedom whose ability to negate and reinterpret remains intact.[41] Beauvoir, whose goal in *The Ethics of Ambiguity* is to distinguish existentialism from nihilism, finds it morally unacceptable that some individuals should be able to reveal *so much more* of the world and of themselves than others can. But although they are opposed, genuine transcendence never entirely escapes immanence.[42] This ambiguity should not be understood in the sense that one remains partly locked in one's 'head' or one's 'ego', but in that the limits of one's world are always uncertain – transcendence must be *converted* through a deliberate choice of oneself and one's meaning for the sake of the other's freedom.

For Hegel, transcendence also involved the expansion of rationality into ever more aspects of reality, whether driven by the consciousness of philosophers or by the immanent logic of practical activity. He too identified consciousness with freedom. Where Husserlian phenomenology located the infinity of the subject/object relationship in the inexhaustibility of possible perspectives, Hegelian phenomenology located it in the subject's self-relation by way of its object – an increasingly complex object that implies the whole human world and even natural history. This is the aspect of 'transcendence' that Andrea Veltman rightly associates with public or productive work in Beauvoir's text.[43] What is transcended, for Hegel, is a state of partial knowledge or ignorance that results in contradiction. But productive labour also alters one's relationships to others; it exists *for* others and thus has an ontological effect on the worker.

Other people or social plurality were implicit in this self-relation almost from the start, and Hegel considered the possible vicissitudes or contradictions of expanding freedom, political and philosophical, in his *Phenomenology of Spirit* [1807]. While Husserl referred to the Other person in his published work as ambiguously 'analogous' to the self in its expressive behaviour, his phenomenology had a strongly Cartesian, almost solipsistic flavour and his suggestion that subjectivity was intrinsically interpersonal appeared primarily in posthumous writings.[44] Hegel, therefore, offered Sartre and Beauvoir very different ways to incorporate intersubjectivity into their accounts of freedom in the late 1930s; for Sartre as a contradiction in the constitution of immanence and for Beauvoir as a promise of support, an assurance that immanence might have exits.

Behind Sartre, Hegel and Husserl, however, we should also consider the presence of philosophers Beauvoir studied prior to phenomenology, such as Bergson and Leibniz. Although the concept of the 'Other' is credited to Lévi-Strauss in the Introduction to *The Second Sex*, in her student diaries Beauvoir also claimed to be obsessed by the 'problem of the Other'.[45] From Bergson, on whose *Time and Free Will* we have some reading notes, Beauvoir got the theme of a possible conflict between two selves, one 'genuine' and one merely conventional or social, recognisable to others but inhibiting true freedom.[46] She expressed a wish to study Leibniz, not, like Deleuze, because she regards him as the originator of the concept of the Other, but because of his notion of the 'identity of indiscernibles':

> I hate the mechanism that, reducing the quality to the quantity, makes the quality disappear. Likewise, to reduce men to similar but diversely combined tendencies explains nothing; whether the difference be in the combination or in the elements, there is always a given that excludes the identical. That is why I feel myself to be not phenomenon but noumenon; quality is a reflection of noumenon on the plane of experience.[47]

Leibniz, whom Beauvoir helped Sartre and his friends study in 1929 and on whom Beauvoir eventually wrote an undergraduate thesis, famously argued that human concepts could only grasp beings from a limited point of view, by comparing them to other similar beings.[48] God's concepts, however, could grasp them – indeed, create them – in their full individuality. For God, therefore, no two drops of water or blades of grass were identical.[49] The whole of a human being's life – for example, Alexander the Great – was contained in his or her singular concept, and contained the entire world from a unique point of view.[50] Beneath the differences that allowed two beings or points of view to be compared and put in a common category, God could always discover hidden *inner differences* defining that being as singular.[51] Later, Beauvoir recalls trying to construct a 'pluralist morality' whose goal would be 'comprehension of the singular' (MDD 322).

In a journal entry from her youth, Beauvoir wrote apropos of her reluctance to freeze becoming through definitive choices:

> I must bit by bit kill off all but one of these possibilities [*possibles*] in me. This is how I see life: thousands of possibilities [*possibles*] in childhood fall by the wayside bit by bit, and so much so that on the last day there is no longer anything but *one reality*; you have lived *one life*. But it is Bergson's *élan vital* that I am rediscovering here, that which divides, letting go of one tendency after another so that a single one can be realized [*realisé*].[52]

The *élan vital*, often translated as 'vital impetus', is Bergson's term for the intrinsically plural and self-differentiating nature of life. In *Matter and Memory* [1896], Bergson conceived of all reality in these terms: matter, taken as a whole by human thought, homogenised differences in a measurable, extended way while living memory or duration implicated the *one who remembers* in the interpenetration of all cumulative qualitative shifts. Early in his career, Deleuze identified Bergson's *intensive* difference, a difference of *kind* that could only differ 'internally' from itself, with a radical singularity similar to Leibniz's essences.[53] Being atheist, Beauvoir was also aware of how difficult it might be to discover and demonstrate one's singularity without the overlay of others' beliefs and wishes, especially those imposed or adopted from love.

This suggests that what Beauvoir means by 'transcendence' is not surpassing a given which would constrain our choices in a certain direction, but something much closer to *differentiation* or *individuation* in the work of Bergson and Deleuze (and Simondon, on whom the latter sometimes draws).[54] For Bergson, like Leibniz, humans experience freedom when their impulses and tendencies are so unified that they do not feel divided from themselves. Such self-unity, of course, may lead them to diverge from the wishes of others and to lose a shared vision of the future. The stablest tendencies and becomings in our assemblages often conflict with *self-representations* and with the inertia of other assemblages. In other words, one's *actions* are not caused by anyone else, to whom we might be opposed, but neither do they take the form of a choice between two alternatives except in retrospect.[55]

'In short', Bergson writes, 'we are free when our acts spring from our whole personality, when they express it, when they have that indefinable resemblance to it which one sometimes finds between the artist and his work' (TFW 172). Thus both Leibniz and Bergson denied the existence of free will in the sense of arbitrary choice; apparently free acts result from the accumulation of innumerable obscure tendencies and causal chains within a single being: 'minute insensible perceptions' like 'so many little springs trying to unwind and so driving our machine along . . . the choice that we make arises from these insensible stimuli, which . . . make us find one direction of movement more comfortable than the other'.[56] The *petites perceptions*, as Joe Hughes points out, *are* the stuff of individuality.[57] In principle, as Sartre would agree, there is no difference between choosing one's intentional objects and choosing oneself, whether or not the self is identified with consciousness or with pre-personal singularities, although unlike Sartre, Leibniz would never believe a monad could know itself completely.

For Bergson, ignorance of these internal processes – comparable to Leibniz's inner differences – can result in actions that seem unexpected and therefore arbitrary, as when one adopts the opinions of trusted friends without sufficient self-knowledge. Our ordinary understanding of free will as choice results from a misunderstanding of this very common situation:

> Little by little they [the opinions of trusted friends] will form a thick crust which will cover up our own sentiments; we shall believe that we are acting freely, and it is only by looking back to the past, later on, that we shall see how much we were mistaken. But then, at the very minute when the act is going to be performed, *something* may revolt against it. It is the deep-seated self rushing up to the surface. (TFW 169)

'In reality', however, 'there are not two tendencies, or even two directions, but a self which lives and develops by means of its very hesitations, until the free action drops from it like an overripe fruit' (TFW 171, 176). The *conversion* later invoked in *The Ethics of Ambiguity* would refer to the affirmation of this deep-seated self over superficial selves, which also, thereby, differentiates the subject from other people. Concepts can also impose false selves and block access to singularity. Despite this language of truth and falsity, the singularity of the self remains potentially multiple, even for Bergson. Self-unity is not something we can 'choose' by sheer force of will.

In addition to the conceptual components adopted from other thinkers, and in addition to conceptual personae drawn from the history of philosophy, every concept links the practice of philosophy with the parallel fields of art and science, and the work of thinking with the work of *living*. For what is revealed by transcendence is ultimately *a life*, irreplaceable and unexchangeable, whose proper name only a god could know. This life appears *impersonally* when the self built through habit, as Deleuze describes in *Difference and Repetition*, breaks down and fails to recognise itself. But the failure of self-recognition need not imply the failure of individuation.[58] Indeed, in the terms of *Difference and Repetition*, individuation is a phenomenon of *actualisation or dramatisation* taking place after the failure of self-recognition *generates* Ideas and problems.[59] The blur of becomings settles into a new stratification of beings according to their actions and passions. If actualisation is a 'counter-actualisation', it will confirm the transcendence/selectivity of something *in* the thinker as well as something *in* the perplexing event that gave birth to problems.

Many contemporary social accounts of individuation come from English and German sources: liberal, romantic and psychoanalytic in their focus. John Stuart Mill, for example, believes that the development of individual personality is a social good justifying a robust tolerance of nonconformist behaviour.[60] Mill's ideas about individualism and personal liberty overlap with the Hegelian and romantic view that inner personality is and should be reflected in property relations and cultural expression or creativity (as well as the prejudice that individuation is less possible and less valued in non-European cultures). Some psychoanalytic theorists, such as Erikson, regard 'individuation' as the stage of psychological development that follows after group attachment and, in early childhood, narcissistic self-absorption.[61] In much of this literature, individuation and individualism are either expected of men to a greater degree than of women or more highly valued in men than in women. Drawing on liberal and psychoanalytic sources, contemporary feminist legal theorist Drucilla Cornell argues that the basic structure of justice in a liberal society can be evaluated on the basis of its ability to provide 'minimum conditions for individuation' for women as well as men.[62]

From the side of the biological rather than social sciences, Gilbert Simondon argues that individuation is a two-step process.[63] First, during any kind of reproduction, two beings emerge and separate from an initial state of unity or undifferentiatedness. The physical or numerical individuation of each organism takes place through splitting, gestation and postpartum nutrition and interaction with other members of the same species or the environment. This may result in the training and development of specific bodily skills and organs. In humans, individuation is followed by *individualisation*, by which people who more or less resemble each other in superficial respects resolve their problems with the natural and human environment by appealing to cultural habits, language and the play of emotions (IPC 126–33).[64] In this way, the individual's potential for 'interiority' is developed and what Leibniz would have called inner differences may emerge and find expression. Individualisation is unending, although male physical individuation soon comes to an end. Many women, of course, individuate themselves physically from the children they bear, in addition to indefinitely 'individualising' themselves.

The moral drama of Sartre's early work is found not in personal interaction but in the relationship between being and nothingness, freedom and facticity, and self-knowledge and bad faith. But Beauvoir and Merleau-Ponty, who refer to these and similar phenomena as examples of an inescapable 'ambiguity', seem not to share his tragic tone.⁶⁵ It is as if they are less involved with mourning obstacles to self-consistency than in taking the measure of differences from others. The specificity and consistency of 'transcendence' as individuation in relation to these conceptual components and associated fields is borne out when Beauvoir references Merleau-Ponty on biology approvingly and says:

> Woman is not a fixed reality but a becoming; she has to be compared with man in her becoming; that is, her *possibilities* have to be defined . . . the fact is also that when one considers a being who is transcendence and surpassing, it is never possible to close the books. (SS 45–6/1:72)

So when Eva Lundgren-Gothlin writes that 'Beauvoir as well as Sartre maintains that human being makes itself a lack of being and that it is this negating moment, when human being differentiates and separates itself from being as not being it, that being also appears', her focus is the *negating* character of this moment.⁶⁶ My focus is on the no less difficult but *positive* act of differentiation and separation that produces it. 'Existentialist morality' is a matter of the ambiguous being's individuation. Through it, Beauvoir opposes *her* concepts to the concepts that have blocked the singularity of her transcendence – and that of others.

Conceptual personae and the pre-philosophical plane

Interestingly enough, the example Deleuze and Guattari offer to illustrate the components of the concept is *Autrui* or the 'Other person', which many philosophers – including Beauvoir – have reworked over time or used as a fulcrum for turning their predecessors' philosophies in a different direction:

> This concept of the other person [*autrui*] goes back to Leibniz, to his possible worlds and to the monad as expression of the world. But it is not the same problem, because in Leibniz possibles do not exist in the real world . . . In short, we say that every concept always has a *history*, even though this history zigzags, though it passes, if need be, through other problems or onto different planes . . . (WIP 17–18/23)

What about the conceptual personae that 'flesh out' transcendence, and thereby contribute to constructing the plane of 'existentialist morality'? Non-philosopher friends, lovers and even literary characters may serve as conceptual personae, representing examples of a philosophical concept *in situ*. Beauvoir almost modelled the character of Xavière in *She Came to Stay* after Simone Weil (PL 252), but basing her instead on Olga Kosakiewicz, might have ended up making her more like a female caricature of Sartrean spontaneity. Beauvoir's novels gives numerous examples of the kind of transcendence described above: for example, as Simons has suggested, when Françoise finally breaks through her well-socialised self-image in *She Came to Stay* [*L'Invitée*, 1943] and acknowledges her own aggression, she *becomes herself*.[67] In *Les Belles Images* [1966], Laurence risks harming herself with a hunger strike to make sure her husband recognises the depth of her divergence from his point of view; and in *When Things of the Spirit Come First* [*Quand Prime le Spirituel*, 1979], Marguerite is forced to accept that her desire for a bohemian life does not depend on the knowledge or whims of her frustrated brother-in-law, Denis, but originates only in herself.

The individuation or individualisation of a singular *person* is different than the construction of a singular *concept* with its plane, but restrictions on the individualisation of the woman philosopher are justified by the philosophical tradition and make it difficult for her to philosophise without reference to her sex. As Deleuze and Guattari explain it, the first rigid stratification imposed by Oedipal societies involves the theft of women's *becoming* – a fluidity then attributed to sexist sense, so that actual women are stuck in the state of *being* – specifically, being *Other* to the Oedipal subject (TP 276/338–9). This split inhibits the full life of the would-be independent woman – who cannot forget herself, that is, forget the *self that exists for others* and is therefore *herself-as-other*.

This is not to say that gender is the *only* aspect of sense that blocks the individuation and therefore freedom of human beings. But it's a major example, and one that affects men's freedom – their capacity to become – as well as women's (ibid.). This is why Deleuze and Guattari say that men, no less than women, must become-women – they do not want men to 'steal' becomings specific to women, or to repeat such a theft once committed, but to restore the becomings whose loss made female 'specificity' into a trap rather than a human being's zone of interaction with the rest of her environment. Individuation is particularly difficult for women because of pregnancy, as will be discussed in the next chapter, but the meaning of old age in contemporary societies poses similar obstacles. Above all, we must note that these factors that obscure and even prevent singularity from developing are *bodily*, not just conscious or conceptual.

In *The Ethics of Ambiguity*, women's social status and colonial oppression are both offered as examples of obstacles to morally significant freedom challenging Sartre's theory of freedom as sheer spontaneity (EA 38/54–5; SS 765/2:576). Indeed, according to Beauvoir's memoirs, this argument with Sartre, which took the woman in a harem as its chief conceptual persona, had been going on for many years (PL 346, 434).[68] This suggests to me that Leibniz's indiscernibles and Bergson's qualitative multiplicity are important components of Beauvoir's concepts, but also that *The Second Sex* needs to be approached as a study of a *particular institution or form of sense* that inhibits the singularity and diversity of women's qualitative becoming(s).[69] It also suggests to me that the colonised, especially colonised women, were among the important conceptual personae for Beauvoir's philosophical development, along with figures such as the complicitous bourgeois woman, the woman destroyed by her adherence to feminine norms, the (more or less successful) independent woman, and the man – whether Sade, Sartre or characters from her novels like Gerbert and Fosca – who exhibits traditionally 'feminine' traits or identifies with women.

While the concept is dramatised through conceptual personae (Descartes's ordinary man, Bergson's runner), and describes a plane of immanence on which its components are related consistently (Kant's universalism, his acceptance of modern mechanism, his obsession with freedom as resistance), the concept is also related to a 'pre-philosophical plane' which one might imagine as comparable to the reserve of sounds or samples from which a particular musical arrangement is composed (WIP 40–1/43–4). Instead of conceptual personae, the pre-philosophical plane is inhabited by symbolic 'figures' and is often structured hierarchically or through analogy. Although one can imagine 'secular' examples of the pre-philosophical plane from which philosophy then begins to create consistency, what comes to mind are the Buddhist mandala or the Great Chain of Being. Figures would include the sage, the trickster, the prophet or saviour. (Perhaps 'the Eternal Feminine' is a pre-philosophical figure for Beauvoir, and 'Man' is one that, according to later anti-humanists, might persist in her thought.) The pre-philosophical plane could also include background beliefs about the world that animate a philosopher psychologically, the foundational metaphors analysed by social scientists like George Lakoff or Hans Blumenberg.[70]

Certainly Catholicism formed part of the pre-philosophical plane from which Beauvoir's thought emerged. Although she soon became atheist, her interest in social justice was nurtured in the Catholic *Équipes Sociales* and she never entirely abandoned the ideal of 'service' (which one imagines was a powerful reason for her admiration and even envy of Simone Weil). Simons has suggested that Beauvoir had psychological tendencies to 'solaltrism' or compulsive devotion to others,[71] but she was far more individualist than the environment in which she was raised. Moreover, Beauvoir's student diaries suggest that debates over religion with her professor Mlle Mercier, who wanted her to remain Catholic, were among the emotionally wrenching crucibles in which her atheism became a scene of loss as well as possibility.[72] This is not to say that Beauvoir's atheism was 'really' Catholic but that her atheism and her (former) Catholicism are *both* elements of the milieu into which she dips when creating concepts.[73]

The value of egalitarianism, which Beauvoir may have adopted from Catholicism but also (to her father's dismay) from the republican ideology of Third Republic France, is unquestioned even when Beauvoir distances herself from specific radical movements. Likewise, the idealism of a thinker like Léon Brunschvicg was part of the environment against which she and her entire generation of thinkers reacted; years later, Beauvoir complained that *The Second Sex* was still too idealist.[74] This means that the residue of idealism – along with some indefinite will to place her work under the sign of the concrete and the material – were aspects of the pre-philosophical plane. And finally, as I have argued elsewhere, the fear of anonymity – which sometimes took the form of a fear of death, but also a passionate defence of singularity against the tyranny of universals – is part of the psychological backdrop against which her thought developed.

What were some of the other concepts that occupied the plane of so-called 'existentialist morality'? Different commentators have argued that Beauvoir's contribution to philosophy and feminist theory consists in the concept of the 'social Other', 'ambiguity', 'oppression', and, despite Moi's objections, 'gender'. But since the *problem* that orients philosophical work is a multiplicity, it is not surprising that the concept, insofar as it has managed to change our way of relating to the world of actualised entities, is also multiple.[75] Remember, moreover, that even if the *names* for these concepts are used by previous thinkers (who contributed components), there is no reason to believe that

Beauvoir's use of 'transcendence' is the same as someone else's, from whom she is presumed to have 'taken' it in an 'unoriginal' act of 'being influenced'.[76] According to Deleuze, the creation of concepts is a relatively rare event, but the *names* for these concepts might be even rarer!

In *A Thousand Plateaus*, Deleuze and Guattari use the term 'machinic phylum' to indicate a flow – a flow of underground ore, of printed material arriving in the mail, of water in a fountain – which combines with other flows (of mining companies, of smelting heat, of readerly attention, of thirsty cells) giving rise to encounters of longer or shorter duration (TP 406–10/507–10). The concept of phylum is part of Deleuze and Guattari's effort to replace Aristotelian hylomorphism, whereby numerically distinct 'things' are matter pressed into some specific 'form', with continuous modulation of becomings and protracted encounters that may have the stability of 'things' to an observer, but less in the sense of an object on the table than in the sense that a current in the ocean or the trade winds have so much stability that mariners can count on their power when navigating. Deterritorialising a concept means removing it from one stratum and using it as an element in another, the way glass can be found among the sand on the beach and then set into a metal frame in order to make an artwork, or iron melted out of the rock and recast as part of the scaffold for a building. Concepts are their own phylum in the practice of philosophy.

There are unquestionably moments when it is impossible to tell whether Beauvoir's use of a concept 'truly' differs from that of Sartre or Heidegger. One might say that Beauvoir's becoming encompasses a becoming-Sartre, a becoming-Hegel, a becoming-Heidegger or Merleau-Ponty. It is also equally clear that the Sartre Beauvoir becomes is not 'everyone's' Sartre, even though she might have wanted to present herself as his 'chief interpreter'. (Beauvoir was deeply disconcerted by Sartre's becoming-Benny Lévy, and was not about to follow suit.)[77] Beauvoir's Hegel is strongly influenced by Jean Wahl and Alexandre Kojève; this is not everyone's way of becoming-Hegel – almost certainly not *Hegel's* way of becoming-Hegel. Those who seek to legitimate Beauvoir as a philosopher by identifying her esteemed precursors or who seek to delegitimate Beauvoir by reducing her philosophy to literature or to her biographical relationships make an error in how they understand both philosophy and *life*. As mentioned, a *life* is not a *chronology*, in which events happen once, have discrete effects and fail to continue happening. Often the most powerful loves and hates in early life are simply blurred sketches – 'obscure and confused', as Leibniz might say – for overmastering events to which the self formed by passive synthesis is not yet equal and which it has not yet been able to formulate in *problems*.

Thus we can see Beauvoir's claustrophobic mother, her adored friend Zaza, her teacher Mlle Mercier, Sartre himself or Olga Kosakiewicz, even the war – not as *causal factors* driving Beauvoir's later work in certain directions, but the first inklings of underground tremors that were eventually to find their proper form – or the best form she could muster – in a certain shape of thought.[78] In the existential psychology of *Being and Nothingness*, Sartre claims that every life is driven by an 'original' choice (BN 598–9). In a larger sense, this choice is always between striving to coincide with being or to acknowledge one's *lack of being*; in the narrower sense, this choice is a matter of *what* to be or *how* to manifest one's lack of being, and against what image of the self, in the eyes of which others, as Genet defined his lack of being through and against his first acts of theft.[79] For Bergson, as mentioned above, a truly free choice is neither arbitrary nor binary but results from the combination of innumerable micro-tendencies that constitute, whether one knows it or not, the actual movement of one's own becoming. But we may not be aware for quite some time which tendencies are our own or in which direction they are pushing us; and it is difficult to say that the event *precedes* its effects; rather it emerges *through* them.[80] If we are to counteractualise certain events, it is crucial to wait until they take a form in which we can meet them halfway.

Beauvoir is often criticised for having an overly 'phallic' notion of freedom; in a world where women must often transgress simply to be themselves, transcendence is imagined as the transgression of norms – where freedom, as for Sartre, is conceived as a 'project'.[81] In fact, although she does not stress her differences from Sartre, Beauvoir's intent is not to stage a contest of wills.[82] Although it takes immense effort to discover who one is, apart from those one loves or hates, this is not the work of the pole-vaulter or soldier on the front lines. For in this vision, there is no common horizon; if we are vaulting, we do so in different dimensions. This is in fact the source of extreme difficulty, for it may be necessary to remain in contact with those against whom one would otherwise define oneself. Difference so easily turns into opposition, as Deleuze complains with respect to the dogmatic image of thought.

Differentiation as conversion is Beauvoir's effort to resist that dialectical tendency. The plane passes *through* those dimensions: its consistency is not the consistency of a common sense, good sense or public space.

Sometimes, far from resulting from energetic effort, the plane is only discovered through *loss*, as when Marguerite is abandoned by Denis (in *When Things of the Spirit*), or when, as Michèle Le Dœuff describes, men discover their own philosophical voice because they are *disappointed* by a beloved teacher.[83] In philosophy or in life, individuation never fails to affect the other persons and entities with which one interacts. For this reason, one can think of loss as a kind of encounter – if only a 'missed' or 'faulty' encounter. How long does it take to decide that things aren't working? Certainly work goes on during that time. In Beauvoir's memoirs, like her literature, we see repeated examples of the *time* it takes to *learn* how to immerse oneself and then detach – from oneself, from lovers, from philosophical views, from cities, from nature.[84] Deleuze writes:

> Learning to swim or learning a foreign language means composing the singular points of one's own body or one's own language with those of another shape or element, which tears us apart but also propels us into a hitherto unknown and un-heard of world of problems. (DR 192/248)

How does the singularity of a life relate to the singularity of a plane of immanence? In other words, as Beauvoir put it, 'who are we' to ask the question of how 'sexist sense' first emerged? 'Men are judge and party: so are women. Can an angel be found?' (SS 15/1:29). Are there any becomings stable enough to be a point of view that would be neither male nor female? No, the problem – and the solution – lie in the fact that *not all members* of those grouped as *women* are affected in the same way: 'Many women today, fortunate to have had all the privileges of the human being restored to them, can afford the luxury of impartiality' (SS 15/1:29). On the one hand, 'we' are professional women like Beauvoir herself, who are able to identify with those suffering from discrimination. Yet Beauvoir goes on to argue that things are not equal even for professional women. Likewise, the desire for lucidity seems to be a qualification, even if it appears against the background of a practical desire for change – but only a paragraph later, Beauvoir is already challenging the terms on which desire and change have hitherto been envisioned, staking the project on 'existentialist morality'. In this way, the Idea-object of the problem begins to have effects on actuality, even the thinker's own actuality, although it remains veiled.

In this case, it is possible that despite a proclaimed 'vocation' for happiness (PL 27–8) Beauvoir did discover her singularity, implicitly, through involuntary separation or loss of others – by *surviving*, as Marguerite survives Denis's betrayal in *Things of the Spirit*, as Fosca refines his values after witnessing the passing of generations (in *All Men are Mortal* [*Tous les Hommes Sont Mortels*, 1946]), or Anne builds a reason to live on and after the enormous losses of the war (in *The Mandarins* [*Les Mandarins*, 1954]). Loss unblocks singularity by destroying the old concept of the self-as-an-assemblage, along with the stability of the entities to which that concept referred. The loss of Zaza, and then for a time, both Sartre and Olga at once – gave her permission or might have made it obligatory to live the life Zaza 'should' have lived; and after the trio, in particular, something in Beauvoir was confident that she would never lack for things to say (PL 478–9).

Notes

1. Moi, *What is a Woman?*, 177–245.
2. Moi, *What is a Woman?*, 10–20.
3. To achieve this goal, Moi draws not just on Austin and Wittgenstein but also on more recent exponents of the ordinary language tradition, such as Stanley Cavell and Lorraine Code. For Deleuze's take on false problems, see DR 207–8/268–9.
4. Moi, *What is a Woman?*, 30–83.
5. Bauer, *Simone de Beauvoir, Philosophy, and Feminism*, 7.
6. Bauer, *Simone de Beauvoir, Philosophy, and Feminism*, 24–5.
7. Hughes, *Deleuze's Difference and Repetition*, 1–3.
8. See also Bergson, *Creative Evolution*, 55: 'The idea that for a new object we might have to create a new concept, perhaps a new method of thinking, is deeply repugnant to us. The history of philosophy is there, however, and shows us the eternal conflict of systems, the impossibility of satisfactorily getting the real into the ready-made garments of our ready-made concepts, the necessity of making to measure.'
9. In *Difference and Repetition*, problems are the objects of Ideas, and 'concepts' are generated as a result of the actualisation or 'dramatisation' of Ideas. Thus Deleuze's focus is really on the creation of

Ideas, not concepts. In *What is Philosophy*, the 'concept' is described in terms that closely resemble the Idea in *Difference and Repetition*. I am relying primarily on that version. See Peden, *Spinoza Contra Phenomenology*, 242–6; and Smith, 'Dialectics', particularly p. 108.
10. Hughes, *Deleuze's Difference and Repetition*, 112–13. The concept of Problem in *Difference and Repetition* comes from Albert Lautman (Peden, *Spinoza Contra Phenomenology*, 241–5). Deleuze's Problem/Idea complex responds to Martial Gueroult, for whom every philosophy is a system/Idea – philosophy never leaves itself or has anything to do with an extra-philosophical 'experience' – as well as to Ferdinand Alquié, for whom such Ideas are never exhaustible and for whom this inexhaustibility *is* an experience (ibid., 193).
11. See Husserl, *Ideas II*, 289–90, for a discussion of the synthesis of the personal ego and its relationship to the synthesis of the transcendental ego.
12. In *A Thousand Plateaus*, Deleuze and Guattari speak positively of Husserl's acknowledgement that some essences were 'vague' – empirically singular and resisting simple capture in a *noema* with the form of a universal (TP 407–8/507–8). See Lawlor, 'The End of Phenomenology', 19.
13. Significantly, it is also what other *women* expect to see. This is a topic I explore elsewhere.
14. In 'Beauvoir's Minoritarian Philosophy', Secomb proposes that Beauvoir's main concept is 'becoming-incarnate'. Her discussion focuses primarily on the plane of immanence, the reterritorialisation of others' concepts, and the image of the philosopher in Beauvoir's work.
15. On questions versus problems, see DR 188/243–4; on the choice of good questions, see also *Nietzsche and Philosophy*, 75–9.
16. In fact, it was Sartre who asked, when she was about to begin her memoir, whether she should not consider how being a woman had affected her life. See *Force of Circumstance* (FC), 94–5. As we will see, not even *noticing* the problem counts as an example of immanence.
17. On the Hegelian aspect, see in particular Lundgren-Gothlin, *Sex and Existence*; on Lévi-Strauss, see Direk, 'Immanence and Abjection in Simone de Beauvoir'. Deutscher points out that these two thinkers may be incompatible sources but shows Beauvoir's desire to cut across disciplines rather than an incoherence (*Ambiguity, Conversion, Resistance*).
18. Deleuze, *Nietzsche and Philosophy*, 75–7. Spinoza, of course, would say that each individual body is composite, and so too is every situation – defined by the relative speeds and slownesses of its components, their unique capacities for action and passion. Spinoza, *Ethics*, Part 2, Proposition 13, pp. 71–6; Deleuze, *Spinoza*, 123–4.
19. Kojève, *Introduction to the Reading of Hegel*.

20. Kail, *Simone de Beauvoir Philosophe*, 138–9.
21. Kail, *Simone de Beauvoir Philosophe*, 149–53.
22. Kail, *Simone de Beauvoir Philosophe*, 151–3.
23. Heidegger, *Being and Time*, 149–63. For discussion of *Mitsein* in Beauvoir, see Lundgren-Gothlin, 'Reading Simone de Beauvoir with Martin Heidegger', 56–63; and Bauer, 'Beauvoir's Heideggerian Ontology'.
24. See chapter 3 of Deleuze and Guattari, *A Thousand Plateaus* ('10,000 B.C.: The Geology of Morals'), for an attempt to reformulate the classic Aristotelian concepts of matter and form in terms of selection, sedimentation and stratification using examples from geology, biology and linguistics (TP 39–74/53–94). The subject of passive synthesis, for example, could be understood as an accretion or formation of a stratum so slowly changing as to seem like a 'being' opposed to becoming – like a snowball thrown in a snowstorm, tangibly dense and vulnerable to melting at a slower rate than the falling flakes. For other examples in context, see Lorraine, *Deleuze and Guattari's Immanent Ethics*, 33–8.
25. Peden credits the idea of experience resulting from two non-communicating series to Spinoza; whether these are Thought and Extension, the infinite and the finite, or Aion and Chronos (*Spinoza Contra Phenomenology*, 225–7). 'For Deleuze, an event, what *happens*, is always qua event incorporeal in itself, much in the way that Heidegger's concept of being effectively *as* time can never be correlated to a discrete corporeal entity. Deleuze's claim is that the irreducibility of *sense* in language to the materiality of its component parts is homologous to the irreducibility of an *event* in existence to the corporeal substance in which it occurs' (ibid., 226).
26. Holland, 'Non-Linear Historical Materialism'. See more extensive discussion in Chapter 6. This line of inquiry has been developed in a remarkable forthcoming article on Beauvoir's debt to Lévi-Strauss by Eva Bahovec ('Between Structuralism and Aleatory Materialism').
27. For an alternate application of this kind of strategy, see Luce Irigaray's use of 'mimesis' in *Speculum of the Other Woman*.
28. Having identified the (problematic) Idea that links two series, whether sense and bodies or the two repetitions involved in selfhood, and having articulated or 'differentiated' (*différentié*) all its components, Deleuze proposes that this Idea can be 'differenciated' (*différenciée*) to produce a series of local solutions or actualisations that relate to one another in a global way (DR 209–10/270–1).
29. Moi, *What is a Woman?*, 227–37; Bauer, *Simone de Beauvoir, Philosophy, and Feminism*, 44, 47.
30. See note 10 above. This feature of Deleuze's thought is Spinozist and mediated by Martial Gueroult, for whom the reality of philosophy takes place purely in philosophy, although he is a pluralist

about the number of philosophical realities or Ideas. Gueroult represents one demand for a 'philosophy of the concept' as opposed to a 'philosophy of consciousness' and lived experience, and thus a philosophical tradition resistant to phenomenology (Peden, *Spinoza Contra Phenomenology*, 60, 71, 79).

31. Beauvoir, 'Pyrrhus and Cineas' (PC); *The Ethics of Ambiguity* (EA) [*Pour une morale de l'ambiguïté*]. See for example, Deutscher, *Ambiguity, Conversion, Resistance*, 7–8; Le Dœuff, *Hipparchia's Choice*, 89–90. For Deleuze, the connotation of 'morality' differs from 'ethics' in significant ways, proposing what 'should' be done rather than what 'might' be done; it is not clear that the distinction has such importance for Beauvoir.
32. For a detailed analysis of the concept, see Mader, *Sleights of Reason*. The concept of 'multiplicity' employed by Deleuze, allowing him to declare all concepts multiplicities, comes from Riemann and is then taken up by both Husserl and Bergson (DR 182/236).
33. Deleuze, *Pure Immanence*, 29–30.
34. Deutscher, *Ambiguity, Conversion, Resistance*, 192.
35. Deutscher, *Ambiguity, Conversion, Resistance*, 14–18.
36. 'A thinker may have perspectives that exceed or even conflict with the perspective she may have as a consolidated personal self with a recognisable character or set of beliefs' (Lorraine, *Deleuze and Guattari's Immanent Ethics*, 23).
37. Schwarzer, *After The Second Sex*, 57–8; Pilardi, *Writing the Self*, 103–4.
38. For an extended treatment, see Parker, 'Singularity in Beauvoir's *The Ethics of Ambiguity*', to which I am much indebted. Earlier analyses which focus on the distinction between moral and metaphysical freedom in *Ethics of Ambiguity* include Arp, *The Bonds of Freedom*, and Kruks, 'Teaching Sartre About Freedom'.
39. PL 346, 434; see also Kruks, 'Teaching Sartre About Freedom'. Debra Bergoffen contends that all of Beauvoir's works are written in two 'voices'; one using the Sartrean language of transcendence and the project, the other speaking about eroticism and generosity or risk (Bergoffen, *Gendered Phenomenologies*, 6–7).
40. According to Andrea Veltman, Beauvoir tends to associate transcendence with work and other activities that are temporally futural, engage the actor in a larger world and leave self-justifying results; while immanent activities are non-productive, maintain life and repeat rather than mark progress in time (Veltman, 'Transcendence and Immanence', 115, 120–1).
41. What seems morally dubious (if unavoidable) is *bad faith*, the temptation to identify one's freedom with some *thing* in the world and particularly the 'self', whether disclosed by reflection or through interaction with others. Beauvoir's *immanence* has some

connotations of bad faith as described in *Being and Nothingness*, but also some connotations of Beauvoir's 'mirage of the Other' (*'mirage de l'Autre'*) – attribution of one's own states to others – described formally by Sartre in *Transcendence of the Ego* (78–9) and autobiographically by Beauvoir in *Memoirs* and *Prime of Life* (MDD 114; PL 86, 141–3, 207–9, 269–70, 272).

42. Commentators who believe Beauvoir is 'masculinist' in various Sartrean ways tend to read *The Second Sex* and its concepts of 'transcendence' and 'immanence' independently of *The Ethics of Ambiguity*; those who think she carves a new path tend to assume that the concept of ambiguity remains relevant even in *The Second Sex*.
43. Veltman, 'Transcendence and Immanence', 120–1. I would argue that productive work 'manifests' the invisible singularity of the worker or slave. In terms of *Difference and Repetition*, it is the 'manifest' or general repetition (particularity) that conceals and expresses the 'latent' or singular repetition (singularity). See Hughes, *Deleuze's Difference and Repetition*, 26–7.
44. See Welton, *The Other Husserl*, 148–56, 236.
45. Beauvoir, *Diary of a Philosophy Student*, 58–61, see also PL 86.
46. Beauvoir, *Diary of a Philosophy Student*, 60; Bergson, *Time and Free Will* (TFW), 169. Some of these ideas about alterity are also found in Beauvoir, 'Notes for a Novel', 327–78.
47. Beauvoir, *Diary of a Philosophy Student*, 279.
48. At that time, Beauvoir was writing a thesis on 'The Concept in Leibniz' under the direction of Brunschvicg (MDD 266).
49. See Leibniz and Clarke, *Correspondence*, Fifth Letter, §23, pp. 40–1.
50. Leibniz, *Discourse on Metaphysics*, 13–14. On singularities in Leibniz, see Hughes, *Deleuze's Difference and Repetition*, 42–5. According to Sylvie Le Bon de Beauvoir, Beauvoir once recounted a longstanding fantasy that 'her singular existence, with all its frivolous incidents and the incomparable taste of mortal instants' was captured on a giant tape recorder (Allen, 'Response to a Letter from Peg Simons', 119).
51. Leibniz, *Monadology*, §8–16, pp. 252–4.
52. Beauvoir, *Diary of a Philosophy Student*, 246–7; Bergson, *Creative Evolution*, 57–60, 97–8. Discussed in Simons, 'Beauvoir's Early Philosophy', 196. On possibilities, see Hughes, *Deleuze's Difference and Repetition*, 12–14.
53. Deleuze, 'Bergson's Conception of Difference'.
54. In *The Ethics of Ambiguity*, Beauvoir distinguishes between a Hegelian understanding of 'surpassing' which optimistically incorporates its negative moment, and her vision, which preserves the negative. 'There are thus two ways to surpass the given: taking a trip is something quite different from escaping from prison', for the latter involves a decisive rejection of the given, as well as the affirmation of alternate

possibilities (EA 84/121, translation modified). I interpret this to mean that all 'transcendence' must involve *difficulty* and further define the actor's becoming in relation to his or her given.
55. As one might imagine, there is a complex dialogue with Bergson in Sartre's philosophy as well. For Sartre, Bergson is the philosopher who most problematically identifies consciousness with the self, an 'interpenetrative multiplicity' comprising many blurring motives and tendencies (Sartre, TE 85; BN 81, 161–2). There are two main principles behind Sartre's opposition: first, consciousness must be *pure*, translucent, and therefore qualitatively unified in any intentional act (intentionality cannot be 'ambivalent'); second, temporal *continuity*, including the apparent continuity of actions, external phenomena and consciousness, depends on the temporalising of an intentionality that is *spontaneous* and does not 'endure' rather than the reverse (BN 192–1, 204–9). Enduring is said of the world and of the objects of consciousness, including the self – but not of consciousness. For Bergson, duration is primary, and temporal as well as spatial distinctions are provisional abstractions introduced by 'intelligence'.
56. Leibniz, *New Essays*, 53–7, 165–6, 188. See Smith, 'Dialectics', 184, 395, n. 25.
57. Hughes, *Deleuze's Difference and Repetition*, 45–6.
58. 'The singularities and the events that constitute *a* life coexist with the accidents of *the* life that corresponds to it, but they are neither grouped nor divided in the same way . . . The indefinite article is the indetermination of the person only because it is determination of the singular' (Deleuze, *Pure Immanence*, 29–30); see also *A Thousand Plateaus* (TP) 261/318–20.
59. Hughes explains how Ideas 'set' or 'block' the concepts in giving them their 'sense' (Hughes, *Deleuze's Difference and Repetition*, 34–8). The blockage of a concept is different from the blocked process of becoming or individuation. Women's becoming is set/blocked at the level of 'sexist sense' by men as well as women who share their *Mitsein* and choose or see no alternative to unfreedom.
60. Mill, *On Liberty*, 69–83.
61. There are many psychoanalytic accounts of separation and individuation, most of which focus on mother–child interaction. In classical Freudian theory, the father represents the real or symbolic third party in relation to whom the child's attention, enjoyment and identification are divided, creating internal ambivalence as well as a desire to master the symbolic world above and beyond his or her bodily needs. Freud addresses the relation between bodily boundaries and ego boundaries in *The Ego and the Id*, the loss of separation in *Group Psychology and Ego Analysis*; Lacan explains the process through his division between the imaginary and symbolic registers of

social being. For a discussion of Erikson from a feminist perspective, see Franz and White, 'Individuation and Attachment in Personality Development'.
62. When explaining her feminist standard for reproductive rights legislation – in this case, insurance coverage for pregnant employees in the United States – Cornell contends that Beauvoir anticipated the difficulty of accepting and incorporating sexual difference prior to all assessments of equal treatment: 'Simone de Beauvoir argued this point when she insisted that a woman is defined as man's other and that as so defined she will be always evaluated as both inferior and not individuated' (Cornell, *The Imaginary Domain*, 63–4). However, Cornell goes on to criticise Beauvoir for failing to 'symbolize the difference of the feminine except within a relational concept of difference'; that is, limiting women's difference(s) from men to their bodily capacities.
63. Simondon, *L'Individuation Psychique et Collective* (IPC).
64. This will be discussed further in Chapter 4.
65. In her review of Merleau-Ponty's *Phenomenology of Perception*, Beauvoir begins by critiquing formal education for trying, albeit unsuccessfully, to replace a child's sense of his or her presence in the world with a universal perspective. 'In spite of ethics, every man knows a mysterious intimacy with a unique existence that is precisely his own and, in spite of science, every man sees with his eyes' (Beauvoir, 'A Review of *The Phenomenology of Perception*', 159). This establishes the importance of individuation. She also praises the book for recognising that 'it is in giving myself to the world that I realize myself, and it is in assuming myself that I have a hold on the world' – rather than, perhaps, by negating the world and detaching from oneself? (160). For consciousness is not 'a pure for-itself, or to use Hegel's phrase, later used by Sartre, a hole in being, but rather "a hollow, a fold that has been made and can be unmade"' (163). Finally, Merleau-Ponty 'suggests that we embrace the very movement of life that is belief in the things of this world and in our own presence' (164). The positive value placed on continuity and flexibility in these phrases is unmistakeable.
66. Lundgren-Gothlin, 'Reading Simone de Beauvoir', 50.
67. Simons, 'Bergson's Influence on Beauvoir's Philosophical Methodology', 126–7; see also PL 269–70.
68. Bergoffen believes the 'harem' was a signature problem guiding Beauvoir's reflection on women's freedom over the years (Bergoffen, *Gendered Phenomenologies*, 37–8).
69. In *Difference and Repetition*, Deleuze proposes that there can be social, as well as linguistic and scientific problems such as ideology (DR 206–8/266–9).

70. Lakoff, *Moral Politics*, and Blumenberg, *Paradigms for a Metaphorology*.
71. Simons, 'Beauvoir's Early Philosophy', 232–3.
72. Simons, 'Beauvoir's Early Philosophy', 211–12, 220–1.
73. Talal Asad points out that secularism is always defined with respect to a given religion; there is no 'secular' in general. See Asad, *Formations of the Secular*, 26–37.
74. Beauvoir, *Force of Circumstance* (FC), 192. Beauvoir, like Sartre and Nizan, detested the neo-Kantian Brunschvicg as an example of a philosophical spiritualism and 'idealism' whose long-term effects on her thinking she deplored. Nizan's *The Watchdogs* excoriated him as representing the ideological function of French higher education in philosophy; Holveck hypothesises that Beauvoir's *When Things of the Spirit Come First* was written as a literary refutation of his philosophy by demonstrating its inability to account for female experience (Holveck, *Philosophy of Lived Experience* 45–6, also 51–3).

    Interestingly, Brunschvicg was an 'elder statesman' for most of the rationalist historians of philosophy and philosophers of science, starting with Jean Cavaillès, who positioned themselves against the new discourse of phenomenology during WWII and led to the approaches called structuralism and post-structuralism, among which Althusser and Deleuze figured. See Peden, *Spinoza Contra Phenomenology*, 32.
75. On Ideas as multiplicities, see DR 182, 186–7/236, 240–2; also TP 32–3/45–6. All Ideas, as multiplicities, coexist virtually.
76. For years, Beauvoir was assumed to be merely 'applying' Sartre's views. The main text revising this assessment from a historical standpoint was Fullbrook and Fullbrook, *Remaking of a Twentieth Century Legend*; more recently, Daigle and Golomb, *The Riddle of Influence*.
77. Cohen-Solal, *Sartre: A Life*, 513–16.
78. Zaza (Elizabeth Lacoin) was Beauvoir's closest friend during adolescence and her training in philosophy. Dynamic, independent and strong-willed, she was nonetheless deeply attached to her bourgeois family; she died around the time that Beauvoir became independent from her own family. Beauvoir describes her relationship with her mother and her friendship with Zaza in *Memoirs of a Dutiful Daughter*. Beauvoir's brief 'trio' with Sartre and Olga Kosakiewicz, a student and long-lasting friend, is described in *Prime of Life*.
79. Sartre's existential interpretation of the playwright Jean Genet's life can be found in *Saint Genet*.
80. See above on Bergson and Leibniz.
81. See, for example, McCall, 'Simone de Beauvoir, "The Second Sex", and Jean-Paul Sartre'; Hartsock, *Money, Sex, and Power*, 287–91;

Lloyd, *The Man of Reason*, 101–2; Grosz, *Volatile Bodies*, 15; Léon, 'Eunuch or Male?'; Chanter, *Ethics of Eros*, 49–50. More examples can be found in Jo-Ann Pilardi, 'Feminists Read *The Second Sex*', 32–4.
82. Pilardi, *Writing the Self*, 102.
83. Le Dœuff, *Philosophical Imaginary*, 107. Beauvoir acknowledges that failure, insofar as it manifests the resistance of the given, can also be an instance of disclosure (EA 81/118).
84. One example would be Beauvoir's reassessment of her naïve nominalism where Jewish identity was concerned, as well as the more controversial case of her effort to produce a 'subversive' radio show for the Vichy government. See Miranda Fricker, 'Life-story in Beauvoir's Memoirs'; Simons, 'Beauvoir and the Problem of Racism'; see also Deleuze, DR 164–5/213–15 on learning.

Chapter 3

Lived Experience

In the Introduction to *The Second Sex*, Beauvoir concludes her reflection on whether male–female relations might or might not resemble various historical examples of Hegel's master-slave dialectic with the observation that 'The division of the sexes is a biological given, not a moment in human history. Their opposition took shape within an original *Mitsein*, and she has not broken it' (SS 9/1:19).

Heidegger would be loath to identify *Mitsein* with a biological given, which seems at first to be the drift of Beauvoir's phrasing. 'Being with one another', Heidegger writes, 'is based proximally and often exclusively upon what is a matter of common concern in such Being.'[1] In fact, the place of the biological body in Heidegger is almost as obscure as the place of being-with, which he generally regards as a distraction from authentic engagement with the activity of existing. But Beauvoir is not suggesting that the *Mitsein* is biological, or *contrasting* biological division with historical division; rather biology (like history) is *also* experienced by human beings within their social form.[2]

> A society is not a species: the species realizes itself as existence in a society; it transcends itself toward the world and the future; its customs cannot be deduced from biology ... It is not as a body but as a body subjected to taboos and laws that the subject gains consciousness of and accomplishes himself. (SS 47/1:75)

Our habits of being-with contribute just as much to the production of sense and emerge from this production as do our private experiences. In Volume 2 of *The Second Sex*, Beauvoir describes concrete situations in which sexist sense produces subjects and objects of immanence; that is, behaviours and experiences corresponding to an unnecessarily and unjustly blocked individuation. This is the form that *Mitsein* takes for men and women in the society of her time – still far too often in our time. There is no reason to believe Beauvoir wants *no Mitsein*; but *Mitsein* should not require women's self-abnegation to function.

Difference and Repetition does not discuss *Mitsein* or similar structures in much detail. One might say it focuses on the dynamic and static syntheses of individual thought; but more to the point, it focuses on the *pre-individual* components of individual and social events rather than on psychological *personalities* and the *meanings* that they attribute to experience. In his writings with Guattari, Deleuze suggests that the very distinction between 'individual' and 'social' is somewhat misguided since *all of them* are assemblages reflecting desires and are best described as such. *Mitsein* would be an assemblage of a peculiar sort – one that seems to be intemporal human nature, although it is made of our everyday practices.

Like Bergson, Deleuze and Guattari believe that thinking and living always *begin from the middle* of a complex, confused multiplicity of becomings, some of which have been identified as *beings* (for example, by habit and representation) because of their stability.[3] Most of the Ideas/concepts Deleuze discusses in *Difference and Repetition* can apply to groups as well as they apply to solitary individuals; moreover, insofar as an Idea (or concept) is a *multiplicity*, it is also a point of becoming through which multiple *subjects* can pass – and find their relations reorganised. Here *Mitsein* is the 'middle' from which we must begin – and it is *in the middle* of other impersonal, but affectively and cognitively significant encounters. In this chapter, however, we will approach habits of interaction between the sexes from the standpoint of 'individual' consciousness.

Consciousness and habit

Throughout his career, as mentioned in the last chapter, Deleuze praised Sartre for proposing that consciousness was a pure field rather than a 'personal' subject. What this means is that consciousness is primarily unreflective consciousness 'of objects', and only secondarily reflection on the phenomenon of consciousness or on its individuality and identity. The consciousness that becomes a (secondary) object of reflection (and thus appears to us as a 'self') is certainly not the *cause* of unreflective consciousness – a view

Sartre attributes to both Kant and Bergson.[4] Sartre's approach was compatible with Deleuze's claim that pure consciousness had the character of a fundamental, pre-personal, or even bodily 'contraction' – a passive synthesis, even though Sartre himself seems to have thought of it as highly energetic and active. However, it seems clear that this consciousness, while pre-personal, corresponds to the boundaries of fully formed individuals.[5] Husserl himself only took up the issue of individuation later in his career.[6]

Sartrean consciousness is always absorbed in sense. In other words, the object of consciousness is not 'neutral' with respect to meaning; it is 'Peter-having-to-be-helped', dinner-to-be-made, and not inert perceptual data (TE 56). But sense, as we have learned, always 'blocks' concepts – sets them in relation to one another, limits their fluidity, and these concepts in turn freeze becoming and singularity at a certain level of generality. If consciousness, after reflecting, takes itself for a personal ego, this is because that ego has a meaning interwoven with the meaning of all other acts and objects in the social world.

In *Being and Nothingness*, this rigidity is ultimately a matter of bad faith or the refusal to accept one's own freedom *along with* facticity, but the Other's expectations can certainly contribute. Insofar as a singular consciousness is seen as a distinct self, it desires to be the *cause* of its intentional acts, rather than a *response* to the world and others. But such consciousness is not differentiated from others except when another person imposes an alien meaning (or sense) on phenomena in a context of conflict. If consciousness is identified with the self, its freedom gets caught in the game of eluding objectification (and simplification) by the intentionality of others. Sartre might say it is a misfortune that the phenomenological subject feels the *need* to individuate.

In *Prime of Life*, Beauvoir makes an ambiguous remark referring to her continued belief in the 'transcendental ego' as well as the self-as-intentional-object (PL 292). Since Sartre believed no 'transcendental ego' was necessary to explain the unity and spontaneity of intentional consciousness, one might surmise that she was trying to say that she believed in Sartre's *critique of* the transcendental ego. But given Beauvoir's proximity to Merleau-Ponty's phenomenology, it might be that she simply attributed to Sartre Husserl's later clarification that the transcendental ego actually implied and involved other egos whose coexistence supported the intentional acts of individuals: in short, that it was a fundamentally intersubjective ego (which can still take the individual ego with its *facticity* as an object).⁷ Either way, Beauvoir's thought about transcendence is distinguished from Sartre's by disclosures that, unless blocked, are continual (ideally mutual) acts of differentiation and individuation from others. Beauvoir seems to believe the individuation of consciousness is more interesting and problematic than does Sartre.

Why? First, the 'mirage of the Other' (MDD 114, PL 86). In *Transcendence of the Ego*, Sartre argues that consciousness allows itself to be controlled through its secondary, reflective image: the ego (TE 78–9, 82).⁸ One could compare to Lacan's well-known concept of alienation in the mirror image, which (like *Transcendence*) was first made public in 1936.⁹ In *Memoirs of a Dutiful Daughter* and *Prime of Life*, Beauvoir discusses alienation in the perspective of others – such as Zaza, Sartre, or Sartre's friend 'Camille' (PL 62–5). Sartre seems to think that pure consciousness knows when its meaning and world are threatened by others, but Beauvoir seems to think that consciousness easily can fall into the trap of identification with the meanings offered by others unless it has some way of differentiating its experience from theirs. This would be a differentiation marked in the 'ego'. In fact, two impersonal consciousnesses can share the same world and objects/meanings and differ only in the emotional tone of their respective intentionality, as when one partner is relieved by a breakup and another is heartbroken.

Second, unlike Sartre, Beauvoir seems to believe that people actually *help* one another by apprehending them as meanings, particularly as moral meanings, rather than as mere obstacles or objects. They do not steal the world from one another; recognition gives and *confirms* each person's right to have a world. In Lacanian terms, it is when the parent confirms whatever the child identifies with in the mirror that the child knows he or she is onto something good. This is a notion that Beauvoir does not develop until *The Second Sex*, where she explicitly refers to Lacan (SS 284/2:15).¹⁰ However, in both 'Pyrrhus and Cineas' and in *The Ethics of Ambiguity*, Beauvoir agrees with Sartre that we should regard the ego or 'reflected consciousness' as secondary to impersonal consciousness – not so much because it is an illusion or risks a 'mirage' as because focusing on the ego as a *transcendent object* and wishing to make it the *transcendental cause* of our consciousness and action blinds us to the rest of the objects and meanings in our world. Indeed, trying to *be* this ego disclosed in reflection rather than trying to *disclose* other things, including other persons, makes it impossible for us to discover the ego's own concretely differentiating contours.

In two unpublished chapters of her first successful novel, *She Came to Stay*, Beauvoir describes a girl's transition from 1) solitary, impersonal consciousness of the world, to 2) intentional consciousness that involves a self-conscious dimension but has no concrete notion of differences from others, to 3) intentional consciousness that involves a reflective moment but also sees others as sufficiently different not to be 'bewitched' by identification with their impersonal consciousnesses.[11] Although the chapters were abandoned, Beauvoir tells this story very successfully in a loose rendering of her own childhood, her absorption in the perspective, interests and opinions of her friend Zaza (the most significant object of her intentional consciousness) and finally her effort to create an 'ego' object that would be able to stand alongside Zaza in her own consciousness.[12]

Again, this is a small but significant difference of emphasis within a common framework: while Sartre believes that consciousness detaches from its objects (some of whom are Other) in reflection, Beauvoir suggests that consciousness differentiates itself from them by *creating* an ego and an Other. In short, although the field of consciousness is impersonal, Sartre seems very sure when he is encountering consciousness of/as an Other. Moreover, he either does not believe his perspective on the world can be shared with others or it does not interest him to the extent that Zaza's perspective, for example, enthralled and frustrated Beauvoir – or, in the finished version of *She Came to Stay*, Xavière's perspective enthralled both Françoise and Pierre. Perhaps Sartrean consciousness does not *notice* relations with others unless they are combative?[13] 'The essence of the relations between consciousnesses is not the *Mitsein*;' he famously declares (paraphrasing the same passage of Hegel that opens *She Came to Stay*), 'it is conflict' (BN 555).

Beauvoir does not go so far as to say that the impersonal consciousness known as Sartre was shaped by a series of contractions and syntheses that are characteristic of male habits. What she does is to show how the contractions and syntheses that produce the consciousness of women in various situations tends to *prevent* them from exploring or recognising their differences from others or moving forward to the formation of problems when they fail to recognise themselves in the third synthesis. 'It is difficult for men to measure the enormous extent of social discrimination that seems insignificant from the outside and whose moral and intellectual repercussions are so deep in woman that they appear to spring from an original nature' (SS 14/1:28). The pre-personal synchronisation of one's habits with those of others does not attract Sartre's attention the way clear-cut oppositions do; what Beauvoir realises is that for many women, the most important synchronisations prevent clear-cut oppositions between self and other from appearing at all.

As mentioned in the last chapter, Deleuze's 'dynamic genesis' of representation consists of three 'passive syntheses' – which means that they are syntheses that *produce* subjects of experience rather than products of an active, synthetic consciousness (DR 71–85/96–115). The first synthesis is the 'contraction' of a habit within matter, an originary activity that defines its own time (one might compare it to the time of a breath, or an attention span that only lasts so long). The second synthesis relates two contractions to one another, producing a *memory* far below consciousness (having done it a few times, the body expects to breathe again; although distracted, my attention retains a trace of my previous focus in moving to a new object) (DR 79–85/108–15). The third synthesis tries to 'contract' multiple syntheses in a unity, matching up the form of the second synthesis – one version of time – with the form of the first – another version of time. But it fails to relate these two series in an image of a complete event (other habits are always interfering, my awareness is always distracted by new material). Deleuze refers to the third synthesis as a 'failed act of recognition', a 'fractured I' ['je félé'] continually distended in time and subjected to time (DR 88, 144–5/119–20, 187–90).

However, as also noted in the last chapter, this quasi-phenomenological account of the creation of concepts (and the genesis of representation) is complemented with an *impersonal* account in which *faculties* rather than selves develop and shape one another in response to unexpected and traumatic sensations. Passive synthesis is *provoked* by the encounter between matter and a stimulus – an imperceptible chemical, for example, in the environment of an embryo or an organism – but the resulting contractions can also be understood as the actualization of a virtual Idea by means of 'faculties' (DR 139–45/181–90). This is Deleuze's variation on Kant and the Kantianism that remained implicit in phenomenology's focus on conscious subjectivity. Indeed, Deleuze thinks of the *Critique of Judgment* as a genetic account of the faculties discussed in Kant's other major works. The topography of faculties, in whose rivalry and collaboration individual personal subjects may feel themselves implicated (for example in aesthetic judgment) replaces the landscape of individual experience.

In *Anti-Oedipus*, Deleuze and Guattari revisit the three passive syntheses using the language of desiring-machines. A first synthesis connects, in order to enable both a flow of libido and a cut in (some other) flow. Repetition, which invariably interrupts or complicates some other repetition, makes a primitive machine. A second synthesis, which corresponds to memory in *Difference and Repetition*, organises primitive machines using binary distinctions; mind and body, city and country, child and adult – ultimately, male and female are part of this system of divisions. One can only be either one or the other. A third synthesis, again, has to do with recognition – but while *Difference and Repetition* specifically targeted recognition as an element of the dogmatic image of thought, one which inhibited the future-orientation of problematisation, in *Anti-Oedipus* recognition is positive but ephemeral. Moreover, it tends to be an *impersonal*, passive recognition that *forms* a momentary subject rather than active self-appropriation.

'So that's what it was!' ['C'était donc ça!'] a machine jubilates (AO 20/27), thereby moving into the subject position for a second – and implying, moreover, that until just then it had *misrecognised* whatever it was. However, the organisation of binary distinctions we call 'Oedipus' tends to prevent us from being recognised at any moment when we don't fit a certain model of personality, behaviour or sociability – when we are, in short, 'becoming' something else or engaging in too much 'becoming' rather than 'being'. 'Oedipalisation' refers to the habits inculcated by European and European-settler societies that train the ego to conform to a certain kind of sense.[14] Such habits take either the body or meaning and language for their target. Like all singular entities, men and women emerge through repetition. Identification as female involves a subject in a particular Oedipalising trajectory, and the opposition between 'male' and 'female', which had a practical (and somewhat fluid) significance in less technological societies becomes a site for subjective interpretation in capitalism.

Are these syntheses elements only of the 'philosopher's' experience as it lurches toward thought? It would seem that everyone is capable of creating concepts (or of being the site where such concepts emerge), but we would be participating in a dogmatic image of thought to assume that everyone wants to think, or that bad will and stupidity are infrequent obstacles (DR 131, 148–53/171–2, 200–1). In fact, even philosophers tend to take refuge in representation – other people's solutions to problems they should have solved themselves. In his later work, Husserl argued that a science like mathematics was only possible if something like writing made it possible to hand down complex conceptual objects and operations from one generation to the next, so that each generation might share in the *same* meanings and problems as the last and contribute to their solutions.[15] He also proposed that philosophical and scientific reflection emerged from a 'lifeworld' of *unreflective* practices that were collective as well as individual.[16] For Heidegger, language itself, meaning etymology and usage, contained the tradition of meanings relevant to the lifeworld that Husserl primarily studied with respect to the history of sciences.[17]

It is not just mathematicians or philosophers who live in the solutions to problems others have posed. For example, in taking a yoga class one practises the habits and poses – the passive syntheses that managed to produce past states of consciousness – for the sake of present enlightenment. The body continually fails to recognise itself in these new time spans, but such a failure is only an example of 'bad will' or stupidity if we are unable to identify these lapses as problems – problems leading someplace new rather than back to a prior breath or distraction. Likewise, many bodies have the capacity to think, but only under the right conditions of challenge and support.

In the sections titled 'Formative Years' and 'Situation', Beauvoir does her best to describe whole *worlds* of interpersonal habits that 'feminise' girls and women. She begins 'in the middle' of lives shot through with potentials for transformation, differentiation and reaffiliation. Each type of 'femininity', each contraction and failed recognition, presents opportunities for transcendence and for complex mutual definition in terms of other humans, institutions, thoughts and nature. That her examples are drawn primarily from the white-majority cultures of Western Europe and North America (particularly France, though she quotes many Russian authors, probably due to their strong immigrant presence in Paris during the interwar years) does not mean that comparable analyses could not be done for other groups around the world.

Unfortunately, most women, like most men, experience this as a world of beings and institutions that are largely fixed and unchanging. These types and behaviours are all *actualisations* of an Idea of gender and society, a solution to someone's problem or to the problematisation of a collective. 'The problem of woman has always been a problem of men' (SS 148/1:216) and it has also offered men a *solution* to some of their problems (SS 212–13/1:309–10). These habits are also potential examples of 'seriousness', 'complicity' or 'oppression'. As such, they are not simply individual, but go to define individuals.

Varieties of immanence

In *Creative Evolution* [1907], Bergson proposes that a parasitic wasp and the caterpillar in which it lays its eggs are not distinct except from the external observer's point of view. They form a single system of repeated activity; wasp paralysing caterpillar and laying eggs that hatch and use it for food – a continuum so seamless for the creatures involved that the wasp seems to 'know' exactly where on the caterpillar's body to inject its venom.[18] Although Beauvoir never uses such a hostile metaphor for relations between men and women, the *Mitsein* is exactly this sort of seamless flow of habits that can be, but rarely is, broken up into individual components any more than someone listening to a symphony consciously focuses on this or that instrument. The player in the symphony knows when he or she is playing an instrument, but this instrument is part of a *whole production of sound* and the player may not be able to *hear* her own instrument separately from the whole. This immersion in a qualitative multiplicity involving the actions and fantasies of others is immanence; transcendence means testing every once in a while to make sure one's horn or violin is still producing sound and capable of producing a sound that differs from the rest, whether or not one wishes to be disruptive.[19]

Beauvoir describes two kinds of immanence in the Introduction to *The Second Sex*: *oppression* and *complicity*. As part of her explanation of the standpoint from which she is writing, 'existentialist morality', Beauvoir claims that

> every time transcendence lapses into immanence, there is degradation of existence into 'in-itself,' of freedom into facticity; this fall is a moral fault if the subject consents to it; if this fall is inflicted on the subject, it takes the form of frustration and oppression; in both cases it is an absolute evil. (SS 16/1:31)

In *The Ethics of Ambiguity*, Beauvoir had already noted white women's capacity for 'seriousness' in adhering to the views of their families and particularly men, which made them sometimes 'harder, more bitter, and even more furious or cruel than their masters' (EA 37–8/69–70). In *The Second Sex*, she argues that women's lack of experience in creating social systems leads them to blindly valorise those that exist:

> they seek to compensate for their inaction by the force of the feelings they display ... power creates the law since the laws they recognize in men come from their power; that is why they are the first to throw themselves at the victors' feet when a group collapses. (SS 642/2:427)

On the other hand, she insists that breaking away from social norms requires women to have some opportunity, resources and education. The sheer spontaneity of intentionality cannot count as morally meaningful freedom if its scope is artificially restricted.

> A freedom wills itself genuinely only by willing itself as an indefinite movement through the freedom of others ... A freedom which is interested only in denying freedom must be denied ... I am oppressed if I am thrown into prison, but not if I am kept from throwing my neighbor into prison. (EA 90–1/131)

The Second Sex describes obstacles to women's opportunities, resources and education in great detail. For example, far too many women are discouraged or forbidden to explore or travel alone and lack (successful) lessons in employing violence (SS 749/2:556). Poverty or the threat of poverty, thus economic limits, add to limits of direct compulsion or control, whether posed by men in their private or public capacities. But she also notes that, particularly for privileged women, oppressors rarely find such complicity among their victims as men do among heterosexual women (SS 10, 754/1:21, 2:561).

According to *Being and Nothingness*, someone who identifies exclusively with either the spontaneous intentionality of pure consciousness or with the 'facticity' of phenomena, including the ego that is discerned through reflection, is in 'bad faith' because both elements are fundamental to human ontology. The world, its meanings and the self do not 'exist' as such except as intentional objects. Sartre gives several famous examples of bad faith. One of these, a woman who allows her date to touch her arm but does not immediately accept or reject the possibility of his interest in further sexual contact, has been devastatingly critiqued by Michèle Le Dœuff and Toril Moi (BN 96–8). Not only is it unclear that the woman is *denying* rather than *postponing* her implication in a possible sexual scene, it is Sartre himself who believes the meaning of certain gestures on a date (whether talking or touching) is given in advance, rather than being constituted again and again as intentional meanings (if the woman is a philosopher, she might be responding sexually by continuing both the touching and the conversation!).

Beauvoir rarely uses the term 'bad faith' to indicate resistance to ambiguity but frequently uses 'seriousness' when inherited names and values are taken for static existence or 'being'.[20] The term is taken from Kierkegaard and, for Beauvoir as for Sartre, means resting content with a universally or externally comprehensible performance of one's religious vocation, rather than seeking an internal and singular trajectory. Immanence, like seriousness, captures a free, unique existent within the uniformity of a belief or a practice shared with others. Beauvoir refers to this as 'making oneself a thing' – but Bauer translates this as a 'massive disincentive for me to make these objects and concepts *my own*'.[21] The serious person abdicates the uniqueness of his or her own becoming to perpetuate a 'being' that can be universally recognised; in this way he or she also freezes the becomings of those to whom he or she is similar or interchangeable. This is a moral fault because 'every subject . . . accomplishes its freedom only by perpetual surpassing toward other freedoms' (SS 16/1:31).

Many women achieve vicarious individuation through the trials and accomplishments of their menfolk, whose performance is enhanced by their supportive presence. In the Introduction, Beauvoir focuses on women's lack of mutual bonds, shut up in the houses of men from varying races, religions and classes (SS 8, 149/1:19, 217–18). For this reason, she fails to note that many of the bonds constraining women's individuation are bonds among women; particularly mothers and daughters, mothers- and daughters-in-law, female employers and their domestic servants, religious models and pious women. But these examples come forward in Volume 2, particularly when she describes how women's lack of opportunities for individuation create competition and jealousy with daughters (SS 295, 631–2/2:28, 413–14).

Universals represent blockages of becoming. For example, Kantian principles evade the reality of ambiguity. Beings that are identified through universals, unlike becomings, must not only fit the definition but are also substitutable and therefore endangered by one another.

> The mother's attitude toward her grown daughter is very ambivalent; she seeks a god in her son; in her daughter, she finds a double ... A woman who took pride in being the Wife and the Mother in an exemplary and unique way will refuse no less fiercely to give up her throne ... (SS 631/2:413–14)

Likewise,

> The prostitute who trades on her generality has competition; but if there is enough work for everyone, they feel solidarity, even with their disputes. The hetaera who seeks to 'distinguish' herself is a priori hostile to the one who, like her, lusts for a privileged place. (SS 616/2:396)

Beauvoir also provides numerous examples of how women lack opportunities for individuation or refuse to take them up, usually from fear of losing others who give sense to their egos or from narcissism; in other words, unwillingness to disclose anything other than their own ego and its supporting meanings. The stultifying family environments described in *When Things of the Spirit Come First*, or Françoise's insistence on sharing Pierre's point of view in *She Came to Stay*, can only lead to anxious and aggressive affects.

In *The Mandarins*, Anne tries to respect her daughter Nadine's freedom, as well as Nadine's enormous grief after her lover was murdered by the Nazis. But Nadine cannot use or *find* her freedom and repeatedly plays the role of predefined *being* in relation to a series of men and vengeful acts. Her sense of individuation depended more on her mother and on her deceased lover than anyone had realised. In *Les Belles Images*, Laurence knows that she finds her social milieu shallow but does not know how to choose anything else. Laurence's mother has built her career through men on whose affection she is dependent. She is no model for freedom. In the end, defending their daughters' independence gives both Anne and Laurence a vehicle for their own self-exploration – a truly utopian image. The worst cases, obviously, are the women like Denise (in *The Blood of Others*), Paule (in *The Mandarins*), or Monique (in *The Woman Destroyed*) who go mad when the lovers, husbands or families on whom they relied for a point of view on the world depart.

One of Beauvoir's interesting observations in both the sections on 'History' and 'Lived Experience' from *The Second Sex* is that except for unusual moments in European history, such as the end of the *ancien régime*, rich women may have more resources and education but not necessarily more opportunities to seize and explore their freedom. Although they are obviously oppressed in the sense of being vulnerable, working women and poorer women have the chance to meet and interact with a wide variety of people and situations (barring, of course, those of the elite), which shapes their self-understanding in crucial ways (SS 114–15, 126/1:168–9, 182–3). Women of any class whose interaction is curtailed for reasons of religion or ability, or who are required to spend most of their time in a small family setting, are unable to 'become' in multiple unpredictable directions. It takes experimentation and loss to discover whose habits it is empowering to share and whose habits stifle or render one's individuality invisible. Rich women may have the resources to explore and to protect themselves against vulnerability if they end up in danger or conflict, but they also have the least incentive to be bold (SS 130, 663/2:188, 454).[22]

It may seem odd that Beauvoir puts 'The Lesbian' in the section on 'Formative Years', as if it were a developmental phase, while 'Maturity to Old Age' is found in the section on 'Situation', as if it were a relationship like motherhood, marriage or friendship and social life. Perhaps she meant to identify lesbianism as *progress*, in many women's lives, toward satisfying sexual relationships after their unavoidable but often traumatic 'sexual initiation' by men; perhaps she saw it as an 'alternative' development and commitment emerging from the homosexual sensuality she suggests most girls share. At the time she was writing, lesbianism marked and continues in most parts of the world to mark a profound break with the 'Oedipal' way of composing a female personality. To choose eroticism with women, even at brief moments in one's life, runs against male *and* female social expectations in a profoundly individuating way.

Beauvoir is careful to detach lesbianism from pathology and from the psychological or moral preference for activity or passivity in life and in love. Some women might prefer men to women 'were the equality of the sexes concretely realized'; but certainly not all: 'most lesbians, on the contrary, seek to claim the treasures of their femininity' (SS 423, 428/2:177, 183). And, although some identify with masculine habits, 'The truth is that for most couples caresses are reciprocal ... They can love each other as equals. Because her partners are counterparts, all combinations, transpositions, exchanges, and scenarios are possible' (SS 432/2:187).

Although some lesbian feminists tried to apply Beauvoir's categories of complicity and authenticity to bisexual women, I think Beauvoir's point is that the very existence of lesbianism proves other formations of psyche and society are possible.[23] 'The lesbian' is not a being, defined by a universal; she constitutes multiple *ways* of being, better yet ways of *becoming*, as Sarah Ahmed has argued, that can be found in many environments.[24] Exclusive or non-exclusive, whether for emotional or physical reasons, a *tendency* to desire other women does not in any way dictate what relationships or culture between those women will look like. Lesbianism may allow women to preserve their individually idiosyncratic desires and to develop practices of reciprocity that are closer to authentic humanity than most hetero couples ever experience. And certainly, in terms of responses to a failed synthesis of recognition, 'so *that's* what it was!' is an anti-Oedipal moment with which many queer and lesbian women resonate.[25]

She does not dwell on this point, but implicit in Beauvoir's whole analysis is the observation that many lesbians are not only *able* but also *obliged* to individuate themselves through regular interaction with the commercial and public world. This is because they are far less likely to be able to rely on male support within a family structure for their basic existence. But insofar as lesbians regard themselves as female – implicitly defined with respect to men in a heterosexist society – they are required to adopt 'affects' or to produce 'affects' in themselves associated with immanence (SS 424–5/2:179–80). Thus lesbians struggle with 'sexist sense' differently than heterosexual women do, although they also indicate the possibility of remaining 'women' in many different senses and combining that sexual and emotional diversity with independence.

To be sure, not everyone may identify with such an abstract portrait of lesbian desire: 'Caresses are meant less to appropriate the other than to recreate oneself slowly through her; separation is eliminated, there is neither fight nor victory nor defeat; each one is both subject and object, sovereign and slave in exact reciprocity' (SS 429/2:184). But, since Beauvoir also acknowledges the potential for ruthlessness in such relationships, the point is that lesbianism contains elements for an ideal *human* sexuality, male as well as female. Ordinarily, complicity would involve seeing this incongruity and refusing to act on it, rather than acknowledging that whatever one does will have the character of an experiment. Here, however, Beauvoir's comment that 'this duality is complicity' seems to imply no criticism (ibid.).

Lesbianism, in other words, holds out a hope that the binary divisions through which society organises and understands its own collective habits *can be changed and multiplied* through a different form of sense, although 'contracting new habits' will, doubtless, initially lead to a synthesis of 'failed recognition'. In 'The Independent Woman' Beauvoir insists against anti-feminists that women's dependence on men is not the only possible expression of sexual difference and that the disappearance of this dependence will not lead to the disappearance of desire.

> Let us beware lest our lack of imagination depopulate [*dépeuple*] the future; the future is only an abstraction for us; each of us secretly laments the absence in it of what he was [*de ce que fut lui*]; but tomorrow's humankind will live the future in its flesh and in its freedom; that future will be its present, and humankind will in turn prefer it; new carnal and affective relations of which we cannot conceive will be born between the sexes; friendships, rivalries, complicities, chaste or sexual companionships that past centuries would not have dreamed of are already appearing. (SS 765/2:575, translation modified)

In a world where women are free, there will be *more* varieties of sexual expression and relationship than are currently available – or than people are currently willing to acknowledge they already practise.

Maternity

Here I want to pause and discuss how individuation is furthered or blocked with respect to two sets of constitutive habits in women's 'Lived Experience': maternity and work. In maternity, women's bodies are literally sites for self-differentiation. Pregnant women are faced with an existential crisis that no man can ever know: 'which one is me?'[26] Pregnancy is a relationship with oneself, with another emerging being, and with the whole biological phylum in which form is never stable and individuality obviously a changing process. As Rosalyn Diprose has argued in the context of debates over surrogacy, the woman who bears a child is a different woman than the woman who became pregnant; in her a different set of tendencies has become stable with respect to the surrounding world.[27] At the same time, she has neither become her child nor has she become 'one' with the species or all other mothers and women; indeed, *both* mother and child are selected in a singular way from their field of potentials.

Beauvoir insists repeatedly that human biology is an object and condition of human meaning, not a given (SS 45, 48, 524, 753/1:72, 76; 2:290, 560). Her discussion of sexual biology focuses on the opportunities for individuation open to different kinds of organisms (SS 31–7/1:51–9). This section shows the influence of Bergson's *Creative Evolution;* but Beauvoir goes beyond in applying its insights to humans. Insofar as men and women are grouped as 'beings' by sex, their potential complexity as becomings is ignored or restricted. Beauvoir undeniably regards reproductive biology as a perceived and real obstacle to women's transcendence. But transcendence is a manifestation of the human being's *freedom* or unique ability to postpone and select from divergent actions rather than remaining 'enmeshed' in habit and matter, even the habitual behaviours of material self-organisation we find in organic life. In 'The Psychoanalytic Point of View', Beauvoir protests against reducing accounts of an individual's symptoms to his or her *past* rather than considering the *aims* toward which he or she strives or tends (SS 60/1:92) – why would she not apply this Bergsonian insight to the realm of biology as well?

What we discover is that individuation and/as *freedom* are more complex for females who must decide whether and how to radically renegotiate the boundaries of their *bodies*, not just their values or projects (SS 38–43/1:61–7). This is why pregnancy should be philosophically interesting to all humans, not just to women:

> Separation into new and individualized forces is brought about by male initiative; he can affirm himself in his autonomy; he integrates the specific energy [that is, the energy of the species] into his own life; by contrast, female individuality is fought by the interest of the species; she seems possessed by outside forces: alienated ... Woman, the most individualized of females, is also the most fragile, the one who experiences her destiny the most dramatically and who distinguishes herself the most significantly from her male. (SS 38/1:61)

In one of her most infamous lines, Beauvoir claims that for hunter-gatherer societies, 'it is not in giving life, but in risking his life that man raises himself above the animal; this is why throughout humanity superiority has been granted not to the sex that gives birth but to the one that kills' (SS 74/1:111). According to Beauvoir, men differentiate and determine themselves by risking their lives in battle or the hunt. Women, to her apparent chagrin, do not participate in this kind of stylised self-differentiation.[28] Even when men do not witness women's struggle to define themselves despite – and in relation to – biological generation, women bear witness to male differentiation.

This is one of many places where Beauvoir draws on Hegel's struggle for recognition between self-consciousnesses to explain relations between men and women.[29] This section of the *Phenomenology of Spirit* became immensely important for the French thinkers of Beauvoir's generation and after because of the idiosyncratic reading of Alexandre Kojève. The struggle for recognition is a way of visualising how self-consciousness gains a content and defines itself through something other than *mere* self-consciousness. The relationship between two self-consciousnesses which are otherwise identical is framed first in terms of 'life' – but if self-consciousness is willing to distinguish itself by *risking* its life, this can only succeed (for a time) if another self-consciousness is willing to distinguish itself by some other activity. The less combative, second self-consciousness plays the slave in relation to a master, working the master's property under the threat of death and thereby turning it into an expression of his or her individuality.

The biological aspect of childbearing is not 'work' in the sense of a conscious expression of individuality; 'to give birth and to breast-feed are not *activities* but natural functions; they do not involve a project' (SS 73/1:110).[30] Of course, pregnancy may threaten a woman's life, be enforced under pain of death, and be claimed as service by some man who considers himself the family's master (SS 42/1:67). Although childbearing, as Angela Davis points out, was *part* of the dehumanising and fully productive labour imposed on slave women in the American south, caring for their own family members was the only African American labour that could be described as *escaping* alienation in any way.[31] However, even if it ends in abortion or miscarriage, pregnancy is unquestionably a process of differentiation and individuation. This process, however, does not result in the clear opposition between living, embodied self-consciousnesses that we find in Hegel – the kind of opposition that, as Deleuze protests, has come to stand for *all* differentiation in the Western tradition (DR 44–5, 49/61–5, 69–70).

If Deleuze protests against the reduction of all difference to *contradiction*, Beauvoir protests against the reduction of all differentiation between humans to one or another form of interpersonal *struggle*. In other words, 'mother' and 'fighter' are gender-specific *beings* that oversimplify and perniciously 'represent' the variety of becomings shared by individual men and women who differ *with* and *from* one another. In a society fixated on struggle, where differentiation seems to require 'recognition', women's differentiation is blocked by social fixation on their potential for motherhood, which is conceived as a uniform state of *being* rather than a difficult condition of modulation, separation and transformation. This alienation was only more extreme for women whose reproduction as well as labour were the literal property of others.

Beauvoir generally describes motherhood in terms of relationships.[32] The crises and achievements of pregnancy result from a mother's capacity to preserve or enhance her distinctness from those around her – or the meanings and fantasies they have vested in universals like 'life' and 'motherhood'. Pregnancy is certainly 'transcendent' in the sense that it disrupts a woman's sense of herself as a fixed being in fixed relationships with herself, her social circle and family, and her potential children. But the *Mitsein* women currently share with men requires them to define and differentiate themselves vicariously through the achievements of partners or children. Too often, older mothers and doctors enforce a narrative and system of habits surrounding 'normal' pregnancy with which it is very difficult to experiment. Too often, new mothers deny that their children's fates must be as separate as their bodies were once physiologically interdependent (SS 556–7/2:326–7).

In short, fertile women's struggle to differentiate is doubly blocked. Like men, they accept that recognition is the essence of differentiated relationship and that struggle is the paradigm of recognition. But a second obstacle to transcendence appears in the form of the cliché that mothers are 'prey to the species' and disinclined to struggle. This is a form of the ideology identifying women with care, relationality and peacemaking rather than conflict or competition. It also seems to reflect a misapplication to human women of the biologist's observation that the female of non-human species 'does not usually seek to affirm her individuality; she does not oppose either males or females; she does not have a fighting instinct' (SS 36/1:58).[33]

This ideology is embodied or actualised in the *habits* of idealised motherhood and childrearing in modern industrial societies, which are often repetitive and do not lend themselves to expressing the mother's evolving sense of her destiny and the destiny of her child as distinct becomings.[34] Maternal biological and caretaking roles can be transcendent when they emerge from specific *activities*. But these roles are doomed to seriousness and immanence if they result from the desire to achieve a state of being. The ideology identifying women as 'naturally' maternal, devoted and *uninterested* in recognition makes the female desire for individuation, if not for overt recognition, seem pathological and forces it into covert, destructive forms. Fertility is romanticised as a plenitude to which independent subjectivity is opposed as a *lack*.

In fact, the relationships women are supposed to unproblematically inhabit and preserve are often the very relationships they must test in order to learn or remind themselves that their participation in a social web is *singular* and not generic. For Beauvoir, contraception and abortion are *part of* the process and the constitutive habits involved with being a generative/fertile individual (SS 524–33/2:290–301). Abortion, she writes, 'is such a widespread phenomenon that it has to be considered one of the risks normally involved in the feminine condition' (SS 524–5/2:291). For many slave women, it was a minimal condition of individual and collective resistance. Just as one can only select certain 'possibles' from the indefinite multiplicity through which one is born, one can only select certain children and certain maternities, one can only become a finite series or set of overlapping processes of mothering. No woman can mother *all possible children* of her womb.

Put differently, maternity is not a matter of 'transcendence in immanence' as Sartre would describe it. Mothers, like all human beings, are not transcendent with respect to a given boundary or border but they transcend by being *separate from each other and from their children* and by remaining faithful to immanence as Deleuze defines it – what he would call a line of flight.

To observers, this conflict between women and their fertility or pregnancies may look oppositional and violent. But this is only an effect of the perspective that freezes becomings into beings, as well as the expectation that maternity involves no violence and that women are required to prioritise the species, a generality, over their transcendence, their singular destiny. In *The Blood of Others* [*Le sang des autres*, 1945], Hélène's choice to sleep with Petrus when Blomart rejects her is a risk. To preserve the self she has affirmed through that risk, however, she has an abortion (from which she almost dies). At the end of the novel, she risks killing a second time (and does die) in order to preserve her country against the Nazi occupation. What she is trying to preserve is neither herself nor her country as fixed entities, but the indefinite futures both contain. Abortion, Beauvoir might as well say, is part of the 'resistance' that every fertile woman puts up towards deviations or misrepresentations of her essential tendencies and need to preserve an opening onto new combinations. It is the law, in its generality, that tends to enforce both a universal image of fertile womanhood and a relationship between women and their foetuses that takes the form of an inescapably violent opposition or *contradiction* rather than a painful process of selection, coexisting with a multiplication and rapprochement that can be quite joyful.

Work

The habits associated with oppressive and liberatory maternity can be compared, following the narrative of Hegel's struggle for recognition, to the habits associated with oppressive and liberatory work. Not only is motherhood barely started with the act of physical childbirth, which is not a deliberate act of labour (though it requires determination and endurance). The conscious acts of labour associated with childrearing do not produce the sort of product or possession in which Hegelian self-consciousness can recognise its individuality. Through their home decorating and upkeep, middle-class women try to make themselves distinctive since respectability prevents them from doing so through acts that alter the external world (SS 481–2/2:243). Housework, some minimal quantity of which is necessary even in the absence of children, can be an act of creativity when it is a setting for creativity (SS 481/2:243). How many artists and writers begin their projects, put their bodies in shape to generate the first sentence or sketch, by cleaning up the physical space, sometimes obsessively for days on end, in which they will grasp the future? But housework can also be a living death if nothing is supposed to emerge from this orderly space but that which has always been there (SS 476–7/2:236–7).

Beauvoir is perfectly aware that many women have factory, retail or agricultural jobs in addition to childrearing and household work. Reference to the labour conditions of working women is scattered throughout the book, including reflections on the 'double shift', the relatively lower wages available to women, lack of public confidence or respect for female professionals, and the difficulties posed by paid work for sexuality and maternity (SS 154–6, 523/1:224–8; 2:289). The poor wages available to women, especially those with small children, and the sexual harassment and rape of domestic servants are reasons for women's entry into prostitution, whose work dangers are also discussed (SS 600–1/2:377–9). For too many women, domestic household work *included* and still includes sex work. Finally, Beauvoir acknowledges that within the middle class, men's work in bureaucratic organisations is anything but 'transcendent' (SS 661/2: 451–2) and that housewives have more autonomy at their repetitive tasks than do men employed in factories (SS 721–3/2: 522–3).[35]

But at least until recently, most men were not required to perform invisible 'emotional labour' in the form of attentiveness or tenderness alongside their productive tasks in order to maintain a salary.[36] Women's work, including the work in their own homes, overwhelmingly aims at producing *affects* that assist in the growth, healing or efficacy of other living beings. Such emotional work is physically draining, but it also tends to reinforce the individuality of the customer or client at the worker's expense and in some cases, as with childcare, nursing and sex work, it makes the worker's physical being into an extension of the person being assisted.[37] A happy mother shapes her child's 'flesh, she supports him, she cares for him; she can do no more than create a situation that solely the child's freedom can transcend' (SS 568/2:340). If it is easy to reduce women to roles like 'mother', 'nurse', 'maid', 'secretary' or 'call girl', it is because the activities involved are so repetitive that they seem to describe *beings* rather than genuine becomings. The workers themselves sometimes doubt that they are irreplaceable; there are so many competitors in a world of scarcity. Women in these lines of work depend on this repetition for their physical preservation, to keep a roof over their heads and food on the table.

Beauvoir's opposition to women's isolation in the household does not, as some have argued, simply reflect a preference for the kinds of male activities that are socially valued. The question is not whether housework or home care, particularly for relatives, should be paid rather than given for free. Nor is the question whether women should choose the 'transcendence' of paid work over the 'immanence' of maternity. The question is whether both childbearing and labour, and especially the labour that follows from childbearing, can involve activities that *allow women to differentiate themselves from their charges* and from the other individuals in their environment, all the way up to the political level. This is evident in the example of black women in the United States and many white women of the working classes for whom paid work and sometimes political advocacy on behalf of their families are necessary aspects of mothering.[38] Today, Beauvoir argues, a woman demands 'participation in the movement by which humanity ceaselessly tries to find justification by surpassing itself; she can only consent to give life if life has meaning; she cannot try to be a mother without playing a role in economic, political, or social life' (SS 568/2:340–1). Pay and formal recognition are necessary, and struggle may be required, but the meaning of transcendence is not to be paid or to win a fight: the meaning is to be able to continue, identify and develop one's trajectory – in relation to the freedom of others.

Beauvoir never lived with Sartre, but accepted his financial support while writing *The Second Sex*; much later, without leaving Sartre, she lived with a younger film-maker whose company she enjoyed, Claude Lanzmann. To be supported and to support someone else are not immanence unless they result from an inability or unwillingness to acknowledge the constant tension of rapprochement and separation. This can only happen if episodes of support are contextualised by *reciprocity*. Women must be able to support themselves if they feel this reciprocity has been violated, which may require that such episodes are sufficiently brief in duration that the majority of their lives clearly reflect and develop their singularity socio-economically.[39] However, the one thing that is clear from *The Second Sex* is the danger women face from work that *isolates* them from other human beings. Here the housework of bourgeois women is vastly more problematic than the work of factory operatives, who have many opportunities for interaction, communication and sometimes collective opposition to the terms on which their work is done. Even domestic servants, as Patricia Hill Collins describes, were sufficiently solidaristic to develop a vernacular social theory about their white female employers, giving them a protective sense of distinction within plurality.[40]

Logically, it would appear that in every case where women have the opportunity to vary their activities so as to express individuality – when nursing expertise is recognised by patients and by the doctors they assist, when sex workers have the opportunity to choose their own clients, when maids or mothers have sufficient time and resources to do the work their own way without being so tired that they are incapable of reflection and selection – then these forms of work can be *part of a woman's transcendence*. 'Hetaeras' and performing artists, according to Beauvoir, are able to control the conditions of their own labour sufficiently to let them test and express their own individuality on a regular basis (SS 741–2/2:546–7). There is a natural overlap between the interpersonal habits assigned to women and those of artists insofar as femininity consists so often in producing affects. The problem is that in the performing arts, which were easier for women to adopt in Beauvoir's time than the plastic or literary arts, the product is almost as 'ephemeral' as the product of personal care, and imposes a constant obligation to be pleasing to others (SS 612, 745/2:391, 551). Moreover, especially in a sexist environment, it is difficult to discern an audience's appreciation for the craft and art mediated by one's person and their physical appreciation for *oneself* (SS 611/2:390–1).

The opinions of others are necessary for improvement (as in all professions) but can easily satisfy narcissism rather than art. Beauvoir notes that the performing arts can reinforce women's obsession with themselves (SS 741–4/2:546–50). We see examples in Beauvoir's novels: Régine (in *All Men are Mortal*), Denise (in *The Blood of Others*) and Paule (in *The Mandarins*) try to pursue artistic success, but their art is a quest for personal justification or love, and suffers *as art*. Elizabeth (in *She Came to Stay*) seems able to keep her desire for love separate from the desire to create, but her ability to identify a genuinely new vision is tarnished by romantic unhappiness. The 'blind' individuating surge of the woman who would pursue independence, according to Beauvoir, is always *divided* by her knowledge that she is an *object* in others' eyes and, therefore, by her tendency to look at herself externally as an object (SS 736/2:539–40). This is not a personal fault, but a result of the historical situation in which sexual satisfaction and maternity are difficult to combine with work, whether creative or simply remunerative. This division is *lived* as a feeling of tension and uncertainty, both physiological and moral.

As Bergson notes, 'a complex feeling will contain a fairly large number of simple elements; but, as long as these elements do not stand out with perfect clearness, we cannot say that they were completely realized, and, as soon as consciousness has a distinct perception of them, the psychic state which results from their synthesis will have changed for this very reason' (TFW 84).[41] When divided, the very quality of freedom changes. Because women cannot forget that they exist from an external standpoint, because they are subject to the 'look' [*le regard*] as Sartre would say, they *watch* themselves work more than they actually work, they report on their dreams rather than on the world that they could shape in common with others (SS 743/2:548). Moreover, they are never sure which they value more, acting or watching themselves act. Even those who are hardworking and rational engage in self-sabotaging utilitarian calculations, and strive excessively to please the witness that they carry around (SS 739, 745/2:543–4, 551). To forget oneself presumes one has already *found* oneself (SS 741/2:545–6); now what Beauvoir means is not the self as an *object* but the 'true self' of a freedom experienced only as qualitative multiplicity, and focused on a goal which has yet to come into existence.[42]

Like Sartre, Deleuze thinks the self of habit and the ego never coincide except as a misidentification or an identification that quickly disintegrates. We might say that such an artist or professional – and the many examples supplied in Beauvoir's novels – gets stuck at the third synthesis of recognition. Michèle Le Dœuff notes that many beginning researchers ask, 'Am I the right person for this?' etc.[43] Instead of a surprised 'So *that's* what it was!' the woman who tries to *resolve* her uncertainty through the quest for recognition ends up wondering 'Who was I anyway?' This is the situation faced by the aging scholar in *Age of Discretion*, who gradually realises that her ideas have become stale but, lacking the courage to grasp the nonsense into which her life has turned and make it into a new problem, tyrannises over her adult son.[44]

Hegel's slave demonstrates that work on an external material under the threat of death can actualise the individuality of self-consciousness. But artistic creativity, while it involves external materials, is more properly work on an object of imagination, a vision, a tendency implicit in the environment than simple production or processing. Artistic creativity actually requires a *more rigorous* process of individuation than Hegel or his proverbial master elicit from the slave. The relationship between the 'true self' and its world can only be disclosed through daring and a willingness to be alone 'with the world'. Thus Beauvoir chides the female artist:

> She may feel alone *within* the world: she never stands up *in front of it*, unique and sovereign. Everything encourages her to be invested and dominated by foreign existences; and particularly in love, she disavows rather than asserts herself. Misfortune and distress are often learning experiences [*épreuves fecondes*] in this sense: it was isolation that enabled Emily Brontë to write a powerful and unbridled book; in the face of nature, death, and destiny, she relied on no one's help but her own. (SS 749/2:556)

The single combat of Hegel's master/slave dialectic exemplifies this experience of solitude, and many men believe creative capacity requires actual disdain for society and the freedom of others. For Beauvoir, who recognises that the 'look' can also be helpful, these conditions can be achieved through travel as well as violence, and particularly in contact with nature. However, the situations presented by Beauvoir's own novels suggest she believes that this solitude is most likely to result when a woman feels abandoned by the Other whose gaze initially formed part of her life's shape.

To 'take responsibility for the universe', as Beauvoir suggests is necessary, is a matter of turning it into a *problem* via an Idea when the 'I' cracks. But madness may also result. And when options for positive connection are not available to a woman artist, when isolation is intolerable, and when the world expects her to achieve nothing on account of her sex, the difficulty can be insuperable. If she becomes *mixed* with the world rather than alone *in front of* the world, the surface of sense tumbles into incoherence.

Narcissism, love and mysticism

Narcissism is one of the three justifications to which Beauvoir claims women turn when they realise the incongruity between their becoming and the demand to play a *being* (the others are love and mysticism). Narcissism responds to the cracked 'I' of the third synthesis defiantly, simply refusing to accept the loss of sense or the inevitability of ambiguity. Beauvoir notes that narcissism can give a young woman the necessary courage to start living, but this will only bear fruit if she actually practises that living (SS 681/2:475). Narcissism is a form of seriousness, and it certainly leads to many women's complicity with structures that are otherwise stultifying. This problem appears in Beauvoir's discussion of the hetaera, who is loosely identified with the world of cinema and show business (SS 612, 641/2:391, 426). The starlet or socialite is already so talented, so beautiful, that she does not need to work or to compete; and like Paule (in *The Mandarins*) she avoids all possible tests of this a priori truth.[45] She does not manage to counter-actualise the *event* with a new problem and its Ideas, in which she could meet herself halfway.

The woman in love [*l'amoureuse*] is the product of habits associated with a largely self-serving male myth; so one might say that she answers to male narcissism whether or not she is herself narcissistic. Love is an affect, usually an affect resulting from a deeply moving relationship, not work that maintains and alters one's own individuality in the world – and the body of the woman in love also has other affects, capacities and needs. The woman in love values herself and is valued, however, for the affects she feels and can provoke in others. What's the problem here? In the simplest sense, the woman in love is numbingly bored in the absence of her beloved; her experience of temporality involves endless waiting (SS 633, 700–1/2:417, 498–9). The woman in love substitutes the experience and production of affects for more lasting connections with the world; thus her sense of self, and possibly her livelihood, crumples when these affects fade. Most important from a moral standpoint, she fails to engage in reciprocity – she demands that her lover allow her to claim transcendence through his activity in the world, without engaging in any worldly activity with whose transcendence *he* could identify.

The absence of reciprocity does not prevent the woman in love from confusing her affects with those of others, particularly if she believes love is a 'universal' phenomenon whose stages are known in advance like the stages by which an organism grows or a volcano erupts and dies down. No conclusions can be drawn from a singular love; although being unable to identify boundaries between oneself and someone else is glorious and energising, boundaries will nonetheless appear someday. Beauvoir's woman in love does everything possible, to the point of psychosis, to deny the event of separation even though that separation may simply be a qualitative modulation in an ongoing love relationship. Heidegger may have believed that the meaning of being was given by our finitude in the face of death, but Beauvoir is concerned that the meaning of women's being is given by her finitude in middle age, when her children are grown or her man leaves (SS 620, 624/2:400–1, 404–5). Meanwhile, her *becoming* seems more and more obscure . . .

For Beauvoir, love is frequently a matter of temporal spans and speeds and slownesses. Because women tend to individuate themselves (even today) through love relationships more than through creative, remunerative or political work, they have more time to devote to reflecting and cultivating the range of ideas and affects involved (SS 253, 707, 758–9/1:366; 2:506, 566–7). Most men have put less time into this entire aspect of existence and so Beauvoir observes that they often engage in the habits associated with romance in exchange for sex, provoking resentment and anxiety in their female lovers, whose connoisseurship goes unrecognised.

The intensity of love is supposed to redeem or compensate for all the other negative affects in a life, even those resulting from the lover's abuse (SS 687–93/2:482–90). Indeed, as a form of the most profound nonsense – a 'lapse in the logic of the universe', as Marguerite Duras put it – it can be the leading thread in a man's or woman's individuation.[46] Like the young woman's helpful narcissism, believing that one's point of view is physically and mentally shared with another person can generate the confidence to put the first words on the paper, to build a new institution or to risk one's prior self-understanding and relationships. But the effort to preserve this affect against change can also lead to deception and dishonesty with others. Many 'struggles for recognition' between the sexes result from the feeling that a common rhythm or point of view has failed, and that one party has got more power at the expense of the other (SS 759/2:567).

If the woman in love puts a particular Beloved in the place of the fractured 'I' rather than formulating a problem along whose path she could be individuated, the mystic puts God in its place. Both the cult of romantic love and mysticism can be ways of accepting and justifying immanence. Both can be a support for narcissism as well as powerful reasons for self-abnegation. In Bergson's *Two Sources of Morality and Religion* [1932], the mystic is one who senses that his or her becoming is intertwined with all the becomings of the universe.[47] Bergson describes mystics as natural beings whose insights lift them outside the species and as self-conscious of their own participation in whatever purpose orients the entire universe:[48]

> In our eyes, the ultimate end of mysticism is the establishment of a contact, consequently of a partial coincidence, with the creative effort which life itself manifests. This effort is of God, if it is not God himself. The great mystic is to be conceived as an individual being, capable of transcending the limitations imposed on the species by its material nature, thus continuing and extending the divine action.[49]

This intuition gives rise to a generosity and carelessness that are infectious; thus great religious leaders, Bergson believes, are able to give followers a tangible sense of their oneness with the universe. Unfortunately, this living kernel of religion usually dies while the habits with which it was associated live on, sometimes in a rigid form.[50] However, these forms can be genuinely creative, particularly in the case of institutions of justice.[51] We never encounter either the group-preserving or the group-expanding forms of religion and morality in isolated form; they are always mixed.

How do we know when these justifications are complicitous with oppression and when they either open or accompany a woman's line of flight? Most women do not want to think of themselves as narcissists, but many have also been deeply alienated by Beauvoir's critique of romantic love and by her scepticism towards the liberatory aspects of female piety (SS 559–60/2:448–50). In many sexist societies, religion – despite its oppressive aspects – is the only official discourse reassuring women of their singularity and capacity for agency and responsibility (see for example Mahmood, *The Politics of Piety*). The Black church in the United States allowed women to engage in continuous advocacy and provide their communities with social cohesiveness. In all-female religious societies around the world, women have oppressed other women, but also offered them safe spaces for work and study, free from the exhausting and repetitive demands of male-headed families. On the other hand, women from oppressed groups are sometimes the primary support for their men and children and welcome the sense of being recognised by a merciful deity who is a leader, not a lover. And even romantic love, as Beauvoir's own case attests, can provide the confidence to sustain other activities that are socially beneficial and intellectually or artistically creative. The prospect of a world without a bodily engaging love is the prospect of a world without sense.[52] In such cases, however, love and mysticism are not justifications so much as they are integral *elements* of a woman's individuation, which is oriented toward and distinguished from the world.

Forms of feminism that set themselves against these 'justifications' assumed, first, that we can function and individuate ourselves without intense affective relations with others, and second, that we are actually *cognisant* of all the others who affect us deeply. As mentioned above, these are assumptions that we would associate with Sartre – who would also, no doubt, count these justifications as forms of facticity and remind us that denial of facticity is also a form of bad faith. But *The Second Sex* gives many examples of the enabling or loving effect of others' attention and its concern with individuation suggests precisely that psychic separation and identification of those who influence us requires a learning process and is not something we know a priori.

One problem with romantic love and mysticism is that they seem to cling to the habits that produced certain affects as if the affects themselves could prevent the breakdown of sense or the need to pose problems. Another is that, whether the beloved is divine or human, these activities do not facilitate a woman's grasp on the world and her ability to know her own boundaries in relation to all it contains (SS 717/2:517). Nor do they allow women to solve the constant problem of economic dependence on others. Men certainly use religion to justify their own goals, but these goals ultimately involve them with other people and institutions, rather than substituting for involvement (SS 660/2:449–50). The way both romantic love and mysticism *postpone* the breakdown of sense resembles the way Deleuze describes alcoholism – attempting to live in the past, or in the present *as* past, by repeating the gestures that produce an overwhelming affect (LS 154–61/180–90).

In *Difference and Repetition*, the suffering entailed by the third 'failed' synthesis of recognition seems almost theoretical. The habits that form a personal subjectivity are way stations in the production of Ideas through processes that are largely pre-personal – whether they involve faculties or larval subjects. In *The Logic of Sense*, the failure of sense is a palpable catastrophe, mixing words and things in ways that poison and corrode boundaries, producing completely chaotic affects, hungers and hatreds (LS 82–93/101–14). From this breakdown of sense, which corresponds to schizophrenia, there will emerge no reorienting Problem and Ideas – and one wonders *how much* sense depends on the sexual *Mitsein* described by Beauvoir. Even if she does not use clinical language, Beauvoir is acutely aware of this possibility when her novels depict women who have 'gone mad' after losing both their love object and their self-respect, such as Denise (in *The Blood of Others*), Paule (in *The Mandarins*) and Monique (in *The Woman Destroyed*).[53]

What would freedom mean if not, as for Sartre, acknowledging one's spontaneous transcendence and refusing justifications? In some ways, narcissism, romantic love and mysticism are clichéd solutions to the problem of an incongruity between one's socially valorised self-understanding and one's sense of inner difference or singularity. What makes them clichéd is that they reterritorialise the flailing subject of thought on existing narratives, relationships or affects rather than seeking to transform those narratives and relationships. They often isolate the subject rather than connecting her to larger social wholes – such as schools of thought, markets or political movements. And they permit, if they do not foster, a lack of reciprocity inasmuch as they allow women to take advantage of men's transcendence without work, loss or acknowledging the freedom of others (SS 706/2:504). There is no reason to believe that in a liberated world or less sexist form of sense we would be without narcissism, romantic love or mysticism. But they would not be ways that women reconcile themselves to a lack of knowledge about themselves and their capacities.

Nor should we imagine that all it takes to refuse these justifications is effort. Effort itself, as per Bergson and Leibniz, is the result of numerous microtendencies pushing in a certain direction, the minute insensible perceptions or 'little springs trying to unwind', as well as sufficient awareness to let those microtendencies have their way.[54] When Hélène acts in *The Blood of Others*, it does not have the arbitrary feel of Françoise's murder of Xavière in *She Came to Stay*. We are not surprised that Hélène takes responsibility for delivering the truck filled with explosives, and yet we are excited by her determination, because it has been prepared by all those microtendencies that we share with her as readers. The point of any novel, as Beauvoir later explained, is to assist readers in the process of transcendence by modelling how it looks and feels to develop a sensitivity to what our freedom 'wants' in us.

Hélène was also lucky to find a single act in which she could focus that energy, although she died from it. The tragedy of Blomart, her indecisive and self-loathing love interest, is that, while living, he never found an act that could counter-actualise the oppressive form of sense he had internalised both from his bourgeois family and from his political comrades. However, as mentioned above, despite Beauvoir's attachment to the Sartrean language of the 'project', most of her characters develop a sense of self through *loss*.

Beauvoir's literary portrayal of female mental illness leads us to ask whether some forms of sense actualised in female bodies correspond to events that are *impossible* for those bodies? Are there habits that give rise to bodies so obviously incompatible with current notions of masculinity and femininity that the surface cracks, not only in individual women's own lives but also in their culture? In *The Logic of Sense*, Deleuze describes Fitzgerald's biographical 'crack' as one with the aftermath of the war and the financial crisis, but it was obviously related to Zelda's own difficulty in living for herself and for her own creativity rather than in relation to her husband's career. Fitzgerald's crack is also a crack opened by the meaning of gender, marriage and creativity in the early twentieth century, denied and distilled. In how many nations is women's suffering from war, sexual violence and forced childbearing invisibly embedded in the habits that shape male consciousness as well as the consciousness of women? These forms of nonsense corrode and vitiate *sense* unless they are turned into problems.

According to *The Second Sex*, it is neither biology, psychology nor history that gives women the traits of character they seem to share (SS 68, 638/1:104; 2:422). These are all meanings and forms of sense embedded in habits. It is never clear which gestures and thoughts go together to form discrete 'habits', except in a few obvious cases, often involving formal education or training (but then, isn't daydreaming part of practising the piano for some people?) In practice, they are all mixed together. Liberal feminism and Black feminism explain the female body and its habits or bodies and their habits differently; as do psychoanalysis or behaviourally oriented therapies. Beauvoir was criticised for seeming to equate feminine character with women's *worst* identifiable traits – though she does write that women escape many bad character traits of self-importance into which men are inculcated.[55] The important thing is that Beauvoir issued her criticisms with the belief that women could exert agency to *change* their practices of habituation and perhaps disclose new forms of masculinity along the way.[56]

However, the habits of collectives are no less important than those of individuals, and just as difficult to identify and articulate amid the chaos of constant activity. This is the other side of *Mitsein*.

Notes

1. Heidegger, *Being and Time*, 159. Sometimes this concern is purely instrumental and does not lead to much community, or even provokes mistrust and competition. 'On the other hand, when they devote themselves to the same affair in common, their doing so is determined by the manner in which their Dasein, each in its own way, has been taken hold of' (ibid.).
2. See Gatens, 'Beauvoir and Biology', and Ward, 'Beauvoir's Two Senses of "Body"'.
3. Rhizomes, unlike hierarchies/trees, can only be grasped 'from the middle' or *par le milieu* – which also means 'by means of their environment' (TP 25, 293/36–7, 359–60); see also Deleuze and Parnet, *Dialogues*, 39. On the connection to Bergson, see Smith, 'The Idea of the Open'.
4. In *Transcendence of the Ego*, Sartre argued that the ego, like other phenomena (chairs or equations), is a *transcendent* object of consciousness; it is not a *transcendental* origin or principle animating consciousness from within. In *Being and Nothingness*, like this early essay, the kind of differentiation that matters is differentiation between consciousness and its world of meanings or objects, including those revealed by reflection, not differentiation between one consciousness and another consciousness within and against the backdrop of a common world. This consciousness (being for-itself) is *situated in* the world within which it apprehends objects and its own states, but also *opposed* to the world (being in-itself) – refusing to be whatever it once was, contrasting objects and meanings with nothingness and defining them through comparison, anticipation and negation.
5. As Sebastian Gardner notes with respect to *Transcendence of the Ego*, 'Impersonal it may be, but transcendental consciousness is nonetheless individualized', posing the problem of how consciousness would even come to hypothesise that it is not the only one of its kind. Gardner, *Sartre's Being and Nothingness*, 135, 14.
6. In *Transcendence of the Ego*, Sartre says it would be just as much an error to assume impersonal consciousness is only *one*, unique, as it would be to assume that it was generated by a transcendental ego (104). The problem of individuation is rather that, even if others can experience my emotions or states along with me, their experience of these phenomena *does* differ from mine, and this is a morally as well as epistemologically important fact. With his idea of 'anonymous' structures linking bodies, Merleau-Ponty seems to have believed Husserl's world had a basically intersubjective structure. See Welton, *The Other Husserl*, 236; Husserl, 'On Static and Genetic Phenomenological Method', 631.

7. See Björk, 'Simone de Beauvoir and Life', 352–3.
8. Sartre returns to this problem in *The Emotions*, 82–3, and comments that 'man is a wizard [*un sorcier*] to man' (84–5).
9. Lacan, 'The Mirror Stage'. It is easier to identify with one's mirror image if one is the only moving figure in the mirror. How the child separates his or her part of that image from the parts that reflect other persons and objects must be a complex process. Worse still, the child imagines that what the parent sees in that mirror image (and in the child him or herself) is the *same image and meaning* that he or she sees. Readers of Lacan tend to focus on the child's self-misrecognition; but the real problem is that the child identifies with the *misrecognition of others* whose knowledge and authority he or she trusts.
10. The citation is to Lacan's *Les complexes familiaux dans la formation de l'individu* [1938]. See Zakin, 'The Drama of Independence'.
11. Beauvoir, 'Two Unpublished Chapters of *She Came to Stay*', 31–76.
12. In *Simone de Beauvoir's Philosophy of Lived Experience*, Holveck carries out a similar analysis of the phenomenological descriptions of Françoise's experience in the opening chapter of the novel's final version.
13. This is a theme in early chapters of *Prime of Life*, where Beauvoir comments that during the late 1920s, Sartre was oblivious to the uniqueness of his own interpretation of reality: 'He made no distinction between his own vision and the actual object he saw, which threw him into some very thorny problems' (PL 30).
14. By contrast to the rather monolithic (despotic) model of subjectivation found in *Anti-Oedipus*, in *A Thousand Plateaus*, Deleuze and Guattari propose that 'signifying' (interpretive) and 'post-signifying' (affective) regimes of signs overcode the modern individual who has been released from lineage-based identities (TP 111–48/140–84). See also chapter 7 of *A Thousand Plateaus*: 'Year Zero: Faciality', 167–91/205–34.
15. See in particular 'The Origin of Geometry', Appendix VI in Husserl, *The Crisis of European Sciences*, 353–78.
16. There are some statements in this direction in *Cartesian Meditations*, but the idea is robustly presented in Husserl, *The Crisis of European Sciences*.
17. Heidegger, *Being and Time*, 188–210; Hughes, *Deleuze's Difference and Repetition*, 18–21.
18. Bergson, *Creative Evolution*, 188–91. In *A Thousand Plateaus*, Deleuze and Guattari suggest that a certain orchid and the wasp who mistakes it for a mate form a similar 'assemblage' [*agencement*] (TP 10/17–18).
19. In *Time and Free Will*, Bergson distinguishes between extensive and intensive quantities (3), and between quantitative and qualitative

multiplicities (121–5). Extensive/discrete quantities – or quantitative multiplicities – differ by degree. For example, a cake can be cut into slices which equally remain cake; a gallon of water can be divided into glasses and remain water. But the very idea of an intensive quantity is misguided for Bergson, because intensity, he argues, admits only of quality.

Continuous/qualitative multiplicities differ in kind (the classic example is temperature, which cannot be doubled or halved without changing in kind). Space, for Bergson, was the very model of quantitative multiplicity; but lived time (duration) was a qualitative multiplicity, for cumulative repetitions change the nature of an experience. An extended musical note no longer 'sounds' the same after a given time as it did at first. Thus Bergson believed that 'intensity' could not admit of increase or degree except by a bad analogy to quantities, just as the lived experience of time could not be measured except by bad analogy to the movement of hands around a clock dial.

Deleuze disagreed; he argued that there were, indeed, intensive quantities that were *expressed* rather than 'analogized' or 'represented' by extension (DR 16–18; 222–4/27–30, 286–90). These intensive quantities or singular multiplicities are the necessary cause of qualities as well as spatial extension. The disagreement with Bergson is found at DR 237–40/305–10 and in the earlier text, 'Bergson's Conception of Difference'. Most of the time, I will use Bergson's language of 'qualitative multiplicity' in this text. See Hughes, *Deleuze's Difference and Repetition*, 146–52; Bryant, *Difference and Givenness*, 238–9.

20. All the same, Beauvoir does use the term, primarily to describe emotionally manipulative behaviour such as sadistic, masochistic or narcissistic attitudes in love relationships and in the careerism of certain performing artists.
21. Bauer, 'Beauvoir's Heideggerian Ontology', 75. 'If the *Mitsein* means that I no longer must find a way beyond the nightmarish Cartesian possibility that I am fundamentally alone, it also means that I must fight for my own identity—and indeed, fight for the courage to have the *desire* to have an identity – in a world in which the path of least resistance endlessly tempts me to just melt into the crowd' (ibid., 82).
22. Hurtado points out that the fact that white women are 'seduced' into compliance by white men while women of colour are actively *rejected* means that white women have a harder time telling themselves and their perspectives apart from those of the men in their communities than other women in the US and possibly around the world (Hurtado, *The Color of Privilege*, 10–15). This accounts for some limitations on the applicability and resonance of *The Second Sex* beyond Europe and other white-majority nations.

23. See the authors discussed in Fraser, *Identity Without Selfhood*, 124–40. Note that as Moi points out, Beauvoir did not consider lesbianism an identity but rather an existential choice (Moi, *Making of an Intellectual Woman*, 197). Although it eventually became known that she engaged in several liaisons with women during the war, Fraser also observes that being *bisexual* was not considered an identity *or* existential choice at the time when Beauvoir was writing or speaking.
24. Ahmed, *Queer Phenomenology*.
25. However, as per Foucault, they risk being reterritorialised on the body of psychiatry and biopolitical administration if they do so, since most queer identities were defined in those institutions. For Beauvoir, the primary danger is the bad faith of over-identification with a kind of 'being' rather than a tendency or becoming.
26. For discussions, see Young, 'Pregnant Embodiment'; Scarth, chapter 5 of *The Other Within*; and Zerilli, 'A Process Without a Subject'.
27. Diprose, *Bodies of Women*, 114–18.
28. Lundgren-Gothlin, *Sex and Existence*, 72.
29. Hegel, *Phenomenology*, §179–85.
30. Among other reasons, this is why socialism has been insufficient to guarantee women's equality (SS 66–7/1:103–4); see also Schwarzer, *After* The Second Sex, 32–3.
31. Davis, 'Reflections on the Black Woman's Role', 205.
32. Scarth, *The Other Within*, 156; Zerilli, 'A Process Without a Subject', 131.
33. Seigfried, '*Second Sex*: Second Thoughts' argues robustly against this aspect of Beauvoir's text.
34. Veltman, 'Transcendence and Immanence', 122–5; Jagger and McBride, '"Reproduction" as Male Ideology', 258–9. In many cases, childcare (which includes education and companionship) is combined inextricably with housework, a far less skilled activity. See Veltman, 'The Sisyphean Torture of Housework', and Miller, 'Saving Time'.
35. Although she mentions the United States when discussing Jim Crow laws, she does not talk about racial differences *within* France or within its empire, which was still widespread in 1949.
36. On virtuosity in the workplace and the shift to 'communicative labor' or networking as essential for survival; see Virno, *Grammar of the Multitude*, 62, 89–91; on the shift not only from a manufacturing to a service/care economy but to an economy in which masculinity is marketable as ornamentation, mimicking women's own association with the ornamental, see Faludi, *Stiffed*, 34–40, 599–600.
37. For example, Rivas, 'Invisible Labors' and other essays in Ehrenreich and Hochschild, *Global Woman*.
38. Collins, *Black Feminist Thought*, 199–200.
39. Honneth, 'Between Justice and Affection'.

40. SS 494–7, 645/2:256–9, 431–2; Schwarzer, *After The Second Sex*, 74–5; Collins, *Black Feminist Thought*, 13–14, 27.
41. In *Transcendence of the Ego*, Sartre objects to treating experience as an 'interpenetrative multiplicity' à la Bergson (85–6). To do so mistakes the *indistinctness* and *intimacy* of the ego discovered by reflection for qualities of consciousness itself. Sartre does allow that the ego, as an object, may relate to the *past* as an 'interpenetrative multiplicity'; but he would not think of consciousness itself as having an indefinite *duration* in which many objects and qualities merge. This position is reiterated in *Being and Nothingness* (BN 81–2, 161–2). See Coorebyter, *Sartre face à la phénoménologie*, 228–30. Other objections to Bergson can be found in Sartre's *Imagination*.
42. In *Patterns of Dissonance*, Braidotti wonders whether women can greet the post-structuralist disintegration of the subject with the same fascination as men, for they have not yet achieved a solid grasp of subjectivity. Braidotti, *Patterns of Dissonance*, 10; see also Hartsock, 'Foucault on Power'.
43. Le Dœuff, *Hipparchia's Choice*, 157–8.
44. In Beauvoir, *The Woman Destroyed*, 9–86.
45. As Moi points out, in French intellectual culture, to have to expend effort is a defect in its own right; thus Beauvoir's assiduousness (earning her the name Castor or 'Beaver') counted against her in the male academic establishment (Moi, *Making of an Intellectual Woman*, 69–72). Anne McClintock argues that the model of the idle wife as middle-class ideal demonstrating a man's ability to hire servants was very hard for most women to maintain; delegitimating the value of female labour and forcing them to share in housework while pretending not to (McClintock, *Imperial Leather*, 161–4). Women with intellectual and artistic ambitions, especially those of the upper middle class, were caught in both these snares.
46. Duras, *Malady of Death*, 50.
47. Bergson, *Two Sources*, 201–2. On Beauvoir's own positive associations with mysticism, see Hollywood, *Sensible Ecstasy*. According to Simons, Beauvoir's interest in phenomenology was provoked by Jacques Baruzi. Among other things, Baruzi was known for being a proponent of a mystical interpretation of Leibniz opposed to that of the Kantian rationalist Brunschvicg – under whom Beauvoir wrote her Leibniz *diplôme*.
48. Bergson comments that women are as intelligent as men but, except maybe for mystics, have less sensibility of the sort that gives rise to ideas, because generally all their emotions go towards their children and towards their practical upkeep (Bergson, *Two Sources*, 36). It seems likely that Bergson's morality of the 'appeal' in *Two Sources* is the origin of Beauvoir's emphasis on the appeal in 'Pyrrhus and Cineas'; this is certainly a morality, for Bergson, that challenges the

identification of humanity with a mere 'species'; and yet he too identifies this humanity more properly with the male.
49. Bergson, *Two Sources*, 209.
50. Bergson, *Two Sources*, 203.
51. Bergson, *Two Sources*, 63–72.
52. This problem will be taken up again in the conclusion.
53. See Holland, *Excess and Transgression*. Monique's fragmented, obsessional prose corresponds to the smears used to indicate the presence of intensities in Francis Bacon's paintings.
54. 'What Leibniz (as well as Bergson, significantly) calls a "free" act will be an act that effectuates the amplitude of my soul at a certain moment, the moment the act is undertaken. It is an act that integrates the small perceptions and small inclinations into a remarkable inclination, which then becomes an inclination of the soul. But this integration requires time; there is a psychic integration and a psychic time of integration . . .' Smith, 'Dialectics', in *Essays on Deleuze*, 184.
55. Schwarzer, *After* The Second Sex, 78.
56. This is where Beauvoir's project indeed overlaps with the account of performativity put forward by Judith Butler, though the latter has been interpreted as focusing on the repeated performance of gendered mannerisms associated with anatomical sex rather than, like Beauvoir, emotional or social habits.

Chapter 4

The Freedom of Others

In the *Politics*, Aristotle identifies community – specifically the political state or *polis* – as part of what it means to be human, as an aspect of the form of being human that develops over time.[1] Aristotle contends that there is no such thing as 'form' apart from specific formed individuals, but it is unclear how the form 'enters' matter; especially in the process of reproduction.[2] Deleuze and Guattari's challenge to Aristotelian hylomorphism involves an alternative account of the *forming and modulating* process whereby various flows and becomings intersect reliably enough to strike the observer as individuals of a certain kind.[3] If we ask about the generation of individual humans, we must also ask about the generation and individualisation of the *social* structures Aristotle considered a necessary effect and environment for human form.

Where does *Mitsein* come from, in other words? For the approach of Deleuze and Guattari implies that what Heidegger calls *Mitsein* is a *process*, not just an ontological condition of *already-individuated beings* whose being is given meaning by time. It cannot be, as for Heidegger, a given or universal; it must be a contingent assemblage – albeit a very common one. In other words, an event. But an event is also defined by a problem and its solutions. In Beauvoir's corpus, particularly *The Second Sex*, *Mitsein* is converted from a given into a problem, because of the way that its sense negatively affects women.

As Beauvoir noted in *The Ethics of Ambiguity*, the problem of Stoicism is that despite its individualism, 'what depends on us' depends on a plurality, not on an individual, and this plurality is riven with conflict (EA 82/119). Human beings, as a group and as individuals, are singular and not just numerically distinct assemblages. Thus, the event the Stoics believe we must counter-actualise involves a heterogenous plurality of bodies with different interests. Beauvoir repeatedly tries to solve this problem by linking the moral freedom of the individual who is in the process of transcending or individuating to the moral freedom of those from whom she separates. This is how the plane of immanence in her thought detaches itself from that of other thinkers and emerges like a crystal in a solution that eventually grows beyond its source and provides an environment for others.[4] In various texts, this plane was oriented by the problem of the Other, by the problem of how to justify the individual's existence within the *Mitsein*, and finally by the problem of the *Mitsein*'s sexist sense.

Beauvoir's solutions, however, are consistently framed in terms of mutual recognition and reciprocity. In *The Ethics of Ambiguity*, for example, Beauvoir praises Hegel's ethics of recognition:

> The essential moment of Hegelian ethics [*morale hégélienne*] is the moment when consciousnesses recognize one another; in this operation the other is recognized as identical with me, which means that in myself it is the universal truth of myself which alone is recognized; so individuality [*la singularité*] is denied, and it can no longer reappear except on the natural and contingent plane; moral salvation will lie in my surpassing toward that other who is equal to myself and who in turn will surpass himself toward another. (EA 104/150–1)

It seems Beauvoir also thought mutual recognition could preserve women against the corrosion by universals that Kierkegaard found so objectionable in Hegel: 'recognizing each other as subject, each will remain an *other* for the other; reciprocity in their relations will not do away with the miracles that the division of human beings into two separate categories engenders' (SS 766/2:576, see also SS 260, 273/1:376, 393).

Doesn't this already pose an insuperable problem for any so-called Deleuzian reading of Beauvoir? It is well known that Deleuze argues against any philosophical strategy we could call dialectical – that is, a strategy involving representation, contradiction and recognition. Although one might attribute this to a historical reaction against the Hegelianism of Beauvoir's and Sartre's generation, Deleuze offers two specific reasons for his opposition. First, contradiction represents a restriction of the varieties and powers of *difference* (DR 44–5, 49/64–5, 69–70). Since Aristotle, only those differences that can be identified between identities captured in *generality* – moreover, those differences that result in clear opposition – count as difference at all (DR 51/70–3).[5] Second, Aristotelian and even Leibnizian difference is 'internal to' some concept and to representation rather than producing concepts (which might not be representations) (DR 30–5, 47–50/45–52, 68–73). And yet if there exist differences whose repetition *gives rise* to individuals, that *differentiate* into individuals, these differences must be less distinct and resistant to conceptualisation than differences between unities or identities. Even concepts, as individuals, emerge from the repetition of differences that *cannot be conceptualised*.

Accordingly, when Deleuze criticises recognition, what he means is subsuming a given singularity under a concept or representation. This is literally a dead end for thinking: once a phenomena is 'recognised', it provokes no further thought; its singularities are no longer interesting except as properties of the concept under which it is brought. 'The form of recognition has never sanctioned anything but the recognisable and the recognised' (DR 134–6/176–8). In cases of recognition 'between people', this amounts to what phenomenologists would have called 'typification' – recognising someone *as an example of* some category, a 'what' rather than, as Arendt would have it, a 'who', an origin of surprises.[6] But further, according to Deleuze, recognition reflects an understanding of *power* as object of struggle between two similarly situated entities, rather than as the tension enabling them to emerge in their singularity.[7] Like Foucault, Deleuze believes power is productive. It is not the *condition* by which one force subdues another, a condition that can be turned into a homogenous entity and exchanged or represented.[8]

Deleuze's task in his early works was accordingly how to ground thinking in becoming and differentiation. In *Anti-Oedipus* and *A Thousand Plateaus*, he and Guattari explore political phenomena from this standpoint – asking (though they do not use this term) how various forms of *Mitsein* are generated and individuated as machines and assemblages rather than taken for granted as 'nature'. Later still, he used this ontology to fight against the social and emotional impact of generalities – against artistic clichés and the late modern loss of faith in the world.[9]

But this isn't Beauvoir's problem. Beauvoir's problem is a *Mitsein* that makes singularity, especially the singularity of women, a philosophical problem.[10] The category of the Other, like the other forms of sexist sense, denies women's singularity at both the conceptual and practical levels. True human singularity also requires opportunities to connect and detach from other humans and aspects of nature, to test the multiple forces of which one is composed against other forces in a constantly changing qualitative multiplicity. Recognition would be one practice involving such combinations of forces, even if singularity always eludes recognition. Thus at the very least, understanding singularity, if not the creation of an independent female human being, requires us to invoke intersubjectivity and history.

According to Holveck, Beauvoir was influenced by Hegel's early theological writings.[11] In the *Phenomenology*, the idea of mutual recognition is found in the section on Conscience, at the point when Morality leads to Religion.[12] However, in 'Pyrrhus and Cineas' Beauvoir also criticises Hegel for reducing 'recognition' to recognition of the 'pure abstract form of the self' (PC 129/339). In *The Ethics of Ambiguity*, moreover, she argues that the conception of time and history within which recognition is supposed to take place abolishes the singularity of the ethical beings who recognise one another (EA 116–17/168–9). Hegel's focus is knowledge, and thus the good life is primarily an object of knowledge for Hegel, not his direct goal. As Simondon might say: *Aufhebung* is not 'solving a problem' for the individual.[13] Recognition thus becomes a superficial repetition, which conceals a deeper repetition according to Deleuze's *Difference and Repetition* (DR 84–5/114–15).[14]

So when Beauvoir eventually adopts recognition as part of her solution, she seems to be changing its meaning despite Hegel, and making it do something that Kierkegaard or Bergson might have wanted (solving a problem).[15] She also takes mutual recognition out of the context of religion. Meanwhile, though Kierkegaard (and Heidegger) do value human singularity, they underestimate relationships.[16] Beauvoir's question is how love can *support* one's relation to the self or the infinite rather than dead-ending it.

Let's put *The Second Sex* back into the stream/context of 'Pyrrhus and Cineas' and *The Ethics of Ambiguity*. Both are about ultimate ends and justification – against the solipsism and nihilism supposed to result from atheism.

'Pyrrhus and Cineas'

'Pyrrhus and Cineas' begins with a reflection on time. The world of this essay is a world in motion, measured in the first instance by Pyrrhus' restless desire for conquest. To Cineas, this restlessness seems to be unjustified or absurd. Combining Bergsonian and Sartrean language, Beauvoir notes that 'reflection cannot stop the *élan* of our spontaneity', but 'reflection is also spontaneous' (PC 91/235).[17] Bergson would question the very notion of spontaneity, since it seems to presume an arbitrary break in temporal flows. But as the essay develops, it seems that what Beauvoir means by spontaneity, even when it includes reflection, may be closer to what Bergson means by the *élan* of an individual existence than to what Sartre means by the recurrent spontaneity of consciousness and reflection. The very notion of absurdity, Beauvoir continues, presumes that the stream of time or action has been broken up or lumped together such that 'only a shapeless incoherence would remain, a pure contingency that would neither outrage nor astonish' (PC 99/261). This is similar to the situation that would result if one were to identify an individual fate with the universal, as, she says, do Hegel and Spinoza (PC 101/265–6).

The real question of this essay quickly surfaces: which acts of spontaneity are *mine*? Which garden is mine, for whom should I cry and to whom am I linked by the situation – the flood of tears – that results? On the one hand, Beauvoir seems to affirm Sartre's pure immanence: 'A project is exactly what it decides to be. It has the meaning that it gives itself. One cannot define it from the outside' (PC 100/261–2). And further on, man's 'freedom is interiority' (PC 107/280). But how is it 'mine' except by contrast to what belongs to others? In fact, it is my presence that breaks up 'the unity and the continuity of that mass of indifference into which I wanted not to be absorbed' (PC 101/265).[18] Humanity is a matter of the *kind of situation* created when we relate to others as free. There is no pre-established harmony between humans and no higher reconciliation at the end of history. At the start, 'freedoms are neither unified nor opposed but separated' (PC 108, 109/282, 285). But do we ever encounter freedoms 'at the start'? How do subjectivities emerge? Perhaps when they are broken apart by the reflection of an outsider, regardless of how they are situated?

Beauvoir gives *Hegel*, not Bergson, credit for the idea that we see a contradiction only when we regard totality from a partial standpoint (PC 110–11/289–90).[19] And surely this is a Hegelian idea – but one that would not be out of place in Bergson's *Time and Free Will*. Unfortunately, Hegel minimises the importance of individual becomings and, on her reading, anticipates a standpoint on totality that would neither be partial nor stubbornly dynamic.

Beauvoir's references to Bergson seem more distinctive when compared to Sartre's own objections against him. We have already mentioned Bergson in the context of individuating consciousness in *Transcendence of the Ego* (TE 80). Sartre reads Bergson's 'qualitative multiplicity' as comparable to the *ego* or *in-itself* as object of consciousness, which he believes Bergson considers, wrongly, an essence or *cause* of consciousness (TE 85–6). For Sartre, to speak of freedom as the emergence of trends within a qualitative multiplicity would be the same as identifying freedom with the *object* that we are for consciousness – however complex an object – rather than with the pure field of spontaneous *consciousness* itself. In *Being and Nothingness*, he protests that this object, which could and must be reformulated every time consciousness negates its objects (BN 71), is mistaken by Bergson for the 'profound self' (BN 81–2).

But what seems to be missing from Sartre's account is Bergson's concern for the way that ideas about simultaneity and quantity *break up* and freeze ongoing processes whose constituent elements are none too clear. Indeed, Sartre objects to the Bergsonian presupposition (shared with psychoanalysis) of conflicting and collaborating tendencies within consciousness over time: he explicitly opposes Bergson's and Leibniz's presumption that *continuity* is primary, for he believes continuity is what must be *explained* (BN 192–6). However, he is then driven to describe the for-itself as a 'quasi-multiplicity', at least insofar as the complex dance of relationships between for-itself, positing, negation, reflecting and in-itself generates multidimensional temporality (BN 195–6, 211).

For Bergson, consciousness is titrated or *drawn off from* a more complex ontological flow, the way oil can be skimmed off salad dressing if it is left to sit and separate, or the way that participants in a discussion gradually start realising that they disagree and must choose their words more carefully to prevent a fight. It is not that the salad dressing as a whole is the *cause* of the pool of oil, or that the group is *causing* tempers to rise. In the salad example, the whole mixture sticks to *all the leaves* (intentional objects) if it is applied properly, but only under certain conditions does oil, or vinegar, or a lump of mustard appear as *distinct* (and then you have an unevenly dressed salad). Insofar as we are pure Sartrean consciousness, we are *neither individual nor plural, neither ourselves nor anyone else*. But insofar as we share goals and enter into conflict with others – or even with ourselves, one consciousness does differ from another, and it is useful and indeed inevitable to map that emergence of synergy and antagonism into the 'in-itself'.[20] The Other is not just an alteration of the way I inhabit and possess the world, the Other is also localisable in the world, and over time.

Indeed, to say that the Other is an alteration of my world implies a *qualitative* not a quantitative change, and this is why Bergson would not allow the sharp distinction between self and Other so familiar from Sartre. The Other does not so much steal my world as *divides* it into a before and after, a here and there, heating or cooling and congealing it, and in so doing alters its felt quality and its awareness of separation (BN 343).

Although time is real and open-ended, Beauvoir insists in 'Pyrrhus and Cineas', it is 'not progress but *division*' (PC 120/317). This might be taken in several different ways. Does she mean that moments and periods are discontinuous and successive, the way the minutes on a clock follow one another indefinitely; or does she mean that they are always blocked off out of a larger whole or flow? I would argue the latter. Actions and perceptions interrupt, pucker and reorganise the constitutive speed of that consciousness Sartre rightly says is not the 'property' of any given individual. It is indicative that Beauvoir, unlike Sartre, uses the word 'duration'. Every object of a project, Beauvoir adds, has a duration, while humans sustain the overall movement of projecting (PC 115/301).[21] What this would mean is that human awareness, separate but sometimes shared, 'outlasts' any object and therefore 'measures' or transcends its temporality while it cannot be transcended. But even this temporality is not uniformly measurable.

In saying this, of course, Beauvoir suggests that we are treating humanity itself as a duration – enduring as awareness, but also (with a different half-life) as object. It is in the *situation*, much like the ego in Sartre's essay on Husserl or the in-itself in *Being and Nothingness*, that we discover the breaks and periods making up a life, or dividing and relating lives to one another, introducing comparisons (PC 119/314–15). The other's will may change; so we cannot predict his or her wishes – or which aspect of the other will turn out to be authentic after a division. The problem with devotion, for example, is that it is a state in which responsibility for the situation is confused; the other's radical separation seems to disappear (PC 120, 126/315–16, 331). The later Husserl cited by Merleau-Ponty would say that without others there would be no possibility of a truly transcendent *noema* (and so the immanence within which there is transcendence, as for Sartre, is necessarily collective). However, whether Husserl did account for the Other's essentially unfinished, 'unfinishable' nature at different phases of his career remains uncertain.[22] For her part, Simone de Beauvoir does believe the other's separation is infinite. Each of our duration(s) extends 'beyond' the duration required to apprehend things, not quantitatively but qualitatively.

This is why 'It is not a matter of making recognized in us the pure abstract form of the self [*moi*] as Hegel believes' (PC 129/339). But recognition will not solidify the actor's being, and recognition cannot be forced. Recognition, too, must have a genesis. In fact, as the section title indicates, what happens is more like partial *communication* by means of shared objects in the world, and we exist only by virtue of the situation that divides us. Moreover, I must recognise others – in their separation – in order for them to be able to recognise *me* in my separation (PC 135/353–4). In other words, we recognise one another on the basis of a division within a larger sphere of temporal existence. Rather than a claim to recognition, the recognition of others is the necessary form of an *appeal*.[23] Thus the genesis of recognition involves an *appeal*.[24]

> In order for our appeals not to be lost in the void, there must be men ready to hear me close by, and these men must be my peers ... I would lose myself in a desert where none of my steps would matter. I must therefore strive to create for men situations such that they can accompany and surpass my transcendence. I need their freedom to be available to use and conserve me in surpassing me. (PC 137/360–1)

The appeal is the form associated by Bergson with a morality whose goal is 'higher' than that of simple group preservation. 'Whereas natural obligation is a pressure or a propulsive force, complete and perfect morality has the effect of an appeal.'[25] The moral appeal does not simply enforce a generality on separate members of a community, but evokes the emotional tone of the members' first understanding of their being with others: it 'becomes more and more cogent in proportion as the multiplicity and generality of its maxims merge more completely into a man's unity and individuality'.[26] Thus the appeal is a tension or quality in a multiplicity. Meanwhile, as we will see, Beauvoir emphasises the importance of communication between separate existents more and more in her essays on literature.

The Ethics of Ambiguity

In *The Ethics of Ambiguity*, the obvious starting point is the notion of ambiguity. Ambiguity means, in short, that 'the meaning of existence is never fixed' (EA 129/186). Not only does it lack a fixed justification, but it is simultaneously mental and physical, collective and individual, eternal and temporal (EA 7/10). In other words, we might say that existence (always singular) involves several different kinds of continuous variation: more physical at one moment (without ceasing to be mental), more collective at one moment (but only because of dimmed attention to the individual).

Ambiguity is one of the concepts Beauvoir takes in a different direction than Sartre.[27] According to Monika Langer, Beauvoir's notion of ambiguity is closer to that of Merleau-Ponty, though she cited Sartre out of loyalty. According to Gail Weiss, however, Merleau-Ponty's notion of ambiguity refers to the formation of gestalt perception while what interests Beauvoir is how people *respond* to the ambiguity of perception – with either a desire to be or with a desire to disclose being. Deutscher acknowledges Sartre as *one* of Beauvoir's sources, but thinks that her use of the concept in 'Literature and Metaphysics' is primarily drawn from Maurice Blanchot.[28] Could ambiguity be doing some of the work associated with the 'interpenetrative multiplicity' Sartre rejected in Bergson? What happens if we push ambiguity in the direction of a qualitative multiplicity – one in which individuals discover their own contours by creating situations in which others are free to discover likewise?

As in 'Pyrrhus and Cineas', this essay deals with the question of justification and its relation to time. Humans are still radically separate from one another, and the extent to which they know this and know *how* they are separate remains murky. Unlike 'Pyrrhus and Cineas', however, this confusion regarding the difference between one's own freedom and that of others is no longer exemplified by devotion. Rather, Beauvoir focuses on the way that children and 'serious' adults accept the meaning of social behaviours as if natural and given. Immanence is collective, and refers to the confusion of self and other (*das Man*, in Heidegger's terms) rather than to the pre-personal consciousness of Sartre's phenomenology. And though she mentions Heidegger less than in 'Pyrrhus and Cineas', she has now adopted his language of 'disclosing' (*erschließen* or *dévoiler*) to explain how it is that humans collectively relate to their situations.[29]

The child does not know that he or she *can* behave differently from others at a level that is more than superficial; the subman [*sous-homme*] refuses to act, and the serious person [*homme sérieux*] deliberately affirms an exterior source of values. Then there are those who are kept in childhood and prevented from discovering which aspects of behaviour are changeable or perishable and which are not; or prevented from acting on their discovery – these, including many women, are oppressed.[30] They need to be able to find out what the real limits on action are – not to take someone else's word for it (EA 48/69–70). Just as the absence of others to hear my appeal diminished the ontological force of my project in 'Pyrrhus and Cineas', so too the intertwined effects of human existences on one another, evident only through the situation we create together, can have empowering and inhibiting effects on freedom.

> It is this interdependence which explains why oppression is possible and why it is hateful. As we have seen, my freedom, in order to fulfill itself, requires that it emerge into an open future: it is other men who open the future to me, it is they who, setting up the world of tomorrow, define my future. (EA 82/119)

What makes a project genuinely free? The quality of the actor's relationship to the end pursued. The subman avoids having an end; the serious person's relationship to that end is marked by social conformity. For the nihilist (and to his or her fury), this relationship is arbitrary; while the adventurer takes pleasure in imposing that arbitrariness. Although Beauvoir cites Sartre's notion of humanity as a deliberate 'lack of being' early in the essay, for the adventurer, the ambiguity or failure of fixed meaning is a positive element of human freedom, *not* a 'lack' (EA 58/84). However, the adventurer fails to appreciate that the situation created by his or her action affects others; and Beauvoir contends that it is dishonest to deny that others are involved in one's own freedom (EA 63/91).

For the passionate man (or woman), the relation to the object is not so much arbitrary as absolute but *mediated by subjectivity* (EA 64/92); and if this object is another person's subjectivity, then the absolute relationship must involve an attitude of wonder and concern for an alien freedom (EA 66/95). True freedom acknowledges and seeks to elicit the singular freedom of others (EA 67/95–6). 'One can reveal the world only on a basis revealed by other men.

No project can be defined except by its interference with other projects ... The me/others relationship is as indissoluble as the subject/object relationship' (EA 71–2/102–4).

One can only support the being of others by having the presence of mind to detach from being, to forget one's own 'being-an-ego' for oneself or others by focusing on something else. Recall that for Leibniz, a monad is defined by its inner differences. For humans, two blades of grass, two drops of water, are indistinguishable except for their spatial location. But ultimately, all these differences are *abilities* to affect and to be affected; the drops of water wet what they touch and are evaporated by steam, the hiker in the countryside cringes during the rainstorm or quickens her pace.[31] To know one's difference from the world, to know that it is raining, for example, one must be aware of one's own differences and those of the things one encounters; perhaps one senses water on one's skin and realises that it hasn't been raining, but that one has begun to cry. Distinguishing one's own affections from the affections of others is the exercise of a distinctive capacity. Disclosure and the desire to disclose are not just exercises of consciousness but examples of abilities to affect and to be affected.

Of all Beauvoir's characters, Fosca (in *All Men Are Mortal*) is the one who learns this best and who gives us the most sustained meditation on what it takes to disclose the world as free in its alterity. Because of his immortality (and his royal male upbringing), Fosca not only believes that his ambitions and abilities reflect the necessary course of the world but that it is also right to impose this course on the world.[32] Again and again, he assumes that his way of disclosing the world is not a disclosure, or that it is the only legitimate disclosure, or that it is a disclosure that he can impose agonistically on other humans without destroying his own sources of meaning and pleasure.[33] What he learns is that by giving others the time to act and cultivating his own capacities for observation, others reveal themselves as unique and thereby give him the opportunity for genuine responsiveness. The 'time' of each individual, each nation and history as a whole are difficult to align with one another.

In *The Ethics of Ambiguity*, Beauvoir finds Hegel's way of explaining the relationship between singular human freedoms radically unsatisfying, and the reason has, in part, to do with time. Hegel's way of situating singular projects with respect to the whole abolishes their singularity. It is as if to say, from a long enough time span – Fosca's immortality, for example – all human projects become commensurable in their futility or their contribution to a goal that belongs to history rather than an agent/subject (EA 116–17/168–9).

Beauvoir believes that struggle between negativities [*négatités*] – Sartre's term for transcendent points of consciousness – is unceasing (EA 118/170–1).[34] This is because our situations are singular, not just our consciousnesses. Moreover, they continually demand further transcendence. But the specific goals of the fighters involved fade, and they will not be resurrected, fulfilled or rendered commensurate in any future, for such a notion of the future implies a break with the present that does not *grow out of* the present (EA 105, 117–18/152, 169–70). On the other hand, utilitarianism – particularly the utilitarianism of political or military calculation – assumes that means and end can be temporally and ontologically separated in such a way that the end will not be poisoned by evil means (EA 125/180–1). No future is possible without roots in the present.

Movement is a real thing, not just a transition. The time of movement is not simply a measure of displacement through an empty and uniform space. As Bergson protests, 'We attribute to the motion the divisibility of the space which it traverses, forgetting that it is quite possible to divide an *object*, but not an *act*: and on the other hand we accustom ourselves to projecting this act itself into space' (TFW 112). Yet this is what happens when, like Hegel, one takes the perspective of universal history: 'the viewpoint of externality wins over that of internality, and the idea of externality carries with it that of quantity' (EA 120, 122/174, 176).

Leibniz's monads do not 'recognise' one another – they can feel and take credit for causing feelings in others, but their only common framework is God. And yet the struggle takes place at least partly *within* individuals whose acts of self-risk can be generous as well as violent.[35] These acts are genuine risks even if the actor ultimately emerges unscathed. Thus it is important to note that recognition (of others) does not limit freedom, as does division from them (EA 91/131). Beauvoir seems to be saying that the quality of a singular freedom is not harmed by its expression in risk the way it is harmed by its expression in oppression. This is a crucial ethical proposition. It also explains why, as discussed in the last chapter, sometimes it is *loss* rather than triumph that allows the individual to discover who she is.

By insisting on a common horizon for all qualitatively distinct singularities, Hegel merely extends the problems posed by Kant's own solution to the incommunicability of Leibniz's monads. Kantian space and time create a common (human) frame by pushing God out of the picture. Sensibility is declared less important than measurable aspects of phenomena or logical universals. But this subjects us all to generality and law. The resulting problems are twofold. First, as Bauer points out, when we want 'recognition', we don't want to be recognised as examples of the 'same'.[36] Beauvoir's view of singularity is closer to Marx's utopianism than to the liberal model of equal exchange or distribution: from each according to his abilities, to each according to his needs. Second, freedom is no longer an accumulation of micro-tendencies as for Leibniz, but conformity with law. Indeed, for Kant the only definition of freedom is *resistance* to what we naturally 'tend' to be doing; following Rousseau, the creation of a 'second' nature. In the later lecture 'What Can Literature Do?' Beauvoir denies that we are monads, for the world *is* the process of mutual affection over time.[37] But this does not mean that we are affected *in the same way* by our affections. Nor, she would add, can we refuse to 'accept the tension of the struggle' enjoined by these affections (EA 96/138).[38]

Against Hegel's rational totality, and Leibniz's pre-established harmony, Beauvoir believes her understanding of ambiguity is compatible with Sartre's idea of a 'detotalised totality' in which 'separation does not exclude relation, nor vice-versa' (EA 122/176).[39] In such a totality, 'Individual forms thereby imply each other without destroying each other' in their common relation to future, and the movement of liberation does not lose its quality by the way it is broken up into means and ends (EA 122, 131, 134/176, 189, 194). Now, 'detotalised totality' is a concept used by Sartre to indicate that the same consciousness that grasps the world, the flow of time or the ensemble of other humans as a whole also breaks them up when it interacts with being in-itself; moreover, other consciousnesses do the same to any unified self with which I might be tempted or forced to identify (BN 339). Sartre's meaning is less important for us than the use Beauvoir makes of it.

In 'What Can Literature Do?' [1964] Beauvoir says 'detotalised totality' means that the world is the same – a singularity – for all of us, but each situation also expresses a singular viewpoint on this world, just as the monads *express* the world in Leibniz's philosophy.[40] But unlike the monads, neither the situations nor the world are closed – totalised – and this is why, she continues, literature is possible and justified. We do, in fact, affect one another, albeit imperfectly, in the absence of a pre-established harmony. And we affect one another most poignantly insofar as we refer to the conditions of separation (such as mortality) to which every individual is subject.

At the conclusion of *The Ethics of Ambiguity*, Beauvoir says intriguingly that 'man is free; but he finds his law in his very freedom' which means that a true liberation movement must allow individuals to live and act within general conditions for freedom, but also to discover the rules defining their singularity, such that, as in the very last line, 'each man [does] what he must' (EA 153, 159/226, 230). One cannot help hearing an echo of the approach to freedom found in Leibniz and Bergson: not a matter of 'choice' but of gradually recognising one's desire. What *is* clear is that all justifications for action are finite, immanent to the situation in which people find themselves acting on and discovering these laws. Hegel, to the contrary, makes History itself a justification for action. But in doing so, he grasps the flow of events from a transcendent vantage point that changes the *quality* of those events and suffocates the freedom of the agents that worked to bring them about. Thus the soothing effect of reading Hegel appears on second thought to be suicidal, akin to accepting the voice of Descartes's evil genius.

Recognition and communication

In 'Literature and Metaphysics' [1946], the question was how to present the reader with an imaginative version of the open-ended movement of one's own freedom, in hopes of seducing him or her to discover a comparable freedom.[41] In 'What Can Literature Do?', Beauvoir is more explicit that in literature the 'confusion' of one's own situation with that of others, which risked becoming unethical in the case of devotion ('Pyrrhus and Cineas') and resulted in seriousness for the actors in *The Ethics of Ambiguity*, has a positive foundational role. 'I abdicate my "I" in favor of he who is speaking, and yet I remain myself' – or rather, I have to *discover myself* once again in relation to the author's world, as I once had to discover myself in relation to the world of given values, and meanwhile I also discover myself in relation to other unknown readers of the same text.[42] Thus literature is the 'privileged place of intersubjectivity'.[43]

Is Beauvoir deterritorialising 'recognition' from the phylum of Hegelian ideas? In *Matter and Memory*, Bergson speaks of recognition as a resonance between a singular present image and one from the past.[44] He distinguishes between mechanical recognition, which seems closest to the 'dumb' recognition deplored by Deleuze, and a more active form which, although below the level of consciousness, inhibits some aspects of present perception so as to allow bodily gestures to suggest associations from memory 'creat[ing] anew the present perception'.[45] This also happens by accident, or at least without conscious intent.[46] Moreover, Bergson thinks of generality as 'tension between particulars and becomings' rather than simple subsumption with no residue.[47] Recognition is more like adjusting a lens for focus or tuning in to a radio station, and selecting from associations that are possibly informative, than it is like naming. Such recognition can be – indeed must be – repeated and reconfirmed, in light of the need to protect other associations or adumbrations that are hidden but might be useful, much as I refer an idea to a certain page of text but include more or fewer page numbers in my citation in case I need to revisit them for further insight.

In Debra Bergoffen's reading of Simone de Beauvoir, recognition involves risk or co-implication. By contrast to the Sartrean language of the 'project', the 'muted voice' Bergoffen finds in Beauvoir's early philosophy is a voice equating recognition with generosity.[48] In 'Pyrrhus and Cineas', Beauvoir proposes that 'lucid generosity' is the only possible response to the other's recognition – unlike a debt, generosity cannot be measured (PC 123–4/324–5). A powerful example comes from *The Ethics of Ambiguity*, where Beauvoir describes the passionate 'man' as renouncing 'all possession, of all confusion' with the object of love (EA 67/96). To love genuinely is to love someone 'in his freedom and in that freedom by which he escapes'.

As Bergoffen notes, this comes very close to Bataille's understanding of communication or 'non-knowledge' (EA 126/182–3).[49] In 'My Experience as a Writer', Beauvoir makes this association three times.[50] For one thing, there's no reason to believe that 'communication' or disclosure of the other and his or her world always takes place in language, much less a single language or medium of communication, or involves the transmission of a representational/ conceptual content. Communication need not be an 'intentional affair', as Aislinn O'Donnell puts it.[51] Touch can communicate, and also smell. One can communicate by framing or pointing to a situation in a way that reveals its significance – even, as in literature, to an imaginary situation.

Let us consider two examples. Beauvoir wrote, 'In the generous atmosphere bred by comradeship and action [Hélène] finally won through to that "recognition," in the Hegelian sense of the word, which preserves men from mere immanence and contingency. She died as a result; but only after reaching a point where death itself could not prevail against her' (PL 429). In describing the novel, Beauvoir looks forward to the ideas of *The Ethics of Ambiguity*. Why is Hélène her model for reciprocal recognition? Because rather than succumbing to narcissism or love, she acts in the world for the sake of others' freedom (including, but not limited to, the freedom of the man she loves). Here 'recognition' seems to mean 'disclosure' – such that reciprocal recognition would mean reciprocal disclosure of the Other as free, concretely free in the act of carrying out an individuating project.

The narcissist and the woman in love devote themselves to revealing someone who does not recognise them reciprocally (the self-as-object, the male lover); they *are revealed* across this act of devotion, which makes them dependent – but even their success is hollow, because they have no demonstrated transcendence to offer as a support to the freedom of whoever recognises them (SS 682/2:475). In fact, the problem of 'femininity' is not exclusive to anatomical women. When he agrees to be Regina's lover but cannot settle on any productive activity, Fosca dramatises the same delicate balance between disclosing the other in her freedom and depending on her revelation for his own *raison d'être*.

Hélène learned quickly. In *All Men Are Mortal*, it took Fosca several centuries to stop leaping in and solving problems for his fellow humans on the basis of the knowledge and skills he had gleaned through immortality. Eventually, however, he began to take joy in observing how other men and women, despite their finite abilities and lifespans, approached problems in their own ways. What Beauvoir shows in this novel is that singularity is difficult to express in a process of individuation, whether at the personal or the historical scale. In both *The Ethics of Ambiguity* and in *All Men Are Mortal*, history helps to give a meaning to freedom insofar as it provides a wealth of explicative detail through which the present and its human inhabitants can be revealed. If Fosca does make some 'progress' in generosity, it is because he has the opportunity to repeat and relive past events – even if, as Nietzsche would say, he is also condemned to do so eternally.

The section of Hegel's *Phenomenology* following the struggle for recognition (the 'master-slave dialectic') addresses Stoicism. But in *The Ethics of Ambiguity*, Beauvoir finds Stoicism inadequate as a response to oppression. One cannot respond to human violence as one can to a natural disaster, for humanity is both the agent and victim of such events – moreover, a divided agent and victim.

> Only man can be an enemy for man ... It is here that the Stoic distinction between 'things which do not depend upon us' and those which 'depend upon us' proves to be insufficient: for 'we' is legion and not an individual; each one depends upon the others, and what happens to me by means of others depends upon me as regards its meaning; one does not submit to a war or an occupation as he does to an earthquake. (EA 82/119)

At the end of *The Second Sex*, Beauvoir returns in passing to the subject of Stoicism. Again, she points out that oppression does not result from the given, and neither does virtue. Sexual difference, she has argued, is not a mere natural 'given' but a relationship within a *Mitsein*. On the other hand, here she can envision sufficient commonalities between humans that a certain form of Stoicism is conceivable:

> The fact of being a human being is infinitely more important than all the singularities that distinguish human beings; it is never the given that confers superiority: 'virtue,' as the ancients called it, is defined at the level of 'what depends on us' ... The same drama of flesh and spirit, and of finitude and transcendence, plays itself out in both sexes; both are eaten away by time, stalked by death, they have the same essential need of the other; and they can take the same glory from their freedom ... (SS 763/2:573)

If they can affirm these commonalities, despite the singularities in which freedom consists, men and women could at least have 'fraternity' in their finitude. One might compare such an affirmation to counter-actualisation, which chooses or discovers something 'in that which occurs' giving the event a new meaning for all participants, regardless of the causes that divide them.

Transindividuality

What Beauvoir is proposing is that we disclose the world – the in-itself, the qualitative multiplicity in which we are all mixed and through which we also grasp that mixture – in such a way that we simultaneously individuate ourselves and the others with whom we share that world. Put differently again, we divide time by acknowledging the other or by withdrawing from him or her into ourselves, and this changes the quality of things. Deleuze would never talk about disclosing the world and Others as free in order to preserve the chance of being disclosed, in turn, as free. This is clearly Beauvoir's innovation. But in order to understand where Beauvoir might have been going in her effort to replace the sexist *Mitsein* with new ideas, let's compare her adaptation of Sartrean ideas and those of Gilbert Simondon, who was an important source for some of Deleuze's ideas about individuation and the metaphysics of form. This comparison is elaborated through an understanding of ambiguity as 'metastability'.

For Sartre, what it means for being to be *metastable* is that the for-itself of consciousness continually collapses into the in-itself of facticity, but continually negates that facticity as well, in taking itself and its environment as an object (BN 90). Simondon refers to any medium with excessive and therefore unstable potentials (including a crystal-producing solution or magnetic field) as 'metastable', and unreflective consciousness is Sartre's supersaturated medium – in which new noeses are continually apprehended and cast aside (IPC 13–14). Simondon is less interested in the momentary relationship between consciousness and its objects than in the *process* through which the eventually conscious living being emerges physiologically from its milieu, which he characterises as 'plus qu'unité', 'more-than-oneness' – as well as the process through which that consciousness distinguishes objects within that milieu (IPC 15, 90–1). Thus metastability means simply that every possible situation contains more potential energy than we find expressed in the stable forms of that situation.

After explaining the process by which individuals are physically formed and *individuated* (from their mothers, in the case of humans), Simondon goes on to describe the ways that such individuals *use* the remaining potentials in their environment to further *individualise* (IPC 126–33).[52] When they do so, it is because they are driven by internal 'problems'. Cultural habits and history are among the residual potentials, which he calls the 'transindividual', that individuals use to solve the problem of their disequilibrium with their environment and further distinguish themselves from others who are similar. I eat lunch to solve my internal disequilibrium and I write philosophy to solve disequilibrium with my community.[53] One might compare Simondon's model to the way that a seed crystal grows in a solution without absorbing all the chemicals in the solution, although changes in temperature and pressure might alter the rate of its growth. His word for such growth is 'transduction' (IPC 23–5).

When Beauvoir says 'no project can be defined except by interference with other projects', one might well think of the act of *disclosing* those projects within a field of interference as an act of transduction. Each individual alters the field but in such a way as to leave the field open for others. For, as Simondon explains, to be ethical means to remain in an open problematic – to 'postpone the arrival of singularity' or what we might call closure/totality. There are values whenever there is a *problem* one tries to resolve. It is almost as if normativity itself is defined by reaching beyond one system to another or making the propagation of a problem/solution possible. The desire for absolute values would put a brake on becoming (IPC 240–1). So instead of poking holes in being, as Sartre might describe consciousness, Simondon watches problems form, like bubbles in boiling water.[54] The Other is not a 'special noetic object' for him but a 'problematic noesis'.

While Simondon does not reference the notion of 'detotalised totality', this is precisely how he imagines the essence of morality. There is 'no contradiction in having multiple systems of norms' because multiple crystals can grow from the same rich solution, just as multiple organisms can grow in a fertile ecosystem and even support one another with their waste products. Immorality, however, means actually destroying potentials of metastability, soaking up all the solution from which any other crystal could draw nourishment, stifling the capacity for further differentiation and individualisation (IPC 243).

> one could say that the free act, or the moral act, is the one which has enough reality to go beyond itself and to encounter other acts. . . . The immoral act, if it exists, is the one that destroys the significations of acts which existed or which could be called to exist; and which, instead of staying inside itself like the non moral acts, introduces a scheme of confusion preventing other acts from structuring themselves as a web. (IPC 243–4)

One might compare this productively to the vision of ethics put forward in Beauvoir's qualified critique of Sade. The problem posed by Sade's life and writing, according to Beauvoir, is the separation between human existents.[55] How can separation be mitigated without negating singularity – or rather, how can both sides of the singularity/separation ambiguity be respected? Sade is *honest* about the reality of separation and conflict. But he seems to think these can only be overcome by intensifying them, and he cannot bring himself to accept any success in the endeavour, or to imagine that his sovereignty remains intact *with* others. He will not allow himself any form of emotional intoxication or solidarity – any 'implication' with his (largely imaginary) victims or fellow citizens. Beauvoir warns that 'If there is nothing in *common* between the torment of the victim and the torturer, the latter cannot draw any pleasure from it.'[56] His characters deny the erotic continuum with others that allows him to make eroticism a recognisable value, and they use the flesh, as Beauvoir puts it, in order to signal his *refusal* of the flesh. They also signify his refusal of the abstract ethical recognition that, as Beauvoir agrees, cannot do it justice. By refusing to risk himself, as Bergoffen has argued, the Sadean character renders the risks entertained by his victims erotically sterile, as repulsive as the suffering of those who were guillotined.[57] Neither torturer nor victim can discover or *disclose anything new* as a result of their encounter.

Beauvoir distinguishes between Sade's life and the logic of his pornographic writing, which is interwoven with that life, and she admits that we know less about the man than about the characters and scenes he used to arouse himself. Sade's compulsive risk-taking (with authorities, for example) is of a different nature than the risks and suffering he imposed on his family and entourage. However, by constructing a 'possible Sade' from the ideas and actions expressed by some of his characters, as well as known biographical details, Beauvoir deduces the plausibility of certain existential impasses. In terms of *The Ethics of Ambiguity*, refusing to use his freedom in disclosing the freedom and jouissance of others, however painful and mechanised a *form* he imposes upon it, ultimately freezes the movement of Sade's own jouissance and his participation in the 'nature' he regards as a mechanism. In Simondon's terms, as seen above, the truly free act would recognise the individuated subject's implication in a common biological *medium* as well as a common pool of charged cultural significations from which *all* beings might feed their individualisation. Such an act could be organised under many different moral auspices. The immoral act, which does not forgo freedom but *damages* it, cuts off beings from these two sources of individuation and individualisation, or attempts to poison them so that so that singularity loses value (IPC 242–4).

The transindividual is more a matter of how we live culture together than of how we combine culture and nature. For Simondon, the solution to a problem must get the troubled individual *out* of his or her own body and into the social field (IPC 19–20). Sometimes this is a problem of incommensurate temporalities: the temporality of society is different from temporality of the individual, and even at that level, Simondon distinguishes between community (habit) and society (individuated individuals). When he says that he wants to understand how moral problems can *arise* and be solved, one is reminded of Beauvoir's claim that 'Existentialism alone gives – like religion – a real role to evil' (EA 34/48). Evil is a problem that pushes for the articulation of existentialism. In his focus on metastability of being and in his way of dealing with emotions, Simondon resembles Sartre, but 'problematising' seems to replace 'choosing genuine freedom' and comes closer to Beauvoir's ethics. 'The problem of choice appears only when nothing is left but the empty form of action' (IPC 256).

Étienne Balibar and Paolo Virno are Marxist thinkers who have explored the relation between individuation and the transindividual. For Balibar, whose primary interest is nationalism, transindividuality refers to the fact (also noted by Hegel) that our singularity is always imaginatively mixed with *identifications* that come from a variety social contexts.[58] Virno's description of the relationship between the individual and the multitude in early modern European political thought – also found in the institutions and national structures that grew up alongside and within that thought – can be compared to the relationship between the individual and his or her environment in Simondon. The multitude is not the 'people' who contract to have their sovereignty represented; the multitude tends to resist unification and incorporation.[59] 'The contemporary multitude ... occupies a middle region between "individual and collective;" for the multitude, then, the distinction between "public" and "private" is in no way validated.'[60] Perhaps Simondon, who distinguishes between community (the individuation of a group through habit) and society (a collection of individualised individuals), should have also considered the temporality of the multitude?

Under the conditions of contemporary neo-liberalism, for which *only* individuals exist, the multitude can be accessed only as an interior 'psychological' phenomenon of the individual.[61] As I am writing, more and more women but also men are caught in the situation Beauvoir attributes to the hetaera – their survival rests on 'pleasing' others, in the service economy if not the sex trade, and on 'branding' themselves:

> The hetaera does not uncover [disclose, *dévoile*] the world, she opens no road to human transcendence; on the contrary, she seeks to take possession of it [*capter*] for her profit . . . Giving herself to many men [or rather, lending: *se prêtant à plusiers hommes*], she belongs to none definitively; the money she accumulates, the name she 'launches' as one launches a product, ensure her economic autonomy . . . No man is their definitive master. But they have the most urgent need of man. (SS 612–14/2:391–3)

What poses the chief problem for contemporary citizens, who have a vague feeling of constant anxiety that they are not (already) sufficiently distinct from their fellow economic agents to assure themselves of justification and material support, is the apparent *absence* of the transindividual element that would 'normally' be available for individuals to draw on for the resolution of their problems or internal and external incompatibilities. We *feel* the problem we cannot think or speak, and run in search of refuge – a refuge that sometimes, as with the American war on terrorism, turns out to be even more oppressively homogenising and endangering than the ostensive object of our fears.[62]

In Deleuzian terms, by contrast to the classic political problem of the individual and the state or community, the 'problem' of the individual and the multitude is really about the right to *become* an assemblage and the right to *form* an assemblage – to crystallise with others and to discover inner facets to one's own existence as a crystal, by reflecting in and through others. One could also say that the entire problem of the individual and the multitude, as an example of the one and the many, is misguided because we are not 'either' one or many, we are on a continuum – sometimes part of the many, sometimes many 'ourselves', sometimes one, whether as a single body or a member of a pack. The concept of multiplicity, write Deleuze and Guattari, 'was created precisely in order to escape the abstract opposition between the multiple and the one' (TP 32/45).

Although solitude may often be as desirable as collective power, multiplicity becomes divided or singularises under different conditions than it solidarises; the question is who controls such occasions. Moreover, a *qualitative* multiplicity does not divide into identical units of the same substance but changes in being divided; interwoven tendencies are not likely to be comparable. We can only ask if this perspective on the one and the many would relieve some of the anxiety Virno describes, which leaves us running for refuge from the vulnerability entailed by our interchangeability with other workers as economic bubbles (another metastable phenomenon) repeatedly collapse.[63]

In *What is Philosophy?* Deleuze and Guattari claim that one can put a signature on concepts: the Cartesian *cogito*, Sartrean *metastability* (WIP 23–4/28–9). However, the problem that motivates the emergence of philosophy takes place *between* people, like the solution in which the growing crystals are suspended. Problems cannot be possessed, and entering into a problem or finding oneself *in a problem* changes who one is (the way someone, impersonally, 'gets into trouble'). Maybe this is one way of moving from the broken third synthesis of recognition in *Difference and Repetition* – the 'fractured I' – to the celebratory third synthesis of *Anti-Oedipus?*

Although sexist sense is actualised in individual habits, Beauvoir problematises the *Mitsein* because she considers the problem bigger than the self, the other as noetic object, the Other as *Autrui*, present or absent – and believes the Other has got to be part of the solutions (EA 72, 82/103–4, 119). The problem is *between* people, in their ratios of affecting and being affected. But identifying a problem, like willing to disclose being, allows people to reveal themselves as free and as separate. It also answers Deleuze's second objection to recognition, namely the reduction of 'power' to an object of struggle.[64] People certainly struggle to solve problems, sometimes they *are* problems for others, and often they want others to share their solutions, but as Foucault might argue, problematising itself breaks up the power relations that have hitherto stabilised a community and its oppositions.[65]

Back to *Mitsein*

What about Beauvoir's Heideggerian side, however? The term *Mitsein* and the ethical task of 'disclosing' being rather than seeking *to be* are Heideggerian. Beauvoir insists that it isn't death that prods us to adopt this attitude toward finitude, but something more positive – the desire for meaning, the creation and preservation of sense (PC 113–15/296–7). I have suggested that the need for meaning – framed as justification – comes from the *Mitsein*, just as the solution involves strengthening and transforming the *Mitsein*. This ideas, however, are mostly found in Beauvoir's literary essays, not in *The Second Sex*.

In *The Inoperative Community*, Jean-Luc Nancy examines *Mitsein* from the standpoint of the value of community. This indicates, first off, that *Mitsein* is not the same as community. If community and myth are linked in the popular and ethnological imagination, it is partly because community is itself the object of a myth, the myth of an age which believes itself fully secular and disenchanted. 'This does not mean only that community is a myth, that communitarian communion is a myth. It means that myth and myth's force and foundation are essential to community and that there can be, therefore, no community outside of myth' (IC 57). This myth was particularly strong in the countries that succumbed to fascism, but it also haunted the countries that tried to 'build' community explicitly on the basis of communist principles (IC 2–3).

Like Beauvoir, Nancy doubts that 'death' is the original meaning of finitude, though connecting it to death makes an otherwise fabricated community seem more solid and inevitable (IC 14–15). Apart from the myths of woman that also hold the *Mitsein* together as a community, fascist or otherwise, there is a fundamental imaginative connection between femininity and death that makes women figures of finitude for men who are supposed to be constructing and grasping the future more or less recklessly (SS 183–7/1:267–73). In the image of woman, as in the image of death, the subject of such a *Mitsein* experiences affects that seem to bind him to other (men) and make him feel part of an impersonal becoming.

In place of myth (and community), Nancy seems to advocate making literature the site of a fundamental *unworking* which gives individuals the *affect* of community without requiring the often bloody efforts of social and political construction (IC 39–41). Heidegger himself said that *Mitsein* was a fundamental aspect of Dasein's being-in-the-world, but he then focused on examples of *Mitsein* that were alienating and homogenising, rather than those that successfully individualise Dasein. After all, even people who do listen to the call of conscience must find some of their cultural conditions supportive. Nancy believes this inability to see a positive role for

Mitsein was linked to Heidegger's advocacy of a 'built' community through the Nazi programme (IC 12–14). Nancy believes Bataille moved explicitly away from such social projects, but Bataille, too, thought that love and sacrifice were 'reliable' ways of getting to the goal of community.

Again like Beauvoir, Nancy points to the heaps of dead individuals sacrificed for the dream of a society in which people would feel unified. Such violent means qualitatively transform and poison their end (IC 14). The affect of community is only possible if there is clear consciousness of separation, but Nancy clarifies (IC 19) that this consciousness is not individual, but pre-personal or transindividual. In other words, you and I are not aware of separation as biographical individuals; in fact, we may be confused about our contours whether or not we believe that we are separate. The *experience* of separation involves the awareness that we are, in fact, outside ourselves in others and that others have made a home in our thoughts or cast us in a protective role.

The spacing or sharing of being *between* humans – the betweenness of being, as Nancy would put it – is comparable in many respects to Simondon's ontology of 'plus-qu'unité', burgeoning with virtualities that have not been actualised in individuals. But for Nancy, like Beauvoir, the critique of unified/rarefied being (the critique of myth and its products) and the invitation to further individuation with and along the edges offered by other people takes place in literature.

> Speaking of the most personal experiences that we can have like loneliness, anguish, the death of the people we love, our own death, is on the contrary a way of bringing us together, of helping each other and of making the world less somber. I believe that this is one of the absolutely irreplaceable and essential tasks of literature: helping us communicate with each other through that which is the most solitary in ourselves and by which we are bound most the intimately to one other.[66]

And in Nancy's version of this critique: 'We are alike because each one of us is exposed to the outside that *we* are *for ourselves*. The like is not the same ... I do not rediscover *myself*, nor do I recognize *myself* in the other: I experience the other's alterity, or I experience alterity in the other together with the alteration that "in me" sets my singularity outside me and infinitely delimits it' (IC 33). Unlike Beauvoir, Nancy would not speak of 'allow[ing] my singular story to take on a universal dimension, so that everyone, while reading my book, could recognize his own personal preoccupations and communicate with me'.[67] Rather, Nancy's literary communist writes to disrupt the reader's sense of the certainty of his or her own narrative – and thus his or her boundaries. The literary communist also inspires a longing for myth, an awareness that the affect of community is desirable, even in the experience of separateness. But I would add that this longing and its ratio to the awareness of separation are different for each person (IC 77–8), moreover, part of what it means to be aware of separation is to be aware that none of us is separate in the *same way*.

In *The Ethics of Ambiguity*, Beauvoir speaks of the problem of communication between existents – a problem that *may be* more or less solved through 'recognition'. 'To make being "be" is to communicate with others by means of being' (EA 71/102) and, although this complicity cannot be sustained for long, Batailléan 'expenditure' is 'a matter of establishing a communication of the existants, for it is by the movement of recognition that goes from one to the other that existence is confirmed' (EA 126/182). The longing for community is one version of a desire for being, but to be aware of this longing along with separation is *already* to disclose being, already to indicate the multiple dimensions along which we are linked and closed off to each other. Literature, in Heideggerian terms, can 'let the reader be' in a non-devoted way, not leaping-ahead. In turn, it inspires readers to 'let being be', not destroying the potentials in their situation but working with them.[68] Men and women need to let one another be in a caring way, where caring means taking responsibility for their own desire to be, their own desire for community, whether one represented by a myth of woman or one brutally enacted through the control and exploitation of women's bodies (see IC 103).

This is the light in which to read not only Beauvoir's philosophical *oeuvre* but also her literary theory.

> Insofar as I am captivated [by a literary situation], suddenly it is no longer I who says 'I.' I am in another world. . . . I still live in mine, but I leave it; there is a perpetual movement back and forth that results in the world of others becoming mine while I am still in my world.[69]

In her three most important essays on literature ('Literature and Metaphysics', 'What Can Literature Do?' and 'My Experience as a Writer'), Beauvoir clearly thinks one writes (among other acts) as a *singularity*, in relation to singular words and scenes that are, however, impersonally shared. Unlike philosophical writing, novels communicate through contingencies rather than through knowledge. Although one can reduce the number of contingencies in real life, the novel can only communicate by offering readers elements that seem to be contingent and thereby provoke their own freedom.[70] Indeed, readers lend the situations found in a novel their own temporality, and presumably this experience of passivity in relation to a new situation provokes a freedom whose use changes the *quality* of that temporality.[71] If they do not risk themselves in this way, she argued in 'Literature and Metaphysics', the novel will fail despite the author's best intentions.[72]

In the tradition of French rationalism, the distinction between personal and impersonal thought is associated with Spinoza.[73] Personal thought is mixed with imagination, but impersonal thought is the thought of nature as a whole. Beauvoir, however, is not interested in Spinozism but rather in a challenging dialogue with Leibniz. Literature is justified because individual situations, including those of readers, are *not* monadic or closed on themselves and the world, far from being a totality, is the *process* of their interaction.[74] In 'Merleau-Ponty and Pseudo-Sartreanism', an essay in which Beauvoir's characterisations of Sartre and Merleau-Ponty are undeniably convoluted and questionable, we can nevertheless see that what Beauvoir would *like* Sartre to affirm, would *value* in Sartre, is the concept of 'detotalised totality' and the notion of the 'inter-world' that Merleau-Ponty, to her mind outrageously, claims is lacking in Sartre.[75]

The words and scenes of literature are not just 'drawn from' elsewhere (as in Balibar's transindividuality); the only place they exist is *between* singularities (connecting them uneasily to a multitude). These words and scenes salve the bite of ontological separation from 'Pyrrhus and Cineas' through Beauvoir's essays on literature in the 1960s and 70s. They make affect manageable, and could make philosophy an affair of feeling as well as thinking. They counter-actualise affect at the level of events that no one owns. As Dan Smith paraphrases Deleuze's Spinoza lectures:

> Just as we may have an Idea of a continuous flow of matter in the universe, of which we ourselves are modifications, so we can conceive of a continuous flow of thought in the universe, of which we are likewise modifications . . . The thoughts that come and go in our heads, of which we are neither the origin nor the author,

are the products of this thought flow. Or more precisely, they are themselves the very movement of this universal flow of thought – a flow that is anonymous, impersonal, and indeterminate, like a continuous internal monologue.[76]

Beauvoir's literary writings stress the *plurality* and the potential *inter-personality* or *trans-personality* of this 'flow of thought'.[77] Like many other philosophers, she rebels against the association of *impersonality* in early modern philosophers such as Spinoza or Leibniz with *affectlessness*. Impersonality need not mean affectlessness; in fact, it might imply a particularly convoluted and overdetermined welter of affects.

In discussing Beauvoir's autobiographies, Miranda Fricker observes that there is a kind of ethical work on the self involved in the very effort to combine younger and older perspectives and to forge a solidarity between them across the span – or dissociation – of aging.[78] How can one be committed to the freedom and therefore longevity of one's past self or future self, whatever their faults or failures? The very project calls into question the 'unity' of the author, whether the author's involvement in external collaborations, like Beauvoir ventriloquising Sartre, or the author's internal plurality. Such plurality makes her capable of separation and reconnection, or capable of honesty about separation as well as about the jouissance of co-implication or com-plicity. Deleuze never wrote fiction, but his experience of co-authorship with Guattari might speak to the way that problematisation and actualisation of *Mitsein* work.[79] It takes time, although it is never present *at one time*, and this is why it is an *event*.

> The theory of proper names should not be conceived of in terms of representation; it refers instead to the class of 'effects': effects that are not a mere dependence on causes, but the occupation of a domain, and the operation of a system of signs. This can be clearly seen in physics, where proper names designate such effects within fields of potentials: the Joule effect, the Seebeck effect, the Kelvin effect. History is like physics: a Joan of Arc effect, a Heliogabalus effect – all the *names* of history, and not the name of the father. (AO 86/103)

Is there a Beauvoir effect onto which feminists and philosophers stumble, a region of potentials in a political or intellectual or sexual situation? Are there philosophies, novels or lives one could say are haunted by the 'Beauvoir effect' – which Judith Butler rediscovers in Kate Bornstein's successive refusal of both genders, or Le Dœuff identifies with the capacity of a book like *The Second Sex* to temporarily lift the curse of loneliness?[80] Following Penelope Deutscher, maybe we could suggest that the Beauvoir effect consists in a conversion, by means of disclosing another being/becoming, of one's own being/desire-to-be into a becoming/desire-to-become. When a writer enters into this process, even when they think they're writing by themselves, one might say they are becoming-Beauvoir in a certain sense, they are entering her event or using it to help counter-actualise whatever nonsense confronts them.

Because the point is ultimately not to describe disclosure or to justify it, as Marx might say, but to *get out there*, even when reading Beauvoir, and disclose her and the world in a way that enhances freedom.

Notes

1. 'And therefore, if the earlier forms of society are natural, so is the state, for it is the end of them, and the nature of a thing is its end. For what each thing is when fully developed, we call its nature, whether we are speaking of a man, a horse, or a family. Besides, the final cause and end of a thing is the best, and to be self-sufficing is the end and the best' (Aristotle *Politics*, book 1, chapter 2, 1252b30).
2. Aristotle, *Metaphysics* book 7, chapter 8; see also *Of Generation and Corruption*.
3. See their account of *stratification* in chapter 3, '10,000 B.C.: The Geology of Morals' and of the *machinic phylum* in chapter 12, '1227: Treatise on Nomadology' (TP 40–5, 408–15/54–60, 507–17).
4. In 'Pyrrhus and Cineas', Beauvoir uses the metaphor of an arch whose stones support one another without pillars. See Beauvoir, 'Pyrrhus and Cineas' (PC), 140/367.
5. Hughes, *Deleuze's Difference and Repetition* 44–5.
6. Natanson, *Anonymity*, 25–9; Arendt, *The Human Condition*, 179.
7. 'In all these cases power is always the object of a representation, of a *recognition* which materially presupposes a comparison of consciousnesses (Deleuze, *Nietzsche and Philosophy*, 80).
8. For example, Foucault, 'Truth and Power', 120.
9. Deleuze, *Cinema 2*, 170–2, 182.
10. See Parker, 'Singularity in Beauvoir's *The Ethics of Ambiguity*'.
11. Holveck, *Philosophy of Lived Experience*, 69.
12. Hegel, *Phenomenology of Spirit*, §670, p. 408.
13. Simondon, *L'Individuation Psychique et Collective* (IPC), 27. All translations from Simondon are mine.

14. Hughes, *Deleuze's Difference and Repetition*, 27–8.
15. Bauer, too, suspects that the notion of recognition attributed to Hegel is not exactly Hegelian. Bauer, *Simone de Beauvoir, Philosophy, and Feminism*, 83–4.
16. For both Kierkegaard and Heidegger, the 'they' of public opinion endangers an individual's relationship to him or herself, and in Kierkegaard's case, to faith and religion. Concern for the opinion of others tends to make us avoid a personal destiny. Kierkegaard, 'The Modern Age', in *Two Ages*; Heidegger, *Being and Time*, 164–8.
17. See also her comment in 'Moral Idealism and Political Realism', 'If man's good is constituted by the élan of human transcendence, and if the result forms a single process with the movement leading to it, then it becomes impossible to disassociate the end from the means' (184).
18. We should probably regard this as an example of consciousness as being for-itself interrupting *society* as an example of being in-itself by imposing its own interpretations and temporality.
19. Recall from Chapter 2: 'Our projection of our psychic states into space in order to form a discrete multiplicity is likely to influence these states themselves and to give them in reflective consciousness a new form, which immediate perception did not attribute to them' (Bergson, TFW 90).
20. In her review of *The Phenomenology of Perception*, Beauvoir contrasts Sartre's 'nihilating power of the mind' to Merleau-Ponty's belief that 'our existence never grasps itself in its nakedness but as it is expressed by our body. And this body is not enclosed in the instant but implies an entire history, and even a prehistory' (Beauvoir, 'Review of *The Phenomenology of Perception*', 163).
21. When Husserl speaks about the unity of 'immanent time' combining a variety of protentions and retentions in its horizon, he seems to be describing a qualitative multiplicity or 'duration' in Bergson's sense, for which the idea of 'succession' is inappropriately spatial. Husserl, *On the Phenomenology of the Consciousness of Internal Time*, 80–3. However, in Appendix VI, 'The grasping of the absolute flow', Husserl more or less *defines* duration as the enduring of an 'external' object rather than the enduring of consciousness, whether or not it is focused on 'mental' objects or its own flow (ibid., 118). See Winkler, 'Husserl and Bergson', for an elucidation of Husserl's claim that 'We are the true Bergsonians.'
22. On this subject, see Part III of *Ideas II*, 'Constitution of the Spiritual World'. In earlier texts such as *Cartesian Meditations*, the infinite profiles of the self are addressed on pages 44–5, while the negative account of the other as 'non-given' from the standpoint of the ego's structure is replaced by a more positive account on pages 105 and 114.

23. See Lundgren-Gothlin, 'Simone de Beauvoir's Notions of Appeal, Desire and Ambiguity'; Daigle, '*The Second Sex* as Appeal'.
24. See Daigle, '*The Second Sex* as Appeal'.
25. Bergson, *Two Sources*, 26.
26. Bergson, *Two Sources*, 27.
27. Langer, 'Beauvoir and Merleau-Ponty on Ambiguity'; Weiss, 'Beauvoir and Merleau-Ponty'.
28. Deutscher, *Ambiguity, Conversion, Resistance*, 47–58.
29. See Heidegger, *Being and Time*, 262–3, 384–401. 'Disclosedness' basically introduces an ontological, as well as an explicitly interpretive, aspect to the Husserlian concept of intentionality. The first mention in *The Ethics of Ambiguity* is credited (on page 12) to Sartre, then discussed on pages 28–32. But Beauvoir uses the concept more often in the relatively short *Ethics of Ambiguity* than Sartre does in all of *Being and Nothingness*.
30. This is a problematic comparison, for colonial oppression and even slavery were justified by Europeans on the ground that other peoples were 'children' from an anthropological standpoint who needed to be educated scientifically and economically in order to participate in modernity. See Mehta, *Liberalism and Empire*, particularly the Introduction.
31. See Simondon, *L'Individuation Psychique et Collective* (IPC), 99–100.
32. Beauvoir, *All Men Are Mortal*, 167.
33. Beauvoir, *All Men Are Mortal*, 183–4.
34. In 'Political Realism', Beauvoir acknowledges that 'throughout history we see wars follow upon wars, revolutions upon revolutions' and can draw no meaning but the meaning invested in them by finite participants; on the other hand, in *The Ethics of Ambiguity* she argues against Hegel's assumption that war is structurally inevitable. Beauvoir, 'Political Realism', 181; Beauvoir. EA 105/152.
35. Bauer, *Simone de Beauvoir, Philosophy, and Feminism*, 232. The importance of risk and generosity in Bergoffen's reading of *The Ethics of Ambiguity* will be discussed below.
36. Bauer, 'Beauvoir's Heideggerian Ontology', 69.
37. Beauvoir, 'What Can Literature Do?', 199.
38. This is a very important point in Ann Murphy's comparison between Beauvoir's ethics of ambiguity and Butler's recent reflections on vulnerability: vulnerability and the capacity for violence imply one another and while violence (for example, in defence of the oppressed) is not always evil, *denying* or *ignoring* that our hands can never be 'clean' so long as we are at risk or at stake in a world of plurality is, for Beauvoir, a kind of evil (Murphy, 'Ambiguity and Precarious Life', 223–5).
39. Sartre uses this concept to refer to the way that consciousness as *reflection* unifies the field of phenomena that consciousness has otherwise

fragmented and brought into relations of opposition through negation. Present, past and future are ways that consciousness simultaneously distinguishes itself from the in-itself and *produces* the in-itself, as necessity (past) and possibility (future) (BN 221).

The term is clustered in Sartre's discussions of temporality, of transcendence, and fleetingly but perhaps most significantly (for us) in his claim that our existence for the Other – individual or collective – does not provide our consciousness with a *ground* but introduces yet another source of decomposition and detachment, as Others are themselves 'detotalising' (BN 339).

40. Here 'detotalised totality' means 'that, on the one hand, there is a world that is indeed the same for us all, but on the other hand we are all in situation in relation to it. This situation involves our past, our class, our condition, our projects, basically the entire ensemble of what makes up our individuality . . . So implicitly enveloping the world does not mean that one knows it, but that one reflects it, typifies it, or *expresses* it in the way that Leibniz spoke of expressing the world.' Beauvoir, 'What Can Literature Do?', 198–9.
41. Beauvoir, 'Literature and Metaphysics', 270–1.
42. Beauvoir, 'What Can Literature Do?', 296.
43. Beauvoir, 'What Can Literature Do?', 201; see also 'My Experience as a Writer', 296.
44. Bergson, *Matter and Memory*, 89–95.
45. Bergson, *Matter and Memory*, 100–1. See Alexandre Lefebvre, *The Image of Law*, where inattentive judgement based on habit memory – simple recognition and subsumption (167–9) is contrasted with attentive judgement (182–9). Attentive judgement begins with lack of recognition of a sensory particular and gradually works toward construction of a new object in light of the data from the past with which, as one forages, it is compared (188–9).
46. Bergson, *Matter and Memory*, 106.
47. Bergson, *Matter and Memory*, 166–9. Thus recognition can also mean something like acting together, which is the sense given to the term by Jessica Benjamin. See Benjamin, *The Bonds of Love*, 18–23, 26–7, 30. For Bauer, genuine recognition means finding one's own boundaries so that others can find theirs (*Simone de Beauvoir, Philosophy, and Feminism*, 233). Neither is a 'conventional' understanding of recognition.
48. Bergoffen, *Gendered Phenomenologies*, 61–4, 96–8.
49. Bergoffen, *Gendered Phenomenologies*, 102.
50. See also Beauvoir, 'My Experience as a Writer', 289, 292, 295.
51. It could be, for example, a 'pre-subjective' intentionality or passive synthesis. See O'Donnell, 'Beyond Sexuality', 232.
52. Note that no individual is ever individuated 'once and for all'; in the case of humans, individuation continues at the level of psychology

and culture as 'individualisation' (IPC 176–7). Groups themselves undergo a second individuation (IPC 188–9).
53. In his book on Beauvoir's philosophy, Michel Kail uses 'transindividual' in a similar way, arguing that individual beings are always incomplete and in need of society/history to fill in (Kail, *Simone de Beauvoir Philosophe*). This is how he accounts for the intertwining of social and biological forces in Beauvoir's chapter on Biology, in which he finds seeds for a philosophy of history.
54. Simondon makes an analogy between ontological individuation, which leaves some potentials in abeyance, and phase change between solids, liquids and gases.
55. Beauvoir, 'Must We Burn Sade?', 45.
56. Beauvoir, 'Must We Burn Sade?', 91.
57. Beauvoir, 'Must We Burn Sade?', 55; Bergoffen, *Gendered Phenomenologies*, 131.
58. See Balibar, 'Homo Nationalis', 25–7; and Balibar, *Spinoza: From Individuality to Transindividuality*.
59. Virno, *Grammar of the Multitude*, 21–3.
60. Virno, *Grammar of the Multitude*, 25.
61. Virno, *Grammar of the Multitude*, 24. See, for example, Foucault: 'The individual's life itself – with his relationships to his private property . . . his family, household, insurance and retirement – must make him into a sort of permanent and multiple enterprise.' Foucault, *The Birth of Biopolitics*, 241–5.
62. Virno, *Grammar of the Multitude*, 31–5.
63. Virno, *Grammar of the Multitude*, 33.
64. Deleuze, *Nietzsche and Philosophy*, 79.
65. 'The work of a history of thought would be to rediscover at the root of these diverse solutions the general form of problematisation that has made them possible – even in their very opposition; or what has made possible the transformations of the difficulties and obstacles of a practice into a general problem for which one proposes diverse practical solutions.' Foucault, 'Polemics, Politics, and Problematizations', 118.
66. Beauvoir, 'My Experience as a Writer', 297.
67. Beauvoir, 'My Experience as a Writer', 283–4.
68. See Heidegger's critique of misapplied 'care' in *Being and Time*, 158; as well as Beauvoir's critique of 'devotion' in 'Pyrrhus and Cineas' (PC 117–22/308–31).
69. Beauvoir, 'My Experience as a Writer', 296.
70. Beauvoir, 'My Experience as a Writer', 289.
71. Beauvoir, 'My Experience as a Writer', 294.
72. Beauvoir, 'Literature and Metaphysics', 276.
73. Peden, *Spinoza Contra Phenomenology*, 66
74. Beauvoir, 'What Can Literature Do?', 199.

75. Beauvoir, 'Merleau-Ponty and Pseudo-Sartreanism', 211, 218.
76. Smith, 'Analytics', in *Essays on Deleuze*, 141.
77. Such a flow, of course, accompanies the flow of bodies and strata even if it also cuts them apart and makes some seem like beings and others like events of transition or becoming.
78. Fricker, 'Life-story in Beauvoir's Memoirs', 220, 224.
79. 'It's just a question of something passing through you, a current, which alone has a proper name. Even when you think you're writing on your own, you're always doing it with someone else you can't always name' (Deleuze, *Negotiations*, 141).
80. Butler, *Undoing Gender*, 65; Le Dœuff, *Hipparchia's Choice*, 57.

Chapter 5

Territories and Assemblages

> A novel is a 'problematique.' The story of my life is itself a problematique. I don't have any solutions to give to people and people don't have to await solutions from me. It is in this regard that, sometimes what you call my fame, people's expectations of me, bothers me. There is a certain unreasonable demand that I find a little stupid because it would enclose me, immobilize me completely in a sort of feminist concrete block.[1]

The Second Sex had enormous international impact. It appeared before the emergence of second-wave feminism, and influenced Betty Friedan, whose *The Feminine Mystique* was responsible for the resurgence of liberal feminism in the United States, as well as numerous feminist ideas emerging from the American activist left, such as those of Shulamith Firestone.[2] Excoriated by a largely masculine literary press on its first appearance in France, it was nonetheless well received by women.[3] During the 1970s, it was once again attacked by French feminists emerging from a psychoanalytic, anti-existentialist intellectual culture.[4]

In the United States, despite a truncated translation,[5] Beauvoir's popularity among activists endured and professional philosophers sought to claim her as one of their own, although she had primarily been regarded as a novelist in France. During the 1980s and 1990s, however, real and superficial improvements in the situation of American women made *The Second Sex* seem out of date to younger feminists, who were, moreover, attempting to understand their place in the history of international colonial and racial domination more accurately.[6] The publication of Beauvoir's letters with Sartre challenged the 'official' image of the couple that had been built up in the media and by her memoirs, while European scholars were busy revising the place of existentialism in the Resistance and immediate post-war period.[7]

As Penelope Deutscher has pointed out, there were tensions in *The Second Sex* between multiple disciplines and conceptual methodologies on which Beauvoir drew to portray women's 'lived experience'.[8] Mariam Fraser, like Foucault, suggests that we do not even have a concept of the human 'individual' except insofar as built up by a plurality of disciplines and scenes of interaction and imagination. What disciplinary and political 'difficulties' in the specific field of Beauvoir's interaction with feminists can be resolved by reading Beauvoir in relation to Deleuze? Let us consider three: Beauvoir's identification as a literary writer, her supposed masculinism, and her apparent cultural universalism.

Philosophical and literary problems

One of the strangest difficulties involves Beauvoir's choice to refer to herself in her memoirs and all public appearances as a novelist or literary writer rather than a philosopher. She 'left the philosophy to Sartre', although the latter was also a well-known novelist. This identification was particularly vexing to North American feminist philosophers who believed her solidarity and prominence would help them make gains in an extraordinarily male-dominated academic field. But given the enormous cultural prestige of philosophy in France, Beauvoir's (dis)identification with the discipline could only seem like feminine deference to Sartre.[9]

In fact, Beauvoir said on many occasions that her distance from philosophy reflected a specific notion of what counted as philosophy – the building of speculative systems (PL 178). This is by no means the only definition of philosophy – and one can reject this definition on thoroughly philosophical grounds. It may have been the definition of philosophy held by the male-dominated academic establishment when she was a student and a young philosophy teacher. But it was still her definition of philosophy, and it explained why she wished to pursue her problems through literature when possible. In addition to Simons, other philosophers (particularly Holveck) and literary critics (such as Moi and Tidd) have recognised philosophical arguments and references in her novels.[10] Much of Beauvoir's writing, including a large portion of *The Second Sex*, is devoted to philosophy of literature in some loose sense.

In 'Literature and Metaphysics', for example, Beauvoir discusses how the novel's way of dealing with 'universal' questions such as human separation (she does not use the word finitude) differs from philosophy by beginning from specific situations rather than from universal concepts. As described in the preceding chapter, literature gives practice in grappling with the fact of singularity by generating a *fictional* singularity, a singular world of the imagination. It provokes faculties beginning at the pre-personal level, prior to 'recognition'. The assemblage formed by the reader, the material support of the text and its fictional world can *do* more, learn more, and compose with more elements than before. In literature, the difficulty of dealing with elements of experience that would seem illogical, absurd or contradictory according to philosophical principles is openly acknowledged, through situations and characters that are themselves shot through with ambivalence and nonsense.

In *Difference and Repetition*, Deleuze's focus is on the genesis of Ideas/problems through *thought*, by contrast to *What is Philosophy?* where he and Guattari define philosophy as a discipline distinct from the sciences or arts by reference to the distinction between concepts, percepts and affects. *Difference and Repetition* presents three examples of Ideas with objects that are problematic but structure a field of experience and knowledge: atomism as a physical Idea, the organism as a biological Idea, and abstract labour as a social Idea (DR 182–6/238–41). He also considers structure as a linguistic Idea (DR 191, 203–4/247, 264–5), albeit one that has been mistakenly reduced to binary oppositions, and considers that structure and *sense* are the same 'with regard to the actual terms and relations in which they are incarnated' (DR 191/247).

For Bergson, evolutionary development over several generations may be described as successful problem-solving, rather than as a series of momentary acts of accidental selection. In other words, selection acts on the lineage rather than the individual, and the lineage is the answer to a problem. For Simondon, the individual is by definition in disequilibrium with its environment and must resolve this problem in its life or, for humans, his or her life. For Deleuze, *a life* is different from a chronological biography in that it is a collection of singularities, many of which are not considered biographically relevant. In *Difference and Repetition*, such problems emerge as a result of incommensurability between contractions of habit and the unity that they anticipate. In a way, philosophy differs from literature in its manner of taking up the problem of all human existence, the problem of the 'relationship between man and man' as Beauvoir wrote in her essay on Sade. But both are also responses to a fundamentally Deleuzian problem: the creation of the 'new' in life and art, and in life by way of art. In literature, the reader must lend his or her flesh to the creation of the problem and its solutions.

Audrey Wasser has suggested that literature can originate in problems and that there are 'literary' problems writers must solve, much as organisms seek to solve biological problems.[11] Wasser is critical of two approaches to literary genesis: one that 'posits that the cause of a work is an idea, intention or social-historical reality that will be reflected in the work once the work has been made' (such that effects resemble causes); and another that 'suspects that the truly new cannot be articulated in advance of its creation' but must be . . . 'the absence of all condition'.[12] Wasser would locate this origin in the 'being of the problematic', where the problem is more complex than any work that results and to which the work offers itself as a possible solution.[13]

Along with the 'true' problems that are the object of Ideas such as abstract labour, according to Deleuze, there are numerous 'false' problems or transcendental illusions such as 'commodity fetishism' (DR 208/268–9). 'All the figures of non-sense appear in the objective field of the false problem'; for some people 'the whole of differenciated social existence is tied to the false problems which enable them to live'. Perhaps sexism is one of these 'false' problems, or racism, a transcendental illusion whose confusing effects are compounded when it is analytically separated from gender; while the 'true' problem might be 'individuation', 'ambiguity' or even 'reciprocity' as an ethical ideal.

True, false or ambiguously folded each inside the other, one example of the philosophical problem posed by sexist sense is the dearth of female conceptual personae in the work of male philosophers.[14] But sexist sense was also a *literary* and a *life* problem for Beauvoir, as it is for many readers. When Beauvoir analyses so many novelists in *The Second Sex*, it's not just because she needs sociological or historical evidence for systematic misogyny – it's because as a novelist herself, she realises that idioms for describing relationships between women from a non-masculinist point of view are lacking, as well as descriptions of male characters from a plausible woman's point of view. In her interview with Susan Brison, Beauvoir suggested that one of her primary challenges was how to carry out an ideal of 'committed' literature while creating female characters whose problems and psychological deficiencies seemed *real* – rather than the cardboard ideals of socialist realism.[15] The absence of idioms in which any of these issues between European men and women could be presented from a non-Western immigrant or minority point of view is yet another problem, one Beauvoir does not even truly recognise – as Deutscher pointedly asks, why were neither Richard Wright nor Léopold Sédar Senghor tapped in *The Second Sex* as male authors whose presentations of women might teach us something about myths of woman?[16]

Sexist sense is not the only literary problem that interests Beauvoir. As a beginning writer, she was fascinated with techniques for depicting point of view, specifically how multiple points of view could present a situation without reference to inner thoughts and motives (PL 88). She reports that at about the same moment that Sartre was first taken with phenomenology, the two of them were also fascinated with American popular writers like Hemingway or Dos Passos.[17] This enthusiasm reflects a practical and philosophical desire to convey 'inner' affect using only the language of outer actions and reactions (PL 113–14). These novels broke ground in striving to reveal a *situation* rather than motives.[18] As such, Beauvoir's literary problems were not just shared by Sartre, in *Transcendence of the Ego*, but also with ordinary language philosophers.

Another problem discussed by Beauvoir is the way that different genres such as the novel, the play and the essay distribute the reader's space and time. In her interview with Brison, Beauvoir tackles the problem posed by *écriture feminine* of the 60s and 70s: namely, language is not an individual initiative and the writer cannot attempt to reinvent language, however noble her political justification for the effort.[19] And finally, there is the crucial problem of how to create an *imaginative experience* for the reader with all the ambiguity of a real experience except that 'invisible' details of emotions and tone are articulated and can therefore be shared by others (PL 431–2).[20] Autobiography poses its own problems: the formation of a self that is *intended* for others' intentionality rather than (primarily) one's own, and the relationship between chronology and intemporal meaning.[21]

As Toril Moi has observed, biography plays a disproportionate role in the public reception of female intellectuals. Too often their work is reduced to their experiences, particularly sexual or romantic ones.[22] This problem continues today, as Ann Murphy has shown, in news coverage of the cinquentenaire of *The Second Sex*.[23] In 1949, the press was scathing in its reduction of Simone de Beauvoir to La Grande Sartreuse, and critics assumed that her novels, like *The Second Sex*, were essentially biographical (and therefore unoriginal). But too often, feminists also focused on Beauvoir's biography – for example, activists were ambivalent about the value of philosophical work given male domination and class elitism in academia. Others were interested in her life for the positive reason that they were looking for models of a viable life as a free woman.[24] Later, the same public discovered that Beauvoir's memoirs were more fictional than she led people to believe, particularly with respect to her bisexuality and her jealousy of Sartre's other lovers. Once accused of lacking originality and simply repeating real life, she was now accused of inventing even real life.

The most obvious way in which even philosophers have threatened to reduce Beauvoir's work to her life concerns the struggle to establish 'influence'.[25] However accurate or inaccurate Beauvoir might have been in stressing her intellectual reciprocity with Sartre, reciprocity was clearly her goal and the idea under which she wished her life experience to be read. Psychoanalytic readings of Beauvoir's literature also threaten to be reductionistic – as if the life itself were not *also* a work. As Beauvoir protested with respect to psychoanalysis in *The Second Sex*, 'the individual is always explained through his link to the past and not with respect to a future toward which he projects himself' (SS 60/1:92).

Although literary problems emerge from problematic relationships in 'life' as well as the textual domain, they are manifest in *relationships* between characters, not in the characters themselves. It would be wrong to see all the characters as autobiographical, as many early critics claimed.[26] Zaza, Sartre, Beauvoir's mother, her teacher Mlle Mercier and even Merleau-Ponty lurk behind aspects of Beauvoir's characters. But individuation, or grappling with death and survivorship, are *problems* that are impersonal and interpersonal. 'If literature seeks to surpass separation at the point where it seems most unsurpassable', Beauvoir writes, 'it must speak of anguish, solitude, and death, because those are precisely the situations that enclose us most radically in our singularity.'[27] The woman who dies from deference to her mother's wishes; the teacher whose lack of self-awareness has disastrous consequences for her students; the survivor who questions the value of life without those who have died; the man who cannot love but uses a woman as a social shield for his independence – these are all conceptual personae from whose characteristic 'affects' the reader is invited to construct his or her own problems.

Some of the characters are victims of clichés; for example, Monique in *The Woman Destroyed*. But those that escape this fate achieve an impersonal plane. Hélène, who rode in the back of the truck with the two Jewish women during the first wave of Occupation (in *The Blood of Others*), repeats and counter-actualises that event in the truck that delivers the bomb and eventually kills her. Henri, who fought to represent the truth of the Gulag despite Robert's objections (in *The Mandarins*), lies in order to protect the singularity of Josette's life, for which there is otherwise no language. Laurence (in *Les Belles Images*) depersonalises in the effort to preserve her sense of the political present within her family – on behalf of her daughter – a transformation which her husband utterly fails to appreciate, seeing it merely as 'strong feelings' she should have expressed earlier. These events put the characters on the impersonal plane, but such transformations could not happen to the characters except by virtue of the relations they have with other characters.

Of course a life has biographical elements, ordinary points on the curve and moments of dramatic transition and transformation (DR 188–9/244–5).[28] However, neither Beauvoir's argument about morality with Sartre in the Luxembourg Gardens (as Michèle Le Dœuff suggests), nor her relationship with her mother (as Moi suggests), nor loneliness and the fear of death (as Marks believes) are *strictly* biographical problems.[29] Zaza's death and Sartre's freedom were both challenges to Beauvoir's *own* freedom, which may indeed have found repeated forms in Beauvoir's later relationships with other women and men. But they were not traumas in the sense of tragedies lacking interest as *problems* in their own right, problems in which others besides Beauvoir were implicated. They were also foreshadows or early sketches of problems with which many other women identified.[30]

Ambiguities of sex

A second and related 'difficulty' involves Beauvoir's supposed over-valorisation of male traits and activities. This criticism has been made by cultural feminists in the United States, psychoanalytic feminists in France, and recently by some African and Africanist feminists. Does Beauvoir, in fact, value autonomy and aggression – traits associated with men in Western cultures – over traits associated with femininity, such as relationality and care? Is it that these traits are less valuable than commonly believed, or, as Nkiru Nzegwu argues, is it that they are less 'masculine' than Western feminists believe?[31] This argument runs in the opposite direction of those who believe Beauvoir should have taken credit for the 'masculine' discourse of philosophy, although it is supported by feminist philosophers who wish to argue for the ethical pre-eminence of care.

It is true that in *The Second Sex*, Beauvoir never envisions men sharing childcare to any significant degree. Shared childcare was a demand of many feminists, particularly in the United States, emerging from an object-relations psychoanalytic tradition to which Beauvoir contributed indirectly through her influence on Jessica Benjamin.[32] Not only would men's participation in childcare free up women's energy for more interesting and lucrative work, if children of both sexes observed equality and reciprocity between their parents in rearing children and engaging with the economic and political world, they might grow up adopting prosocial traits of both sexes and valuing men and women equally. Beauvoir's words are ambiguous: 'Maternity leave would be paid for by the society that would have responsibility for the children, which does not mean that they would be *taken* from their parents but that they would not be *abandoned* to them' (SS 760/2:569).

A generous interpretation reads 'maternity' as an institution and a social function that cannot be reduced to biological birth – an event that, as she comments in an earlier chapter, always requires assistance among human beings (SS 547–8/2:317). But the institution of maternity will still mean something different in cultures where children have always been raised in more extensive collectives.[33] Without believing in the success of the Soviet experiment, Beauvoir probably assumed that some of its goals would become widespread. Collective day care was a goal shared by other modernist projects such as the progressive reformism of Charlotte Perkins Gilman and the Zionist kibbutz. So if men were not anticipated to share childcare in the private family home, they might have been expected to care for children in educational and recreational institutions, as they have long worked in other institutions.

For Beauvoir, all activities – whether sexual, educative, political or economic - are *human* activities, not male or female. Thus it would be less a question of 'allowing women' to participate in traditionally male domains[34] than of *removing* artificial barriers on women's access to work that could earn them economic independence, as well as removing barriers to men's participation in childcare and housework – such as sequestration in factories, initially imposed to discipline impoverished male wage labourers. In the case of women of colour who were long expected to work outside the home, removing economic barriers to care for their own children might be equally important. Although sexist sense may be an event that 'did not happen', moreover, there were certainly historically identifiable dated events that contribute to the impression of its inevitability.[35] In the European case, women participated in the French Revolution, like so many others, and many expected to share in the new Republic's governing structures – until laws were passed to prohibit them.[36] Likewise, poor English women performed heavy labour in coal mines alongside men until the male union movement excluded them from this work. This exclusion was affirmed on humanitarian grounds, and on the grounds of improving family life, but it entailed the destruction of working white women's awareness of their own physical strength and its recognition by society on the same terms as white men's.[37]

More important, as Kathryn Gines points out, although Beauvoir contrasts the 'non-event' of women's subordination to the historically identifiable events of capitalist or colonial domination, such events were certainly turning points in the histories of the women from dominated communities, who made up the vast majority of humankind.[38] For example, being forced to take care of white men's sexuality or to nurture children they had with white women certainly marks a historical change for black slaves and colonised women. Last but not least, *men of* colour and sometimes poor white men also assisted with housework in white colonial homes – but only after a fairly precise historical moment.

If one conceives any individual as a qualitative multiplicity on Bergson's model, only gradually individuated over time with respect to other individuals and to themselves, then one can also see that the division of social traits and socially productive activities by sex is artificial.

> In fact, man is, like woman, a flesh, thus a passivity, the plaything of his hormones and the species, uneasy prey to his desire; and she, like him, in the heart of carnal fever, is consent, voluntary gift, and activity; each of them lives the strange ambiguity of existence made body in his or her own way. In these combats where they believe they are tackling each other, they are fighting their own self, projecting onto their partner the part of themselves they repudiate; instead of living the ambiguity of their condition, each one tries to make the other accept the abjection of this condition and reserves the honor of it for one's self. (SS 763/2:573)

Reading ambiguity as *multiplicity* or *assemblage* suggests that every individual possesses capacities for affecting and being affected that can be combined to form *many* masculinities and femininities. But the individual human, whatever his or her sex or personality, never exists apart from a series of social units or assemblages that give these traits meaning. We would not be male *or* female outside of assemblages that give sexuality and reproduction a social meaning.[39] No man or woman, no masculinity or femininity should be reduced to bare anatomical facts. Such a reduction, like women's exclusion from the public and economic sphere, is a falsification and freezing of the complexity of human becoming.[40]

Human freedom never abolishes ambiguity. Transcendence as Beauvoir conceives it is *always* disclosed in relation to immanence, just as any qualitative aspect of an experience is distinguished, spatially located, and disclosed in relation to a complex and shifting whole. The process of individuation does not erase or resolve the multiplicity at the heart of each individual or that individual's immersion in the flow of social habit. This is why individuals are forced to resolve their internal and external disequilibrium *with others*, in action and in the realm of imagination. Ambiguity does not mean 'imprecision'; to the contrary, it means a state that is *too precise* and *too volatile* for the categories that individuals and groups bring to it. Just as assemblages always have one aspect that tends toward change and another that tends toward stability or stasis, so human freedom is caught between transcendence and immanence.

For Beauvoir, as for Merleau-Ponty, this tension between change and stasis is lived as a *bodily* condition and imaginatively represented in terms of the crude comparison between two sexes.[41] In some significant cases, sexual intimacy presents individuals with opportunities to reimmerse themselves in a qualitative stream whereby everything seems new and up for grabs. Each partner, if only briefly, offers his or her vulnerability as a point against which the other's transcendence can define and rediscover itself. Sexuality is a matter of affects; the capacity to affect others and the capacity to be affected – the latter is understood as vulnerability and sometimes shamed as a *lack* of capacity. But it is indeed a capacity, and becoming unable or unwilling to be affected is no less an amputation of the human personality than losing the ability to affect others. Because women are excessively identified with their own sexuality and with the object of male sexual interest in a masculinist society, regardless of their intellectual or economic activities, the reciprocity of heterosexual relations or lack thereof becomes a point of special interest in Beauvoir's study.

Reciprocity

According to Penelope Deutscher, Beauvoir actually invokes many kinds of reciprocity in *The Second Sex*.[42] In addition to the Hegelian reversal of perspectives, these include

> mutual need or dependency; legal and economic equality, particularly of the kind that allows one to enter into a contractual relationship on a fair footing; mutual obligation; . . . the idea of a constant tension produced by the mutual attempt to subordinate, without this necessarily producing the entrenched subordination of any individual or group, a tension that can be seen in both friend and enemy relations; and the mutuality of generosity and friendship between subjects.[43]

We have already considered the model of reciprocity Beauvoir claims is widespread in lesbian relationships. It is also helpful to read the discussions of sexual reciprocity in *The Second Sex* alongside Beauvoir's essay 'Must We Burn Sade?'.[44] In *The Second Sex*, Beauvoir is clear that she does not object to practices of pain, submission or even passivity associated with 'masochism' and as a result she cannot logically object to the roles men play in satisfying such women's needs (SS 411–14/2:163–6). What she does find objectionable is the temptation to relinquish one's own struggle for individuation in a sexual relationship or to conclude from such sexual practices that all human relations involve the objectification of others *without* a corresponding recognition that the ambiguous 'object' of desire also has a subjectivity of his or her own. In connection with 'masochism' as she defines it, the words 'bad faith' and 'inauthentic' appear surprisingly often.

Sade is particularly guilty of concluding that human beings neither can nor should seek to disclose one another's freedom.[45] Formal justice rests on a lie 'because each is enclosed in his own skin'.[46] On the other hand, Sade goes further in asserting that one *should* obey a pitiless version of nature, rather than merely abstaining from virtue. Is nature not just as impersonal as the law? If nature were capable of confirming human individuality, or doing so better than humans, would Sade not be back with the God whose existence he so ardently denied?[47] Sade makes his own body – or literary versions thereof – into material proof that reciprocity is impossible, and tries to make other bodies into signs of his own impassivity, his own immanence.

In *The Second Sex*, Beauvoir observes drily that the conditions under which almost all women were sexually initiated according to her research and informal experience could be considered rapes, and remarks repeatedly that women must often put in a great deal of *work* to meet the male imagination of female passivity halfway. She comments several times on complexes 'making [men] consider the love act a battle' (SS 411, 726/2:163, 528); and remarks that too often they insist on 'taking' what women were trying to offer them (SS 731/2:533), as if the very capacity to be *affected by* or *accept* women's energy and desire were a weakness to be hidden behind bluster. Nor is Beauvoir particularly forgiving of women who are disdainful of men's ambiguity and immanence, like the Violette Leduc character who detests men when they are sleeping (SS 697/2:494), or women who masochistically cling to immanence and are disappointed with men's inability to be purely dominant (SS 731/2:534).

However, Beauvoir does not root men's social and economic domination of women in these sexual roles, fantasies or habits (SS 753/2:560). Rather, if women are tempted to regard themselves as passive and to suppress their transcendence, it is because ultimately they are forced to depend on men for their economic survival, and often agree to do so. Like a Spinozist body, an assemblage is defined by its speeds and slownesses, the ratio of motion to rest between its component parts and its environment. In *The Second Sex*, men's experience and evaluation of time is vastly different from women's, because the former have social and professional interests that compete with their love life for attention, whereas women too often give love (and the lover) central existential importance. She spends hours and days waiting for something significant to happen while he gives significance to projects by the time he allots to them. Her events are deprived of history until men are involved, and often even the events in men's lives are not considered significant unless they are violent. Both men and women are oppressed by the rigid distribution of gendered traits and by the lack of mutual recognition (SS 754/2:561–2); men, Beauvoir argues, would be relieved of mistrust if they had no reason to fear women were manipulating them (SS 755, 758–9/2:562–3, 566–8).

But doesn't Beauvoir imply that men's sexual existence is simpler and therefore preferable in its own right, not least because it is easily compatible with a professional or labouring life?[48] In being very critical of women for agreeing to the form(s) of femininity offered by late modernity, Beauvoir does sometimes imply by her focus on female passivity that men embrace transcendence, seek out significant projects and accomplish them on a far wider scale than we know to be the case from everyday experience. Just as she mixes comments about women's 'enslavement to the species' with reminders that humanity is not a species, she intersperses celebration of male anatomy, 'neat and simple, like a finger' (SS 39–41, 397/1:62–6; 2:147) with reminders that men, too, do not always have very successful careers, are not always comfortable with casual sex, write many mediocre books for reasons unrelated to sexism, and feel awkward when they are objects of the female gaze (she does not even begin to discuss men's discomfort at being looked at sexually by other men!).

Thus improvement in the quality of heterosexual relationships, particularly women's experience of such relationships, is one benefit that can be expected from liberation. But it should be noted that the principle of reciprocity, in which each partner supports the freedom of his or her partner or partners, and which rests in turn on the conditions of a just political and economic system allowing everyone to earn a living as individuals, is not limited to sexuality but to all human relations.[49] For sexuality to support an individual's freedom means that it allows her or him to distinguish him or herself without losing contact with others.

Sexual violence, by contrast, is a practice characterising an assemblage divided into at least two unequal parties, one in motion and one frozen. The interlocking assemblages of families, schools, advertising and courts that create meaning for practices of sexual violence make it difficult for women to become and to recompose themselves while remaining connected to others; indeed, rape is a kind of event whose *sense* damages women's faith in the possibility of human comradeship, even if they do not personally suffer an assault.[50] And if one thinks of racial categories as part of the deployment of sexuality, as Foucault implied in the late 1970s, then colonialism and slavery imposed a whole series of freezing hierarchies – what Olúfẹ́mi Táíwò calls 'sociocryonics' – wherever

European populations encountered Asians and Africans, male and female.[51]

For the other side of white women's 'enforced' immanence in the home and in childrearing is the violence against men and women of colour for which it served as an alibi in Europe, their colonies, and white majority societies around the world. By contrast to the idealised helplessness of elite white women, deserving of protection, women of colour and working-class white women were considered lascivious and dangerous, while men of colour were represented as sexual predators. The models of 'masculinity' established by such dynamics, hypersexualising men whose lives involved intense productive labour but who were utterly 'immanent' in their political agency, were and still are impossible for men to sustain. For men in racialised situations, like those under wartime occupation, time is organised by a different kind of 'waiting' – waiting for surveillance or abuse to descend without warning from employers, police or military officers, while the latter build lives of their own.

Multiplicity

The masks we wear for others are difficult to distinguish those that divide us from ourselves – or manifest our multiplicity. 'Oedipalisation' is one example of this problem, for it requires that individuals locate themselves in a system of binary oppositions and suppress any aspects that don't fit or 'leak'. In *A Thousand Plateaus*, Deleuze and Guattari develop a more nuanced account of structural oppression, 'faciality', which imposes a hierarchy of identities and insists that the individual internalise what does not fit as a *psychological, affective problem*.[52] *Anti-Oedipus* largely focused on what *A Thousand Plateaus* would call the 'despotic' regime of signs, a regime inherited from the feudal era but undergoing drastic reorganisation through capitalism starting in the nineteenth century.[53] By contrast to Oedipus, 'faciality' is an effect of the 'signifying' and 'post-signifying' regimes of signs characterising capitalism and the systems of normalisation pervading capitalist societies.

Mariam Fraser has argued eloquently that many of the discussions of Beauvoir's bisexuality, both those that assume she was hetero and those from lesbian perspectives, participate in this structure of 'faciality'.[54] According to Fraser, Beauvoir's existence as an 'individual' arises from the overlap of three 'topoi' in media presentations: those expressing fascination with bohemianism, those centred on existentialism, and those dealing with 'café culture'. Bisexuality responds to none of these interests, and therefore resists and marks the breakdown of the public representation of Beauvoir as 'individual'. On the other hand, Fraser follows Deleuze in suggesting that this is not a huge loss, as bisexuality can name the affects of a pre-personal assemblage and bisexuals have plenty of things to do besides 'represent' and 'be represented'.[55] The lesson we should take from both Deleuze and Beauvoir is that we should have the right to be and to be recognised as *assemblages*, not units – 'hetero', 'lesbian', 'bisexual' and 'otherwise' – all at once, in different proportions, ratios and intervals – and to create new relationships *as* assemblages.

So on reflection, it seems that despite the apparent evidence of her frustration with other women, Beauvoir does not identify the values she adopts as 'male'. The chief value upheld by *The Second Sex*, apart from individuation, is reciprocity. But both individuation and reciprocity are complicated by the fact of internal multiplicity, which would be one way to understand ambiguity. A more elaborate treatment of this internal multiplicity, which manifests itself affectively as 'ambivalence', could have prevented misunderstandings.

Does Deleuze, who does theorise this multiplicity in great detail, understand reciprocity as an aspect of freedom? In *Proust and Signs*, Deleuze states that 'to fall in love is to individualize someone by the signs he bears or emits . . . the beloved expresses a possible world unknown to us, implying, enveloping, imprisoning a world that must be deciphered, that is, interpreted'.[56] In this text, as in Deleuze's very early article on Sartre and 'woman',[57] the subject is clearly presumed to be male. Despite Deleuze's critique of representation in later works like *Nietzsche and Philosophy* and *Difference and Repetition*, here the subject himself seems not to be altered or individualised by the encounter that individualises the beloved woman. 'The pluralism of love does not concern only the multiplicity of loved beings but the multiplicity of souls or worlds in each of them', he writes; but as a 'possible world', the female Other quickly becomes a stereotypical figure of inaccessibility and mystery (as she does for Lévinas).[58] In *Difference and Repetition*, the object of desire is a *virtual* pole in whom partial objects and compensatory fantasies are unified in the course of the child's individuation, not a centre of differentiation in his or her own right.[59]

The give and take desired by Beauvoir, in which each partner discovers new connections and aspects of him or herself because of the challenge posed by the other's ambiguous accessibility, seems absent here. Deleuze does not imagine the essence of human relations is conflict, as Sartre does. But whether or not the virtual event of *Mitsein* is actualised, he does not seem to consider it a powerful provocation to thought. This is because Deleuze is less interested in the typical combinations of singularities that go to make up humans as 'personalities'. And creativity is more a matter of building connections to an Outside than to an Other; the Other only enters the picture as such once impersonal singularities have been formed into a subject.[60] The singularities that go to make up an Other, of course, are also impersonal and provokes affects prior to any 'recognition'. Deleuze does, moreover, take stupidity – by which he means *insensibility* – as a concern in *Difference and Repetition* (DR 150–3/195–8). Perhaps reciprocity would enter Deleuze's picture as an example of resistance to stupidity.

In *A Thousand Plateaus*, love is both an affect (a relation among bodies) and an expression or sense whose meaning depends on whether it appears in a despotic or a passional post-signifying regime (TP 147–8/183–4). Like the orchid and wasp, lovers form an assemblage as well as being assemblages in their own right.

> What does it mean to love somebody? It is always to seize that person in a mass, extract him or her from a group, however small, in which he or she participates, whether it be through the family only or through something else; then to find that person's own packs, the multiplicities he or she encloses within himself or herself which may be of an entirely different nature. To join them to mine, to make them penetrate mine, and for me to penetrate the other person's. (TP 35/49)

The state and church would prefer to take the assemblages formed by heterosexual lovers as ontological substances, but Beauvoir argues for taking them as scenes of further individuation. Perhaps this is Deleuze and Guattari's understanding of what it means to *disclose* the other's freedom through carnal desire.

Many feminist discussions of Deleuze, however, centre on the concept of 'becoming-woman' found in *A Thousand Plateaus* (TP 275–81, 291–4/337–44, 356–61).[61] Becoming-woman is one example of the 'flight' or leakage of every stable identity, especially those defined in binary terms. As such, it is different from feminism as 'molar' politics on behalf of those who either affirm or are assigned a stable identity as women (TP 275–6/337–9). 'On the one hand', there are 'multiplicities that are extensive, divisible, and molar; unifiable, totalizable, organizable; conscious or preconscious – and on the other hand, libidinal, unconscious, molecular, intensive multiplicities composed of particles that do not divide without changing in nature' (TP 33/46). Every individual has aspects of both tendencies – toward stability and change, toward being and becoming – and so too does every society, an observation implicit in the sociologist's distinction between classes and masses (TP 35, 213/48–9, 259–60).

According to Deleuze and Guattari, the human and animal, the male and female, the European and colonised, are binaries producing entities whose repressed becomings hover around them like a cloud of virtual events. In *Anti-Oedipus*, pre-modern despotic sign systems were responsible for most of this repression, which capitalism has deterritorialised. But kinship identities are now subject to the axiomatics of the capitalist market, as well as the axiomatics of rights-based political systems that have evolved along with capitalism. Insofar as it functions as a norm, the Oedipal European model of adult masculine heterosexual humanity can be compared to a layer or stratum that solidifies through historical pressures as sand solidifies into sandstone. In this approach, characteristic of *A Thousand Plateaus*, becoming-woman and becoming-child are the most obvious forms of 'destratification' or deviation from the norm, while other forms such as becoming-molecular or becoming-imperceptible are more subtle because they refer to processes that have never been captured in fixed identities. Becoming-imperceptible would thus mean becoming a *percipiendum* who provokes thought in others (TP 279–82/342–6).

Elizabeth Grosz, among others, criticised Deleuze and Guattari for taking this term 'woman', essential to women who are still trying to change their social situation, and using its connotations to name a kind of becoming that seems to mostly affect men.[62] 'In a way, the subject in becoming is always man', they write, on the rationale (similar to Beauvoir's) that male identity is dominant and functions as the norm, even if men are not in the numerical majority. 'Man is majoritarian par excellence' (TP 291/356). However, women are clearly also stable subjects, distinct as such from men, and capable of their own becomings. So one cannot help wondering, if 'becoming-woman or the molecular woman is the girl herself' and this does not mean she is becoming a molar woman, does this mean that the molar woman who enters becoming become a girl? How is she to name or conceive of her own molecular aspects?

In other words, *which* woman or women does someone become? Deleuze and Guattari compare becoming-woman to becoming-Jew, but surely this becoming is different for Christian white women, Hindu women and Jewish women, not to mention Jewish men.[63] Just as no one lives entirely in one form of sense or state, neither does anyone live in a single signifying regime (despotic and pre-signifying, signifying or post-signifying, or governed by European Oedipus). Perhaps becoming-woman is a line of flight for men in a society politically and economically stratified by gender, such as Beauvoir describes. But this is not necessarily the case for a society in which men and women have their own political and religious institutions. Some African feminists would argue that becoming-woman or becoming-minoritarian only represent lines of flight for women, especially women of non-European descent, insofar as they have internalised the racist, sexist sense deployed by colonialism (as Fanon describes, for example), in which the becomings of women and non-European men represent fixed, limited poles of direction in the imagination of the ruling minority.

In *Family Matters*, for example, Nkiru Uwechia Nzegwu argues that western feminists who made claims about the universality of male domination (including Beauvoir) relied on anthropological data about African societies gathered during the colonial era and after those societies had also suffered massive disruption and transformation due to the intra-African slave trade (FM 28–30). Prior to the slave trade, at least some West African societies such as the Igbo had female monarchs (as well as male ones) (FM 11). The power to define membership in extended families and to identify legitimate 'paternity' rested in the hands of older women and in the group of brothers and sisters born from the same mother (FM 45–6). Moreover, the social and political institution of motherhood was not necessarily coeval with the status of wife and did not necessarily mandate sexual exclusivity (FM 30–7, 40–7).

However, complex extended families with real female power or multiple power centres were disparaged by colonial France and England, particularly by the Christian missionaries from those countries, and these families and political structures were replaced under pressure by the northern European model of nuclear families headed by husbands, in which the husband's family, occupation and male heirs made all of the important decisions for a household – not to mention those for the nation.[64] Assuming that men held all power in Africa as they did in Europe, European anthropologists did not bother to ask African women about their own institutions, including their occasional role as 'husbands' or *idigbe*, and thus they helped to entrench men's self-serving description of male roles and institutions as the only sources of legitimacy (see particularly chapter 2, 'Legalizing Patriarchy').

Nzegwu acknowledges that European and other white feminists may have an accurate understanding of the power dynamics in their own communities, that the category of 'gender' may be analytically fruitful in their countries of origin, and that equality can only mean 'equality to men' when social power has always meant 'male' power. The concepts 'gender' and 'patriarchy' may also be essential for women of colour living in white majority societies and for some African feminists, particularly in the urban middle class, whose family structures and legal systems have become very similar to those of the former colonisers (FM 12, 17–18). Nzegwu does not deny that there are many aspects of African women's lives in which male dominance is evident (FM 10). However, she strongly rejects the notion that this situation has always held everywhere in Africa, that the worst forms of inequality were always those associated with gender, and that the political goals formulated by European and American feminists in terms of gender – such as relief from the 'burden' of maternity and conquest of equal access to work associated with men – should necessarily be the primary goals of African women who face discrimination within historically layered and mixed legal and economic systems (FM 9–10, 196–7).

Nzegwu's study reminds us that in the post-colonial world, but even in Europe or the United States, men and women are shaped by *multiple* events, multiple 'states', regimes of signs, or forms of 'sense', in ways that are different from Deleuze and Guattari's overlapping regimes of signs. For the Igbo, as Nzegwu describes them, masculinity may not represent the majority/norm and becoming-woman has little to do with becoming the social Other, in Beauvoir's oppressive sense. Inheritors of a society in which women had political and economic power *as a molar group*, women nonetheless lost much of this power when the men of their communities adopted European Christian standards of sexist sense.[65]

As Deleuze says in *The Logic of Sense*, the event/expression of sense moves simultaneously in opposite directions: 'Alice becomes larger', but 'By the same token . . . she becomes smaller'; the becoming-woman of a man may also be the becoming-male of a woman with whose molecules he composes his own molecules. In other words, they share a common 'zone of indiscernibility'. But when a woman who cannot or does not wish to bear children assumes the role of social 'husband' in relation to a mother, is this necessarily becoming-male? Why not say becoming-*idigbe*? The leakage or flight from molar categories cannot be contained by their binaries! A man's becoming-woman also corresponds to a change in the becoming of masculinity itself, including his own masculinity.[66] A man who adopts European norms becomes-European without ceasing to be African or Asian, as Fanon analysed it, but in doing so his Africanity or Asian identity also mutates and does so for those around him. Indeed, Beauvoir became more obviously white when she made awkward analogies between racism and sexism, but this has only become obvious as feminists of colour have insisted that white feminists become-minoritarian, at least in their epistemology.[67]

Women in sexist societies have fewer names for these becomings (since they *are* the name) and therefore move very quickly to becoming-molecular or becoming-imperceptible – so quickly and unimaginably that they suffer from ontological and psychological rigidity and fragility (see TP 215–17, 276/262–5, 338–9). Moreover, one could conclude from Deleuze and Guattari that women of non-European descent must live their own ethnic heritage and its molar identities in a mode of perpetual transformation just as they must deviate actively from the molar categories of European cultures. This would obviously be controversial, for the same reason that Fanon was outraged at Sartre's implicit demand that the authors of *négritude* speed up their identification with the universal proletariat. Overly rapid destabilisation, however, is a recipe for fascism because it provokes a reactive investment in binary categories and destroys singularities rather than allowing them to connect and evolve. We have seen these reactive tendencies on all sides within societies experiencing struggles over gender *and* anti-racism, including among feminists themselves.

Penelope Deutscher has suggested that ambiguity might be a way to think about what American black feminists in the 1990s came to call 'intersectionality' – the fact that no human is ever 'just' or 'primarily' gendered, raced, classed or aged but all these at once in problematic ways that compound or compensate for one another's disadvantages.[68] It remains an open challenge how and whether concepts of multiplicity like assemblages, events and becomings enable us to think about intersectionality in a more fluid way. Kyoo Lee tries to escape the implicit binarism implicit in the notion of the 'second sex', where 'second' means 'other'. She suggests that as the problem of sexist sense is revealed to be *implicated* in ever more historical trajectories and struggles against domination, 'third', 'fourth' and yet more sexes are revealed or *explicated* on the feminist 'body without organs', none of which can claim priority in an absolute sense for the multiplicities – the becomings or assemblages – formed on its surface and expressed in its Ideas.[69]

Both Deutscher and Lee imply that there is no one 'problem of the age', such as sexual difference, but *always* a plurality of points from multiple geographical and historical locations – whether or not individual feminist thinkers manage to tap into all of them in a single life.[70] Moreover, Beauvoir's problem is not the *only* problem out there and she is by no means the only theorist with whom contemporary feminists should compose themselves; all Ideas, as Deleuze says, intersect and 'perplicate' one another at the virtual level (DR 187/241–2).

But laying out a new transversal block of becoming between the affects and speeds of white women, Asian women, indigenous American women, women of African descent in their various mixtures and contexts requires two things. First, the opportunity to form effective unions with others who have similar affects and aspirations. Second, the *will* to seek out unexpected affects and to let oneself be recomposed by them. This second requirement corresponds to Beauvoir's desire to *disclose* rather than to *be*, although it can only be carried out, Deleuze would say, by pre-personal singularities below the level of 'consciousness'. *A Thousand Plateaus* calls this process 'perceptual semiotics' (TP 23/34). This second requirement also brings Deleuze's concern about stupidity – *insensibility* to that which can only be sensed because it challenges the totality of our cognitive categories – together with the concerns of feminists of colour regarding the systematic epistemological blindness of white feminists.

Universal or just common?

It may seem that we are far from Beauvoir and *The Second Sex*. But in fact the relationship between molecular and molar identity, or supra-individual and infra-individual, macro-political and micro-political components, allows us to approach a crucial question: what does or could 'reciprocity' mean if we interpret ambiguity in a Deleuzian way? This relationship enables us to imagine a mutual becoming whose *quality* and affects would constitute, as Beauvoir wishes, a *Mitsein* of *reciprocity*, especially one in which, as Bergoffen stresses, one has no need to insist on an economic equalisation and reckoning of the respective value of male and female affection, care labour, sexual pleasure and time.[71]

Beauvoir has been accused of proposing a single image of women's situation for all cultures, as well as cross-culturally valid solutions to the various predicaments women face – of failing to 'disclose' in a potentially reciprocal way. Criticisms have been aimed at her anthropological sources and her reliance on literary and anecdotal accounts of women's lives that largely reflect white middle-class French experience.[72] A Deleuzian reading helps respond to these problems in two ways. First, the term 'woman' need not refer to a universal, although it may refer to situations that many people have in common (including trans women). Second, women never individuate (or face oppression) as 'bare women' but always in combination with economic, sexual, political and racial assemblages; i.e., as connected with other women and men.

The universal is often a militant weapon; it conveys a compulsion similar to the way Arendt says mathematics implies compulsion in Plato.[73] Political universals often reflect the aspirations of particular groups and rarely achieve truly universal application.[74] Insofar as Beauvoir could be considered universalist, it is because she aligns herself with a left-wing tradition in France that is not only republican but also strongly inflected by Hegel and Marxist-Leninism. For Hegel, historical change is always the concrete instantiation or comprehension of a universal, which was concealed by partial interests or false oppositions; for Lenin, historical change is made by grasping the point of ultimate opposition or contradiction defining the singularity – or concrete universality – of a given historical moment, and enabling a political vanguard to push awareness of that contradiction to an unbearable tipping point for the population as a whole.

Thus several generations of liberationist philosophy, including feminism and anti-colonialism, sought to identify the conflicts that would reveal and transform a contradiction in which the world as a whole could be lived, and not simply *thought*, as a concrete universal. Ironically, Beauvoir's feminist critics from Psych et Po had a similar 'vanguardism'.⁷⁵ Considering all language complicit with male domination, they appealed to extra-linguistic forces such as the female body and imagination to bring about complete symbolic revolution. From Beauvoir's standpoint in *The Ethics of Ambiguity*, this is the deliberate imposition on individuals of a truth that is defined by *opposition* to 'mere' individuality. An indefinite movement of expansion that tries to make some opportunity as *widespread* as possible, on the other hand, seems less noble but may achieve just as much.

Are problems like the right to reproductive autonomy, free choice in marriage and sexuality, education and access to paid work 'universal' women's problems?⁷⁶ Is there a universal form of sexist sense one might call 'patriarchy'? In the Introduction to *The Second Sex*, Beauvoir argues against nominalism as well as against essentialism where 'woman' is concerned (SS 3–4/1:12). She defines 'womanhood', both physically and culturally, as a *situation* in which these aspects are inextricably intertwined. How similar or common are the situations identified as feminine? Spinoza argues that although common notions truly apply to multiple particulars, it is a mistake to conclude that they are universals.⁷⁷ Beauvoir becomes the target of critique, even self-critique, when the common notions she generates based on her reading are interpreted as universals.⁷⁸

Indeed, Beauvoir would have agreed that *The Second Sex* was too 'idealist' (FC 192–3) but she also thought universals were essential within and between given situations.⁷⁹ The thing is, if freedom means individuation, everyone can't possibly do it the same way – or oppress each other's individuation in the same ways. Many women around the world were inspired by *The Second Sex* to combat forms of gender oppression in their own societies that Beauvoir did not understand or represent accurately.³⁰ Just as *The Second Sex* motivated several generations of historians to excavate the changing causal forces and differences in Western women's lives, so too it prompted critical Western and non-Western reflection on the masculine biases of anthropology and economics. Some feminists were critical of Beauvoir for failing to offer a sufficient blueprint for change; but perhaps there was generosity in offering a foil against whom other women could resist and articulate their demands.⁸¹

Regardless of Beauvoir's views, a problem can be urgent without being 'universal' *or*, even if universal, requiring a single universal solution. Insisting on singularity does not imply the kind of relativism that Michèle Le Dœuff finds so offensive when French women who have never undergone excision excuse the practice on the grounds that they cannot judge another culture or, worse yet, on the basis of their fantasies about that culture.[82] It is not a matter of *blinding oneself* to the pain that one imagines another woman suffering.[83] It is rather a matter of recognising that this pain is relative to an entire set of other affects to which the excised woman has access or hopes to have access.

Women who work abroad for long periods to support their children also face a kind of amputation. Women who put up with unwanted sex to keep their home and livelihood might not be able to survive if they reinterpreted those acts as rape. Because she is an assemblage and belongs to multiple assemblages, excision, unwanted sex or migrant labour are never the *only* events defining a woman. In France, citizenship may be a more urgent human right than freedom from these other evils because it gives her the means to protect herself as well as to be protected by others, including the state. In Africa or Asia, ethnic or religious discrimination, domestic and military violence from men, difficulty gaining access to land, and adequate education and health care may be her primary concerns. The most important thing is that neither the assault on her sexual possibilities nor the definition of 'woman' to which she aspires should be isolating dead ends.

But no comparison can be made until a woman from one situation finds her *problem* illuminated in the literary or philosophical description of another situation, the way Beckett seems to have figured out how he wanted to connect characters, symptoms and the look of specific rooms after entering into Proust's novel as if it were his own virtual past.[84] Referencing Stanley Cavell, Moi has persuasively argued that using oneself as an example is not the same as speaking for others, but encouraging others to make the language of one's experience their own.[85] For Deleuze, who says that 'the misfortune in speaking is not speaking, but speaking *for others* or representing something' (DR 52/74), speaking would not mean using oneself as an 'example' – a particular in relation to a generality – but laying out a *singularity*, mixing fiction and concepts, creating affects that would provoke problems and ideas in the reader.[86] Even if the end result in terms of legislation looks very similar to the result of universalism, the 'universal' will include a whole range of 'virtual' meanings and possibilities that are specific to a given woman's *interpretation* of her culture and that are different from the meanings important to the mainstream.

Despite the inadequate anthropology consulted by Beauvoir, it is to her credit that she refused to cite even more of the numerous nineteenth- and early twentieth-century studies that were clearly racist. She did not propose to 'save brown women from brown men' although this might have made her book much more popular in Europe.[87] She does describe the dehumanising effects of *multiple* oppressions, both indigenous and colonial, in sweeping terms that do not encourage readers to seek out the singularity of non-Western women's lives (or men's, for that matter). For example: 'For Arabs or Indians, and in many rural populations, a wife is only a female servant appreciated according to the work she provides, and who is replaced without regret if she disappears'; while 'in modern civilization, she is more or less individualized in her husband's eyes' (SS 570/2:342). And yet with no sense of contradiction she also describes the Kafkaesque routine of European factory workers and prostitutes who are 'reduced to the level of a thing' (SS 610/2:389).

What about Beauvoir's use of metaphors and comparisons for the situation of privileged women that are drawn from the actual and historical lives of multiply oppressed women, such as 'slavery' and 'holocaust' with a small 'h', as Kathryn Gines asks in 'Comparative and Competing Frameworks of Oppression'? While rhetorically attracting attention to the women whose situation she describes, primarily white women, these tropes tend to neutralise or generalise the specific suffering endured by women from enslaved or persecuted populations. Metaphors comparing adult (European) women to children or to slaves also tend to reinforce a longstanding European equation of slaves and colonised peoples with (European) children who must be restricted and tutored until reaching maturity; this is a context in which domination is justified as loving and praiseworthy.[88] And finally, they distract the reader's attention from those numerous cases in which oppressed non-Europeans rebelled, dissimulated, fled, negotiated, and risked their own lives and the lives of their communities in defiance of European-made values and institutions – exhibiting courage quite unlike the affects Beauvoir associates with European female 'immanence'.[89] Intentional or not, these turns of phrase produce affects around a specific narrative of (white women's) oppression that actually flattens *everyone's* capacity to be moved by the obstacles to individuation faced by groups of women other than their own.

All these difficulties are exacerbated, however, by thinking of feminism as a subject of representation and judging Simone de Beauvoir as a 'representative' of feminism rather than simply one becoming among others. As one of a very small number of female public intellectuals in her era, Beauvoir was adopted as a role model by movements with changing identities. Her influence was enhanced by her access to publishers in a culture even more monolithically white-dominated than our own. But too often, discussions of her work are implicitly governed by the presumption of a moralistic cult of personality – should we live, love, philosophise, travel or sign petitions like Beauvoir? Is Beauvoir's work irrelevant given that these activities are neither desirable nor materially possible for most women, while the concerns and tools within their reach were often unknown to her? These kinds of questions assume that a writer *represents* rather than thinks, and in doing so, *represents* members of a class or constituency, who will be moral if they strive to imitate the ideal representative.

Fraser speaks of Beauvoir's individuality as a 'composite' of various genres and scenes rather than an organic entity. Moi's intellectual biography of Beauvoir situates her life with respect to the academic *habitus* which built up her capacity for sense as well as identifying and formulating problems. When media and academic institutions change, this means that Beauvoir's 'individuality' also changes in a way that is not obviously historical or chronological. More important, Beauvoir's life is a text on which people to try out their own ideas about how living should work and how it should incorporate writing. Her relations to lovers, to her mother, to younger women and to writers were singular. How did she form problems from her crises, so that we too can form problems rather than getting caught in anxiety?[90] The point is not to extract a theory from her life and work, but to see how individual experiments worked out and how one might improve and adapt them in the future.

Nor should one necessarily break all relationships that may be contaminated with 'sexist sense' – there is no reason to think all relationships with men involving compromise are toxic, and many women face political and economic challenges requiring them to combine with whatever and whomever can make them stronger, including with men.[91] As Deleuze writes in *Difference and Repetition*, if the Other represents a possible world allowing my *own* world to cohere and to be individuated, it is nonetheless important 'not to explicate oneself too much with the other, not to explicate the other too much, but to maintain one's implicit values and multiply one's own world by populating it with all those expresseds that do not exist apart from their expressions' (DR 261/335). We could understand this as a warning in light of Beauvoir's intuition as a student that 'thousands of possibilities [*possibles*] in childhood fall by the wayside bit by bit, and so much so that on the last day there is no longer anything but *one reality*; you have lived *one life*'.[92]

Perhaps what this means is that we should avoid Beauvoir's 'mirage of the Other' – leave the Other her own 'possibles' and not insist on an overly homogenised and common world, lest we 'use up' our own possibilities.[93] Despite the reality of interdependence, one's world also contains many possible connections, contestations and exits that allow loss to be endured. Simone de Beauvoir is allowed to disappear behind her texts, including those written about her. We have to ask what kind of event she is *for us*, rather than focusing too intently on the events that happened to her. In this sense, she is like any other woman who could be an event for us – singular and yet provoking thought and action.

Notes

1. Beauvoir, from the film *Simone de Beauvoir* by Josée Dayan and Malka Ribowska, quoted in Simons, Benjamin and Beauvoir, 'An Interview', 332.
2. See Simons, *Beauvoir and* The Second Sex, particularly chapter 10: '*The Second Sex* and the Roots of Radical Feminism'.
3. These reactions were collected in Ingrid Galster's '*Le Deuxième Sexe' de Simone de Beauvoir*.
4. See Stavro, 'The Use and Abuse of Simone de Beauvoir: Re-Evaluating the French Poststructuralist Critique'; and Delphy, 'The Invention of French Feminism: An Essential Move'. Two of the key texts in this shift were Kristeva, 'Women's Time', and Spelman, *Inessential Woman*.
5. *Le deuxième sexe* was published by Éditions Gallimard in 1949. In 1952, it was translated into English by H. M. Parshley. Significant cuts were made to the length, particularly in sections dealing with women's history, at the behest of the American publisher, Alfred A. Knopf; moreover, French philosophical terms were not translated with recognisable English equivalents. After Margaret Simons drew attention to the situation in 1979, feminist academics and Gallimard placed regular pressure on Knopf to authorise

a new translation, but were unsuccessful for several decades. See Simons, 'The Silencing of Simone de Beauvoir'. In 2009, the parent company of Knopf, Random House, allowed its British subsidiary Jonathan Cape to commission a new and complete translation by Constance Borde and Sheila Malovany-Chevallier, which was then issued in the United States under the Knopf imprimatur.

6. The impact of multicultural feminist struggles on Beauvoir reception in the United States often took the form of an analysis of Beauvoir's reflections on race relations in *America Day By Day* and in *The Second Sex*. See Simons, *Beauvoir and* The Second Sex; Deutscher, *Ambiguity, Conversion, Resistance*; Gines, 'Sartre, Beauvoir and the Race/Gender Analogy'; and Gines, 'Comparative and Competing Frameworks of Oppression'.

7. Beauvoir's 'myth of harmony' with Sartre is on full display, for example, in the interviews with Alice Schwarzer. See *After* The Second Sex, 37, 51–60. Early discussions of the discrepancies revealed by the letters include Le Dœuff, *Hipparchia's Choice*, 180–94; and Allen, 'A Response to a Letter from Peg Simons', 113–36.

8. Deutscher, *Ambiguity, Conversion, Resistance*, 13–14.

9. See, for example, Simons, Benjamin and Beauvoir, 'An Interview', 337–9; Le Dœuff, *Hipparchia's Choice*, 136–7; and Moi, *Making of an Intellectual Woman*, 37–72.

10. For Secomb, this is one of the respects in which Beauvoir is Deleuzian. See Secomb, 'Beauvoir's Minoritarian Philosophy'; Moi, *Making of an Intellectual Woman*; Tidd, *Simone de Beauvoir, Gender, and Testimony*.

11. Wasser, 'What is a Literary Problem?'

12. Wasser, 'What is a Literary Problem?', 115.

13. Wasser, 'What is a Literary Problem?', 116–17. Her examples are Proust and Beckett, whose works seem to actualise similar structural relations between events and characters, and which, in Beckett's case, seem to be have been inspired by reading Proust, but only in the sense that Proust *awakened* the problem. The problem is a genetic element in addition to the solution/work (ibid., 121).

14. See *What is Philosophy?* (WIP 222, n. 7/67 n. 7) where Deleuze and Guattari cite the 'woman philosopher' as a conceptual persona for Michèle Le Dœuff (in *Hipparchia's Choice*), along with the Couple for Klossowski and the Friend for Blanchot. In *The Philosophical Imaginary*, Le Dœuff argues that the sex of the philosopher forms part of the pre-philosophical plane and tends to distract from, or compensate for, anxieties and defects of argumentation in the history of Western thought (Le Dœuff, *Philosophical Imaginary*, 108–12).

15. Brison, 'Beauvoir and Feminism', 193–4.

16. Deutscher, *Ambiguity, Conversion, Resistance*, 136–7.

17. See Beauvoir, 'Short Articles on Literature', 98–123.
18. After all, as Hughes points out, the *petites perceptions* making up a situation *would be* the singularity of the character him or herself – as well as part of the reader's singularity. Hence the affinity between people shaped by the same literary works. Hughes, *Deleuze's Difference and Repetition*, 45–6; Beauvoir, 'Short Articles on Literature', 116–17.
19. Brison, 'Beauvoir and Feminism', 193–4.
20. See also Beauvoir, 'Literature and Metaphysics'.
21. Fricker, 'Life Story in Beauvoir's Memoirs'.
22. Moi, *Making of an Intellectual Woman*, 77–81.
23. Murphy, 'Ambiguity and Precarious Life', 211–12.
24. Hurtado, *The Color of Privilege*, 109.
25. Key texts in this discussion include Simons, 'Beauvoir and Sartre', in *Beauvoir and* The Second Sex; Fullbrook and Fullbrook, *Simone de Beauvoir and Jean-Paul Sartre, The Remaking of a Twentieth-Century Legend*; Sonia Kruks, 'Simone de Beauvoir: Teaching Sartre About Freedom'; and most recently, Daigle and Golomb, *Beauvoir and Sartre: The Riddle of Influence*.
26. Moi, *Making of an Intellectual Woman*, 79–80; see also Beauvoir, *All Said and Done*, 122–5.
27. Beauvoir, 'What Can Literature Do?', 205.
28. As Dan Smith comments, making reference to *The Fold*: 'One could say that these are the two poles of Deleuze's philosophy: "Everything is ordinary!" and "Everything is singular!"', Smith, 'Dialectics', in *Essays on Deleuze*, 115.
29. Le Dœuff, *Hipparchia's Choice*; Moi, *Making of an Intellectual Woman*; Marks, *Encounters With Death*.
30. After the trio with Olga, one wonders if she did not discover Zaza anew, as well as relive the loss of Zaza, suggesting that there would be a third, a fourth, including forms she herself could create. Nor would it be that Zaza or Sartre were mother-replacements; rather, her mother might have been an early and inadequate partner in the kind of friendship she glimpsed with Zaza and Sartre. Feminist critics who believe Beauvoir unthinkingly subordinated herself to Sartre do not seem as concerned when Beauvoir reports in the memoirs that she was first bowled over with fascination by Zaza and, to a certain extent, Simone Jollivet, another of the young Jean-Paul's girlfriends.
31. See also Signe Arnfred, 'Simone de Beauvoir in Africa'.
32. See, for example, Benjamin, *The Bonds of Love*. The object-relations tradition is associated with Melanie Klein and Donald Winnicott; the most well-known feminist appropriation of this tradition is Nancy Chodorow, *The Reproduction of Mothering*.
33. Schwarzer, *After* The Second Sex, 74–6.

34. This is how Nkiru Nzegwu reads Beauvoir in her hypothetical interview between modern white feminists and pre-colonial female authorities in the Igbo part of Nigeria; see chapter 4 of *Family Matters* (FM): 'The Conclave'. A cursory and informal review of passing citations to Beauvoir in recent books by feminists around the world on Google Books reveals that this is still a very widespread impression of Beauvoir's feminism.
35. See Eugene Holland, 'Non-Linear Historical Materialism' for a discussion of the ways that 'laws' of economics for a given mode of production can be reconciled with the belief that any given mode is historically contingent. Capitalism, for example, required the simultaneous appearance of a 'critical mass of so-called "free" labor available for hire' and a 'critical mass of the liquid wealth available for investment' (19). Once these conditions are met, like the conditions for a chemical reaction, a stable situation results whose functioning can be understood in a lawlike manner until some other instability prevails. The Althusserian concept of 'becoming-necessary is meant to emphasize (among other things) the importance, the omnipresence, the contingency, and the fragility of system reproduction' (ibid., 20).
36. Landes, *Women and the Public Sphere*, 139–50.
37. McLintock, *Imperial Leather*, 113–18.
38. Gines, 'Comparative and Competing Frameworks of Oppression'.
39. Deleuze and Guattari's views at the time of *Anti-Oedipus* were influenced by reflections on Proust: 'We are statistically or molarly heterosexual, but personally homosexual, without knowing it or being fully aware of it, and finally we are transsexual in an elemental, molecular sense' (AO 70/82; TP 277–8/340–1).
40. Toril Moi argues that the specific reduction called 'pervasive femininity' was the chief target of *The Second Sex* (*What is a Woman?*, 11–12). Anthropologist Igor Kopytoff observes that western European and affiliated societies are somewhat unique in their expectation that *all* of an individual's social capacities and affects will *express* his or her sex identity, even if they are not determined by it (Kopytoff, 'Women's Roles and Existential Identities', 77–98). On women's 'overloaded identity', see also Le Dœuff, *Hipparchia's Choice*, 206–7.
41. Anti-black racism often involves a repudiation of part of the white personality which is then simultaneously disparaged and envied in the black 'Other'. See Young-Bruehl, *The Anatomy of Prejudices*.
42. Deutscher, *Ambiguity, Conversion, Resistance*, 163–6. Bergoffen's model, rooted in generosity, is only one of these; and Deutscher notes that Beauvoir does not use the term 'reciprocity' for the ideal outcome of race relations, although she invoked it for intergenerational relations. See Deutscher, *Ambiguity, Conversion, Resistance* 190–2 for connections to Derrida's notion of the gift. Bauer's views

on reciprocity are found on 167–72 of *Simone de Beauvoir, Philosophy, and Feminism*. According to Moi, 'reciprocity' basically means 'concrete' as opposed to 'abstract' equality (Moi, *Making of an Intellectual Woman*, 209).
43. Deutscher, *Ambiguity, Conversion, Resistance*, 163–4.
44. See Bergoffen, *Gendered Phenomenologies*, 113–38.
45. In *Coldness and Cruelty*, Deleuze argues strongly against mistakenly thinking that 'sadism' and 'masochism' express the same psychological tendency; nor do they have a common political logic. Masochism represents the eroticisation of contract, while sadism eroticises a non-consensual legal institution. However, there is no reason to think that these types or syndromes are ever found *unmixed* in social and psychological life.
46. Beauvoir, 'Must We Burn Sade?', 93.
47. See the problems laid out in Klossowski, 'The Philosopher-Villain'.
48. See Moi, *Making of an Intellectual Woman*, 174.
49. On reciprocity, see Schwarzer, *After The Second Sex*, 56–7 in addition to earlier citations from *The Second Sex*.
50. Hengehold, 'When Safety Becomes a Duty'.
51. Táíwò, *How Colonialism Preempted Modernity*.
52. See chapter 7 of *A Thousand Plateaus*: 'Year Zero: Faciality', 167–91/205–34.
53. See chapter 5 of *A Thousand Plateaus*: '587 B.C. – A.D. 70: On Several Regimes of Signs', 111–48, particularly the summary on 135.
54. Fraser, *Identity Without Selfhood*, 151–4.
55. Fraser, *Identity Without Selfhood*, 170.
56. Deleuze, *Proust and Signs*, 7.
57. Deleuze, 'Description of a Woman'.
58. Deleuze, *Proust and Signs*, 120.
59. 'Our loves do not refer back to the mother, it is simply that the mother occupies a certain place in relation to the virtual object in the series which constitutes our present' (DR 105/139, see also 85, 99/115–32).
60. Thanks to Brent Adkins for clarifying this point.
61. Feminist engagement with Deleuze includes the work of Rosi Braidotti (*Nomadic Subjects* and *Transpositions*), Elizabeth Grosz (particularly 'A Thousand Tiny Sexes: Feminism and Rhizomatics' and *Volatile Bodies*), Dorothea Olkowski (particularly *Gilles Deleuze and the Ruin of Representation*), Tamsin Lorraine, *Deleuze and Guattari's Immanent Ethics*, and the essays in Colebrook and Buchanan (eds), *Deleuze and Feminist Theory*. Of course, 'becoming-woman' is far from exhausting their range of concerns.
62. Grosz, *Volatile Bodies*, 163, 172–3.
63. Grosz, 'A Thousand Tiny Sexes', 188–90.
64. Oyěwùmí, *The Invention of Women*.

65. Even within the Nigerian context, as one might expect, there are disagreements over this interpretation of the historical record and its contemporary significance; see also Bakare-Yusuf, 'Yoruba's Don't Do Gender'.
66. See Faludi, *Stiffed*, for an extended study of changes in the meaning of American masculinity during the 1980s and 90s.
67. Grosz suggests that encouraging white men to 'become minoritarian' would be offensive, but it seems to me that the meaning of all ethnicities shifts as each one shifts, insofar as they have no 'being' in themselves but refer to experiences and interests that others are unlikely to share. Grosz, 'A Thousand Tiny Sexes', 189–90.
68. Deutscher, *Ambiguity, Conversion, Resistance*, 140–8.
69. Lee, '(Un)naming the Third Sex'.
70. On the other hand, certain aspects of non-European cultures might move to the fore as models for *everyone's* thinking around the globe. Models of personality that assume every human is inhabited by multiple ancestors, found among South Africans as well as in the Caribbean diaspora, have been used to explain and legitimate the power of women's sexual attraction to one another. For example, Morgan and Reid, 'I've got two men and one woman' (cited in Cornell, *At the Heart of Freedom*); Wekker, 'What's Identity Got to Do With It?'. Models of motherhood that socially recognise the transformations of pregnancy as *ontologically* significant result in two new beings rather than one continuous being who underwent a temporary change and one new being, the child. Igbo society grants mothers distinct powers, psychologically and politically, compared to women who have never given birth (Nzegwu, FM 51–5).
71. Bergoffen, *Gendered Phenomenologies* 40, 62–3; Deutscher, *Ambiguity, Conversion, Resistance*, 190–2.
72. The best known critique is chapter 3 of Spelman, *Inessential Woman* (57–79). Judith Okely's generally positive assessment of Beauvoir's legacy is also critical on this score (Okely, *Simone de Beauvoir*).
73. Arendt, *Between Past and Future*, 107–10.
74. Landes, *Women and the Public Sphere*, 43–5.
75. For a description of Psych et Po, the psychoanalytic feminist group most critical of Beauvoir for her refusal to recognise sexual difference as foundational (thereby provoking twenty years of theoretical debates over essentialism) see Duchen, *Feminism in France* and Brison, 'Beauvoir and Feminism', 198–200.
76. In her interview with Susan Brison, Beauvoir gives an affirmative answer, although her context seems limited to France (Brison, 'Beauvoir and Feminism', 196).
77. The strongest argument against generalities is in *Treatise on the Emendation of the Intellect* §99–101, p. 27; the explanation of common notions is in *Ethics* Part 2, Proposition 40, Scholium 1–2, pp. 89–90. Balibar points out that the *Treatise* is ambiguous: never

clearly permitting us 'to decide if [common notions] are defined *theoretically* as axioms of natural reason or if they are defined *practically* as the perception of utility, similar for all men, at the heart of the imagination' (Balibar, 'Spinoza, The Anti-Orwell', 9).
78. This is inevitable if every concept points simultaneously towards a singular Idea/problem and towards a generality; we the readers are responsible for not tumbling into generality. This might be one sense in which Emily Zakin refers to the universal as a 'temptation'; see 'Beauvoir's Unsettling of the Universal'.
79. Schwarzer, *After* The Second Sex, 45.
80. Some examples, one American and one Congolese, are Hansberry, 'Simone de Beauvoir and *The Second Sex*'; and Chiwengo, 'Otherness and Female Identities'. See Ortega, 'Phenomenological Encuentros', for a detailed account of Beauvoir's reception by Latin American thinkers.
81. Bauer, *Simone de Beauvoir, Philosophy, and Feminism*, 234–5.
82. Le Dœuff, *Hipparchia's Choice*, 289–99.
83. See also Kruks, *Retrieving Experience*, 164–70.
84. Wasser, 'What is a Literary Problem?'
85. Moi, *What is a Woman?*, 226–33.
86. See also the dialogue with Michel Foucault, 'Intellectuals and Power', 208–9. For a nuanced evaluation of this attitude and the positive and negative forces that can inhabit or deploy it in feminism, see Linda Martín Alcoff, 'The Problem of Speaking for Others'.
87. See Spivak, 'Can the Subaltern Speak?'
88. See Mehta, *Liberalism and Empire*.
89. Davis, 'The Black Woman's Role in the Community of Slaves'.
90. Simondon, *L'Individuation Psychique et Collective*, 111–14.
91. Schwarzer, *After* The Second Sex, 33–6.
92. Beauvoir, *Diary of a Philosophy Student*, 247.
93. 'In every psychic system there is a swarm of possibilities around reality, but our possibles are always Others' (DR 260/334, quoted in Hughes, *Deleuze's Difference and Repetition*, 13)

Chapter 6

Virtual Conflicts

According to Deleuze, philosophical problems persist covertly in the actualisation of solutions.

> It is an error to see *problems* as indicative of a provisional and subjective state, through which our knowledge must pass by virtue of its empirical limitations . . . [a problem] is solved once it is posited and determined, but still objectively persists in the solutions to which it gives rise and from which it differs in kind. (DR 280/359)

For one thing, the solution of a philosophical problem in the social and political domain involves its actualisation in a field of institutions and actions, which inevitably face contingencies and obstacles. For another, the event of perplexing sensibility that gives rise to the problem occurs in a field of other ideas and events with which its effects are intermixed. With what other events is the problem/solution complex of *The Second Sex* intertwined? What problems might we expect to emerge from the actualisation of Simone de Beauvoir's implicit Idea, from a Deleuzian point of view?

Three potential problems come to mind. First, whatever its initial goals, *The Second Sex* was historically actualised by a 'molar' feminist movement to which Beauvoir eventually lent support. Can movements dedicated to the defence of those who affirm or are assigned to a certain identity support their becoming beyond that identity? Second, *The Second Sex* is consistently egalitarian, and assumes that all humans should prefer equality to hierarchy – including equality between the sexes – whether or not this is their empirical desire. But is equality always preferable to inequality? Finally, in writing *The Second Sex*, Beauvoir did assume that history would and should follow a roughly linear progressive path towards the institutionalisation of equality and freedom. Even if it was hard to account for the present existence of sexism using such a linear narrative, given Beauvoir's belief in the artificial nature of gender hierarchy, she seemed to believe that such hierarchies would eventually be abolished along with those of class and race or nationality. These aspects of Beauvoir's project have either given rise to historical problems for feminists or might be expected to do so.

Ethics and politics from the *milieu*

Beauvoir later acknowledged that her vision for the future of sexual difference was very vague and generally optimistic.[1] All the same, she had cautioned that it was insufficient to change either institutions, education or family structure without changing all three at once (SS 761/2:570). Feminism is both an ethical and a political project. But Beauvoir does not write about the relation of ethics to politics directly in *The Second Sex*; readers must infer that relation from her earlier *The Ethics of Ambiguity* and her historical involvement with struggles related to women's rights. From *The Ethics of Ambiguity* and 'Moral Idealism and Political Realism' (written shortly before in 1945) we find two relevant meta-principles that might govern the actualisation of Beauvoir's idea of a world in which women are independent and the sexes relate with reciprocity.[2] First, neither ethical *nor* political action can be deduced a priori from a general principle, as Kant would insist. Second, violence can never be ruled out a priori. In *The Ethics of Ambiguity*, this is because projects clash over scarce resources, including the resources of recognition and power. However, neither can violence be considered *inevitable or necessary*, as many conservatives (on both right and left) conclude from the permanent *possibility* of conflict.

When Beauvoir says that freedom cannot be a matter of individual spontaneity but also depends on the situation and the will of others, this means the same circumstances that can be approached ethically can and sometimes also *must* also be approached politically. But what makes an action political as opposed to ethical? Politics is located somewhere between institutions (with their violence, even legal institutions) and the pure structure of law. If human ambiguity is both individual and collective, this means that action always involves more than one person, even if institutions are less predictable than individuals. Such action involves power relations, abilities to affect and be affected, rather than codes or violence – although it can always draw on these latter for support.[3] Arendt, for example, characterises *action* by consensus and dissensus-formation around common projects. Action is neither purely instrumental nor purely concerned with justice, but reveals both the group and the actor as particularities, as infinitely self-disclosive answers to the question 'who?'[4]

Could we say that for Beauvoir, politics is about creating the *conditions* under which individuals and groups disclose the world and *one another's* projects as becomings? Better yet, about projects that make it possible for individuals and groups to develop certain individualising habits or ways of life? This need not prohibit the sort of visionary action preferred by Arendt, because conditions for disclosure are not just *given*, any more than projects are: they have to be disclosed and shaped in turn. The phenomenon of *choice* among ends and among means, including their consequences, does seem to play a greater role in political action for Beauvoir than for Arendt. Despite their common focus on disclosure (inherited from Heidegger), Beauvoir neither laments the rise of the 'social' like Arendt nor does she assume that law and material security exist prior to politics in the 'proper' sense. She is deeply concerned with the role of *failure* in even the best-executed political action and with the difficulty of *accepting* failure – even, perhaps, in our definition of 'the political'.

In *The Ethics of Ambiguity*, Beauvoir identifies three forms of ambiguity that tend to ensure no political project will completely achieve its goals. First, humans are both individual and collective; their individuality is generated and preserved by their connections to others (EA 7/10). Second, political means and tactics are not independent of ends; no end is absolute, justifying any end, and as mentioned in the preceding chapter, the meaning of every end is altered by the means (EA 124–5/179–80). In some cases, for example labour strikes, the spirit of freedom and cooperation born from the means has value in itself, even if the end of higher wages could be attained more quickly by simple technocratic decree.

Taken together, these principles imply that a collective action that ignores the desires of individuals or treats them as means to an 'external' goal will alter and degrade that goal's quality or meaning. This is true whether the goal is stability or change, hierarchy or equality, independence or belonging. However, despite all the pacifist care one might imagine, (and this is the third form of ambiguity), the liberation of some individuals to shape their own lives will almost surely require treating those who would oppress them as means (EA 99/143). Violence cannot easily be avoided. People individually and collectively *do* have projects that require scarce materials and build different meanings from the same givens. These are the conditions that eventually pose difficulties to Beauvoir's implicit solution to the problem of sexist sense in *The Second Sex*.

Beauvoir later believed both *The Ethics of Ambiguity* and *The Second Sex* were too idealistic, focusing on the tasks and achievements of the individual personality and not enough on the ways that individuals are 'situations' for one another, often struggling with or reinforcing scarcity (FC 67–8, 192). The first book, however, was written shortly after Nazi occupation and the Vichy regime, during which the most respected European institutions were actively complicit with oppression and genocide. In the essay 'An Eye for An Eye' [1946] Beauvoir defended her refusal to sign a petition asking for the post-war pardon of Robert Brasillach.[5] Brasillach was a literary figure and editor of a fascist magazine in which the names and pseudonyms of French Jews were published, facilitating their systematic deportation and eventual murder.

The essay begins by observing that many French who would have deplored the violence of the justice system and its role in the enforcement of economic inequality were now eager to use it for vengeance. This shows that the author of *The Second Sex* was fully aware of the ways that, even when it was not hijacked by fascists, bourgeois law protected owners while leaving workers exposed to misery and injury. As a proto-feminist, she was also aware that all institutions including the private family colluded in denying women's transcendence. During the Occupation, she had lost her job as a philosophy teacher due to an abuse of the legal system by a student's parents;[6] but many other women had been punished by the pro-natalist policies of the Vichy regime and abortion became miserably difficult and dangerous, as shown in her novel *The Blood of Others*. Unsurprisingly, it took some time before Beauvoir began to think more hopefully about the institutions that actively imposed sexist sense or that could realise her ethical vision on a mass scale.

For Deleuze and Guattari, as for Walter Benjamin, violence can both preserve and destroy states.[7] But in *A Thousand Plateaus*, the state is one (static) pole of a political process that also tends towards change under certain circumstances and from certain points of view. In other words, violence can reinforce stasis as well as force change. Surely this is relevant for the institutions that would be required to implement those aspects of *The Second Sex* that cannot be left up to the individual will to disclose others' freedom. Neither *The Ethics of Ambiguity* nor *The Second Sex* is sufficiently detailed to ask how phenomena can be governed by one institution instead of another, moving from one regime of governance to another, or how it can move in and out of institutional focus, as when domestic violence becomes a concern to the state and medicine or when homosexuality ceases to be such a concern. Such institutions are referenced obliquely throughout the text: schools, churches, factories and business enterprises, the legal institutions that give a meaning to marriage or sexual violence, the biological and medical institutions that reduce women to a materialist vision of maternity or regard the body as an instrument for realising a woman's life and relationships, including but not limited by maternity.[8]

Institutions, like all assemblages, are singularities – much as we may be tempted to regard them from a distance as 'examples' of a universal, a cookie-cutter concept. However long-lasting and stable, like glaciers, they are also in motion and changing. Institutions are *both* bodies in depth and effects of sense. Finally, *both* the stabilising and destabilising aspects of institutions are capable of wreaking violence on the singular becomings they encounter in the environment – either by blocking their becoming (as when oppressed people are the victims of homogenising stereotypes) or by decomposing their ratio of motion to rest (as when they are imprisoned, assaulted or forced into disabling work).[9] No sharp distinction exists between these two kinds of violence. Male domination is a feature of institutions in many societies, to such an extent that it can be regarded as an institution in its own right, but usually it is not treated as an effect of sense in a way that allows it to be acknowledged, much less counter-actualised. *The Second Sex* is an attempt to grasp this singular institution, in its multiplicity, in a way that would allow for counter-actualisation.

Sometimes, moreover, male domination is part of an institution's tendency to change and sometimes it is a source and effect of an institution's stability. For example, anthropologists Sharon Hutchinson and Jok Madut Jok studied the ways that attitudes towards the treatment of women in all parts of life changed during the Dinka/Nuer war in South Sudan during the 1990s, as each side was willing to use increasingly violent tactics against the other.[10] Although Beauvoir does not discuss this problem, surely the violence required to defend the freedom of the oppressed would also be legitimate in defence of women (and not only women from colonised or persecuted populations): even when no blood is shed, many men do feel the restriction of their right to dictate women's lives and the loss of women's unquestioned support as a kind of violence. Thus in her interviews with Alice Schwarzer, Beauvoir observes that men have become more aggressive in everyday interactions as they feel their assumptions and habits are under assault from women.[11]

When Deleuze and Guattari refer to 'the State', they do not simply mean the administrative, military and legislative apparatus that appeared in Europe during the seventeenth century. As Foucault has pointed out, many different structures have been called 'the State' over the course of French history, let alone the history of other cultures.[12] 'The State' is one way of grasping institutions or sedimented relations of power – with respect to their stability – that can also be grasped as a 'war machine' with respect to their potential for change. The institution need not be an actual government and the war machine need not be an actual armed body; it can be a philosophical or artistic movement, or even a tendency to destabilisation and polyvalence within a text (TP 422–3/526–7). One might even think of the state/war machine relationship as a form of ambiguity characterising collectives.

Deleuze and Guattari add, however, that *war* itself is best understood as the capture of a 'war machine' by the state – in other words, an institution's deployment of its radical potential for change in defence of its own stability against internal or external challenges (TP 417–18/521–2). Of course, overly rapid transformation undoes the internal relations making an assemblage – such as a community, a family or a human body – capable of its characteristic affects and actions. In their view, fascism is best understood as the state deployment of a war machine in ways that tend to destroy the state as well as its own and neighbouring populations (TP 421, 214–15, 230–1/524–5, 261–2, 281–3).[13]

But fascism was a system of power for enforcing gender and family relations as well as economic and racial hierarchies. Many of these habits remained intact or were even enshrined as 'tradition' after the end of World War II, and it was these assumptions about maternity and femininity – retooled for the post-war antifascist era – that Beauvoir's text was responding to. Two essays from *Privilèges*, 'Must we Burn Sade?' [1952] and 'Right-Wing Thought Today' [1955] touch on the way that literary figures, if not politicians, glorify militarism and the cult of fashion and thereby justify women's subordination.[14] In describing the suicidal nature of fascism, Deleuze and Guattari minimise its gendered aspect, though later theorists like Klaus Theweleit have suggested that the very association of femininity with 'becoming' and transformation – a kind of spectral war machine on the horizon of early twentieth-century capitalist culture – motivated fascist states to deploy their (captured) war machines in defence of a masculinity whose speed was ultimately suicidal.[15] In sum, the relationship between states and war machines in most institutions is profoundly important for the actualisation and counter-actualisation of sexist sense.

One might imagine at least three ways that institutions could be 'at stake' in women's struggle to achieve a transcendence such as men take for granted. The model of liberation in *The Ethics of Ambiguity* is drawn from the resistance to European fascism, which was waged by Allied national armies as well as by the guerrilla Resistance. It is also drawn from the model of revolutionary communist struggle against states whose legal system protected the owners of private capital and from the anti-colonial insurgencies against European commercial and military domination in Asia and Africa. This is the model of the 'war machine' versus the 'state' in the empirical sense from which the ideas of Deleuze and Guattari are drawn, and insofar as many early second-wave feminists in the older industrial countries became politically active on the left or in movements for minority civil rights, they analogised and metaphorised this struggle to anti-fascist, anti-capitalist, or anti-colonial warfare.

However, in *The Ethics of Ambiguity*, Beauvoir noted that the communists imposed a statelike rigidity of organisation and ideology, even within their efforts at insurgency (EA 147/212). In most countries where the 'war machine' on behalf of oppressed peoples won out over the capitalist or colonial state, that machine's own 'statelike' tendencies came to the fore and communist or post-colonial governments became remarkably repressive in their turn.[16] This is an example of the inevitable 'ambiguity' of political conflict, particularly liberatory conflict. The disciplined habits of militancy and clandestine warfare are not those of legislation and administration; when administration is turned over to former guerrillas, the result is easily a police state that interprets every expression of dissidence or delinquency as renewed warfare by the ousted elites[17] – which, of course, it sometimes is.

While insurgents can defend the freedom of those who are oppressed, just as they can commit violence in the process, it *must be possible* for states and courts to defend that freedom, just as they once meted out judicial violence on behalf of owners and elites. In 'An Eye for an Eye', Beauvoir acknowledged that a defeated oppressor is free (as consciousness) to repent of his former deeds. He is also a vulnerable object of pity for those who have triumphed over him.[18] Nonetheless, the legal system has the right and the duty to put him to death in order to assure those he once threatened that *there does exist* an institution supporting their freedom through the freedom of others. And finally, the new regime must be able to defend that freedom, however imperfectly, against 'reactionary' violence by those former elites, as well as by new economic agents such as corporations with the power to co-opt states and to pay for secret militias.

Beauvoir engaged with the courts as a political site at least twice more. During the Algerian War, Beauvoir opposed the quietism of public opinion and the French courts' collusion with military atrocities by writing in *Le Monde* on behalf of Djamila Boupacha, an Algerian militant accused of planting a bomb and raped during interrogation by the French army.[19] Having signed a confession under torture, Boupacha was on trial for her life. Boupacha's case was complicated by the fact that rape might prevent her from becoming married even if independence proved successful. She did not convince the court that she had been unjustly treated, but the accusation of terrorism was dropped with the Évian Accords. The FLN forced her to return to Algeria, where she did however eventually marry.[20]

The Algerian War was the culmination and test of Beauvoir's views on the necessity of violence against oppression, aired many years earlier in *The Ethics of Ambiguity*.[21] In that case, as in the later (Bobigny) court case which resulted in the legalisation of abortion, the legal work was done by Gisèle Halimi, lawyer and – after Beauvoir – second president of Choisir la Cause des Femmes. Halimi was later an important figure in the creation of the law attempting to assure parity between male and female candidates for public office. Beauvoir, however, created an association to support the Boupacha case, met with court officials, and risked bomb threats for her involvement. Beauvoir had already succeeded in persuading judges to soften a death sentence against one of her former philosophy students who had married an FLN supporter in Algeria.[22] A decade later, in the article 'In France Today, Killing Goes Unpunished' [1971], she clearly felt that the courts had a role to play in punishing employers who imposed deadly working conditions on women.

The last kind of conflict to consider is the one arising, not between the state and external or internal war machines, but between the war machine aspect of multiple institutions. This is the kind of case one finds in zones where multiple independence movements claim the right to defend those who live on a certain territory, or in conflicts between economic and religious forces that are simultaneously expanding, being incorporated into, and resisting citizens' daily habits. After independence, insurgencies continue to seize the assets of former colonisers, to establish ethnic domination or to claim independence for subregions. In both the Algerian civil war of the 1990s and the wars in the Democratic Republic of Congo from 1995 to the present, rape and kidnapping for domestic or sexual service have been used to sustain militias and terrorise populations. Arguably, this means that rape and domestic violence are part of the 'state', the normal stable functioning of institutions in a male-dominated society, as well as violent habits preserving those institutions against destabilisation.[23] The state chooses where to spend its energy, and few states pursue domestic batterers with the energy these crimes deserve, granting most men impunity in advance.[24] But like terrorist actions, they are also 'anonymous' and private, often illegal; states, parties or religious organisations rarely claim them as a source of power.

Women's resistance to such violence at the level of social opinion or legal reform is its own war machine, which since the 1970s has developed its own 'state' apparatus of advocacy groups, laws and legislative strategies, and enforcement mechanisms up to the level of international criminal courts.[25] In fact, institutions now claim a certain amount of feminist activism and scholarship as a progressive legitimating 'front' in conflicts that also deeply influence men's freedom and ability to affect and be affected. Just as Beauvoir notes that countries colonised by the Allies were reluctant to support them against the Axis because their own independence took priority (EA 98–9/142), men from ethnic minorities or organised labour have often claimed that feminism is a 'diversion' from the struggle they consider most important.[26] The human rights of women in the colonial and post-colonial world have been used as an excuse for interventionism by the wealthy industrial countries, although this does not mean that those women and their struggle for human rights is any less important in itself.[27]

Must Beauvoir's own idea in *The Second Sex* be actualised or dramatised through 'molar' politics? After all, I have argued that Beauvoir does not want to freeze the becoming of either men or women. In terms of *The Ethics of Ambiguity*, the transcendence of each individual rests on the will to disclose the transcendence of all others, regardless of sex, race or nationality. And this transcendence, I have argued, implies a willingness to identify with sub or supra-individual singularities rather than with one's current composition, to the extent that this is possible without seriously damaging the individual's functions. In terms of *Anti-Oedipus*, it implies a refusal to give in to a 'paranoid', segmented interpretation of one's desiring-production. In terms of *A Thousand Plateaus*, it implies a willingness to act in a molecular rather than a molar way. Yet Beauvoir unquestionably appeals to those individuals who find themselves in the situation labelled 'woman' and proposes to set society in motion and change beginning from this identity.

As she says in the Introduction, regardless of the 'molecular' possibilities and the meaning each individual gives to being sexed and sexual, it is quite certain that the world is currently divided into two gendered categories (SS 4/1:13). Politics is about *power*, not just the *desire* to be or to disclose. Although it is not a concept Beauvoir analysed, *power* is a relationship within and between groups and can limit or direct the disclosure of one's own freedom and that of others. Power is found both in bodily assemblages and in the incorporeal events that make them capable of interaction. Whether or not it counts as *oppression*, power currently divides the world into two molar sexes loosely associated with anatomical difference. In *The Second Sex*, Beauvoir was willing to envision the partial decomposition of sexed subjectivity into the class consciousness required to reorganise the economy for workers' benefit, but she was not prepared for the ways her own Idea led 'woman' to be called into question.

The potentially 'molecular' aspect of Beauvoir's call to disclose the freedom of all others as a condition of one's own freedom can help feminists deal with the 'intersectionality' of oppressions mentioned in the last chapter. Intersectionality poses an obstacle for effective 'molar' politics. If being a woman is a function of being in a certain situation, nonetheless there is no one 'situation' that makes someone a woman; there is a complex range of situations varying by race, age, religion and economic standing. However, to the extent that it *is* molecular, Beauvoir's Idea of freedom and reciprocity fails to present an image with which women in many different feminising 'situations' may identify *as individual psychological selves*. Much feminist activism and scholarship in the 1990s was motivated by this paradox; as women came to more and more successfully individuate themselves and develop capacities to affect and be affected, forming small identity-based groups, the *movement* itself could no longer be analogised to a single subjectivity, still less one that was recognisably 'female'.[28]

Tamsin Lorraine notes that identity, the physical or imaginative grouping with others who form a 'molar' pack, may facilitate the preservation of many people's defining speeds and slownesses. This is the context in which 'visibility' becomes a fraught existential as well as political issue for many women. In addition to the identifications of race, class and religion that form around the primary visible categories of modern and late modern 'faciality', every human being is involved with a host of 'molecular' and less visible becomings that *might* form points of identification if they encountered a critical mass, as well as less visible becomings that elude identification with other humans altogether. 'Imperceptibility', for Deleuze and Guattari, refers to the coextensiveness of one's singular line of flight with beings of non-human nature, with sound and light, and with concepts. Becoming-imperceptible does not mean becoming invisible to others, but of recovering one's 'invisible' dimension and finding a home in experiences that are not named or visible to others, and that, for better or worse, do not make one into an easy subject of 'recognition'.

Equal how?

Although Beauvoir often states that her goal is reciprocity or reciprocal recognition between men and women, *The Second Sex* also uses the familiar republican language of equality to make her case. This is clearly *part* of her driving Idea: 'it seems most certain that [women] will sooner or later attain perfect economic and social equality, which will bring about an inner metamorphosis' (SS 764/2:574). Meanwhile, as long as their equality is not concretely grounded in social and economic institutions, 'it is very difficult for a woman to act as an equal to a man' in sexual matters (SS 598/2:375). Inequalities are responsible for women's alienation from their bodies (SS 329/2:67) and for hypocrisy in the institution of marriage: 'as long as the man has economic responsibility for the couple, [equality] is just an illusion' (SS 521/286–7, also SS 758–9/2:566–7).

As mentioned earlier, her use of analogies between women's inequality to men everywhere and the racial hierarchy between whites and blacks in the United States obscures the question of *which* women are seeking equality to *which* men. Harriett Taylor Mill, for example, wanted white women of the upper class to be equal to white men of the same class so that they could participate in the rule of white (and presumably black) populations of the working and rural classes.[29] Similarly, Elizabeth Cady Stanton tried to use arguments of class and racial superiority to procure the vote for American white women before it was granted to American black men.[30] Given Beauvoir's critical comments about colonialism and slavery in *The Ethics of Ambiguity* and *The Second Sex*, it seems clear that she would like to dismantle those hierarchies as well, but has not clearly thought through her strategy and its implications, or researched it from the standpoint of colonised women, non-European women in France, or African American women. What exactly does equality mean, and what problems might egalitarianism entail from a Deleuzian standpoint?

Feminism emerged from modernising and democratic movements as well as from the increased focus of Western medicine and administration on the political significance of sexuality. Colonial and racial discourses were part of this matrix and were challenged in a significant way after World War II, the period when Beauvoir was writing. As an institution of sorts, feminism both challenged the state and came to form part of its legitimising discourse, which Étienne Balibar has characterised as 'equaliberty' (*égaliberté*).[31] Most 'modern' governments, but French republicanism in particular, were justified through the assumption that formal equality, if not substantive equality, promoted freedom and that any residual inequality could be justified by the freedom it made possible (an idea associated with John Rawls). With variations, all forms of feminism, Marxism and economic democracy inhabit this space of reasons. Reciprocity and recognition are part of the discourse of equaliberty – its subjective side. Sometimes this discourse coincides with biopower – the practices through which, starting in the eighteenth century, states drew legitimacy from their skill at fostering life, often with the help of families – and sometimes it functions as a limit on biopower or counteracts it.[32] If, in fact, the kind of transformation characterising and orienting the long durée of international politics is not adequately described by *égaliberté*, then Beauvoir's idea is going to run into trouble.

Balibar himself suggests that not all political problems resulting from difference can be resolved with the equality model, and gives sexual difference as a possible example.[33] Moreover, drawing on Spinoza, he argues that there is an 'incompressible minimum' of freedom of thought that no political arrangement can control. This incompressible minimum is the ideational correlate to speeds and slownesses that seem to express a being's *conatus* or desire to continue existing. While relations between the sexes are hardly 'natural' or immune to change, they often come to *represent* that 'incompressible minimum' for men and women – particularly men – who feel that their freedom is being unacceptably 'compressed' in other domains.[34] Thus societies undergoing political or economic destabilisation seem to experience shock waves of intense investment in rigid gender roles and supporting religious or social ideologies. Recognition may, but need not, point to this 'incompressible minimum' or register it symbolically.

For Beauvoir, equating transcendence with individuation means advocating the freedom of individuals rather than the freedom of couples, families or peoples except where these benefit the freedom of individuals (SS 16/1:30). Transcendence is a relation to oneself as well as to others and to one's surroundings. Reciprocity is unquestionably a relation to others, but differs from equality insofar as those who engage in reciprocity can be unequal in one or more domains while being equal in others. As Michael Walzer points out, equality must always be judged relative to a specific social good, and many of these goods circulate simultaneously.[35]

For Foucault, the primary social good during the modern period has effectively been a matter of biological security and flourishing. 'Power would no longer be dealing simply with legal subjects over whom the ultimate dominion was death, but with living beings, and the mastery it would be able to exercise over them would have to be applied at the level of life itself.'[36] Women's bodies were the focal point of multiple strategies enhancing the vitality and productivity of a racially defined population until shortly after World War II. But when biological security is equated with increased market competition, as in neo-liberalism, then individuation becomes mandatory for those who wish to escape the worst inequalities, which are thereby intensified.

But there are problems with equaliberty from a Deleuzian standpoint. Although they engage primarily with utilitarianism, all contemporary discussions of egalitarianism inherit the connotations of justice given to it by Aristotle.[37] This means that equality is a function of comparing like entities who possess a common form and treating them identically, or at least similarly. Equality would be impossible between beings who cannot be compared, or possible only with respect to those properties that can be compared and either found or made more, less, or identical. Unequal beings can be compared by virtue of analogy. Thus in Aristotle's *Politics*, leadership within the state can be analogised to male domination within the family. For the medieval tradition following Aristotle, God's properties can be analogised to those of imperfect created beings; and an artwork can be moving in a way that is analogous to a musical piece, albeit in a different sense. But insofar as we are singular, or *becoming* and therefor partly 'unformed', we are incapable of equality in Aristotle's sense. Thus feminists who protest that women do not want the opportunity to be equal to men 'on male terms' understate the problem. It is not that women and men are too different to be compared, but that all humans *differentiate* themselves precisely along the paths of their incomparability.

According to Deleuze, being is not the sort of thing that can be attributed to entities in 'different senses'; the being of a piece of music, a philosophical theory, a person or a historical period must have *one and the same* sense. But since each of these entities is only the *effect* of multiple differences, in Deleuze's thought being is only said of *that which differs*, insofar as it differs. Only differences can be equal. 'The words "everything is equal" may therefore resound joyfully, on condition that they are said *of* that which is not equal' (DR 37/55). Or: 'When two divergent stories unfold simultaneously, it is impossible to privilege one over the other: it is a case in which everything is equal, but 'everything is equal' is said of the difference, and is said only of the difference between the two' (DR 125/163). In fact, it can only be said of that which *becomes*, insofar as it *becomes different* from itself and others.

Moreover, these differences are never given simultaneously, are never equal at a given moment (of census-taking by the central government, for example) but only *over time*, as each difference becomes equal to *its own implications* or, in the terms of *Nietzsche and Philosophy*, 'what it can do'. These are the two ways that Deleuze thinks about equality: equality of differences and equality *to* the event, 'a becoming-equal to the act and a doubling of the self' (DR 89–90/120–1). These differences, however, are unquestionably 'below the level' of psychological and legal subjectivity, or even units such as political and religious communities – the identities he and Guattari refer to as 'molar'.

Later feminists castigated Beauvoir for supposedly assuming that equality with men meant equality in those social goods that men valued and by which men in Western societies systematically distinguished themselves from women.[38] The fact that she pointed out the biological and social handicaps imposed on many women by pregnancy, and did not herself become a mother, seemed to support this interpretation. At the time when Beauvoir was considered basically Sartrean, her use of 'transcendence' was taken to mean the act of an aggressively independent ego, rather than a self always in the process of disconnecting and connecting to other changing humans and a changing world. It also seemed to be a male value, opposed to connection and perhaps to reciprocity. Of course one can imagine a Sartrean or Hegelian interpretation of transcendence making equality very difficult, as all parties vie to surpass and surprise one another agonistically. But equality remains elusive, because it is a goal that links one individual to others who are also moving and changing. Maybe this is the spirit in which we must interpret Beauvoir's cryptic claim on the penultimate page of *The Second Sex* to the effect that 'those who talk so much about "equality in difference"' (thereby implying that women's inequality should be considered mere difference), 'would be hard put not to grant me that there are differences in equality' (SS 765/2:576).

Finally, not all women want equality to the same extent and in the same sense that Beauvoir or most feminists desire it. This problem is most important for Beauvoir when it involves women's *complicity* with male domination, but it also extends to women's support of class and racial domination, and finally to their acceptance of dependency as one dignified state among others.[39] The movement valorising sexual difference that Beauvoir refers to as 'neo-femininity' presents another challenge to her egalitarianism.[40]

Complicity basically means acknowledging inequality and seeking to attach oneself and identify with the stronger party rather than to neutralise it. Although Beauvoir rarely touches on it, men's dependence on women is systematically obscured in a masculinist culture and masculinism retains its prestige in part by degrading dependency. Men respond violently when their dependence on women is merely made explicit, not to mention when it is threatened. And women, as Beauvoir points out in the introduction, seldom wish to risk violence over making this dependence explicit – not just because they are afraid of dying, though millions of women die at the hands of intimate partners, but because they do not want to have to kill, seriously harm or humiliate those they also love. This is particularly true for women in minority or marginalised populations, who recognise the obstacles their men face in the wider political body.

Complicity may also involve, prior to any possible action, a *refusal to think* about inequality, lack of reciprocity or blocked transcendence – in one's own case as well as the case of others who may be more severely oppressed. Deleuze would not be surprised at this refusal to think, for he believes that it is only due to the good sense and the common sense of representational philosophy – Cartesianism – that we assume human beings of either sex 'ordinarily' desire to think or that thinking begins and ends with peace (DR 131, 150–3/171–2, 196–8). It is only compulsion – the imposition of a stronger force – that shakes us out of clichés and settled habits, often at the cost of great distress. Sometimes, Deleuze allows, the stupidity of others or one's own struggles with stupidity are thought-provoking in their own right (DR 153/198–9). Inevitably, true thought changes who we are or have been striving to become. For women who are trying to live up to 'femininity' the hope of success is a kind of positive force, although their attachment to male-dominated institutions that promote it has never made them stronger.

Beauvoir approaches these problems obliquely in the essays from *Privilèges*. Sade, for example, exemplifies both the unrepentant champion of the right of the stronger and the cause of sexual liberty.[41] 'Would it be possible', Beauvoir asks, 'to satisfy our aspirations to universality without renouncing individuality? Or is it only through the sacrifice of our differences that we can integrate ourselves into the collectivity?'[42] More problematically, can there be reciprocity between singularities that does not involve homogenising them?

Sade is condemnable because he can only grasp the violence of singularity when it is reflected in the literal suffering of an unwilling victim, and because he denies that *anyone* manages to do otherwise – which is, in itself, another gesture of homogenisation. Although thinking may not happen without violence, neither legal nor extra-legal violence can ensure that a victim thinks, as Beauvoir already acknowledged in 'An Eye for an Eye'.[43] She admits having felt this violence, the fear that it could justify a will to power in the mob, and the sense that it will never be satisfied.[44] Beauvoir also believes that Sade identifies with his most violent women characters,[45] thereby reminding us not only that masculinity and femininity are partial attitudes that exist only in mixtures, but also that women, too, can be oppressors, directly and without complicity, at least in principle and under select circumstances.

From Deleuze's point of view, why *shouldn't* a weaker force deliberately affirm a stronger force and thereby experience an expansion of its own powers, if only its power to be affected? 'Every phenomenon refers to an inequality by which it is conditioned' (DR 222/286). This would be Saba Mahmood's interpretation, for example, of women who adhere actively to a religious tradition in which sexual inequality is sanctified.[46] It would also be the attitude of women who exploit traditional gender attitudes and sexual power to take unconventional positions within a corporate structure or to achieve social mobility.[47] In *The Ethics of Ambiguity*, Beauvoir might have objected that complicity enhances the freedom (of movement) of some at the expense of others. In terms of *The Ethics of Ambiguity*, it restricts the scope of potential witnesses or contributors to one's own freedom, and inevitably provokes a backlash that may be violent. In *The Second Sex*, complicity seems to be a moral wrong whether or not it is met with violent resistance.[48] But contemporary political and economic institutions often make individualisation seem possible only on terms that require the support of those who are stronger, if not the betrayal of others' freedom.[49]

I do not believe Beauvoir conceives of equality on male terms.[50] She would be likelier to hope that the activities and affects associated with masculinity and femininity will be present in different proportions in the becoming of *both* sexes and should be equally free to *develop* in both sexes, probably in as-yet-unforeseen combinations. But equality among women is also an elusive goal. Women's differences from one *another*, particularly at the global level and particularly where wealth is concerned, constitute paths to individuation that are just as significant – and fraught – as their differences from men. European, American and other white feminists are caught in events and histories that that are not primarily 'white' and in which, at the global scale, their own whiteness is both a potential for becoming and a source of resistance to change or connection.

The experiences of women who have been educated and those who have not, those who have borne children and those who have not, those who have authority and independence in the workplace and those who are their female employees, those who suffer racial discrimination and those who are free from it, or suffer from a different kind of discrimination, as the singularity of Latinas and Asian women in the US is denied differently than that of African American women, are manifestly difficult to compare, much less equalise. For Deleuze, every assemblage/becoming is defined by its differences of power from other beings (DR 222/286). This means, drawing on Nietzsche, that although active forces may not seek to challenge one another, constituting tacit equality, more often equality is a *representation* through which weak or reactive forces try to limit the power of stronger forces. Indeed, the easiest way for those who are subjugated in different ways to conceptualise equality with one another is in terms of their common lack of power vis-à-vis some third party.

One possible solution to the limits of equaliberty might come from asking, as Arendt does, whether freedom involves *lack of external constraint* or *internal* organisation and action.[51] During Greek antiquity, freedom was a political and not a metaphysical phenomenon; a free person (generally a man) did not have doubts as to whether or not he was free, if he could live and move as he pleased. Freedom in the sense of being able to demonstrate that one was the origin of one's own action was a later development, a philosophical freedom that even a slave whose actions were governed by others could exercise in private, but having enough in common with the 'self-mastery' expected of elite free men to become a definition of freedom with potential universal scope. Following Spinoza, Deleuze is more likely to define freedom in two ways: as maximum capacity to affect and be affected, which is influenced by the other things one is combined with, and one's ability to resist destructive external forces.[52]

Freedom is more than simple independence, but it is not necessarily *measured against* the capacities of others. Beauvoir's strategy in *The Ethics of Ambiguity* is not to use the freedom of any one group (such as men, or white men and women) as the norm, nor to conceptualise freedom in terms of the individual's own needs, but to tie every individual's freedom to the freedom of all others. I suggest this would not mean recognising each individual as an identical subject of individuation, but disclosing individuals in such a way that their forms retain a *margin of indeterminacy* from which new becomings might yet appear.

Looking at these problems in this way also makes clear the kinship between Deleuze's principle of grasping problems 'from the middle' (TP 293/359–60) and Beauvoir's claim that awareness of ambiguity is essential to ethical living. In the history of Western thought, the idea that all representations, entities or assemblages are grasped only partially and temporally is associated with finitude, whether Kantian or Heideggerian. In short, it is because we are not God that we cannot know things from all possible angles. For Deleuze, rather, this is impossible because things are multiple and in motion, and so are we. There is no view from everywhere, but neither is there a view from just one place, one 'mode of existence', to use Latour's term.[53] Every grasp of a situation has tendencies to stabilise perceiver and perceived, as well as tendencies to disrupt or deterritorialise both of them. Ambiguity does not just refer to the fact that we can be thought and body, individual and collective, attached and detached, but that at any given moment we are always becoming either more or less one or the other.

Despite her statement in *The Second Sex* that 'it is institutions that create monotony' (SS 765/2:576), Beauvoir clearly believed socialism of some sort was *among* the conditions required to solve women's oppression (as well as the oppression of men who are poorer or racialised). But she cannot hope to achieve institutions that support greater economic equality in the classic Marxist way, by identifying an 'ur-problem containing all problems', rooted in an ideal point of contradiction. Although Deleuze obviously has his own critique of capitalism, particularly elaborated in the works co-authored with Guattari, he cannot accept the levelling of different social forms, institutions, assemblages and becomings into a single plane on which difference – particularly the *complex* difference(s) of social inequality – would take the clear form of a contradiction.

Whose history? Which event?

In the Introduction to *The Second Sex*, Beauvoir asks how sexism emerged historically. The account she offers has been critiqued and significantly complicated by later anthropologists and historians who point out, among other things, that the sexism Beauvoir encountered in France during the early twentieth century differs from the sexism African American, African, Chinese, Native American or Arab women might have experienced, not to mention French women one or two centuries earlier. Her question has structural affinities with the inquiries made by other mid-twentieth-century historians into the origins of capitalism – except that, as Deleuze and Guattari point out, the hegemonic form of capitalism seems to have clearly started in Europe and spread worldwide through colonialism, remaining 'one' in some significant sense, while each society seems to have produced indigenous forms of sexual hierarchy that only superficially seem to follow a global logic such as 'Othering'.

Beauvoir argues that Marxism misses the causes – and the political significance – of male domination, but her approach resembles Marxism in looking for a single global pattern. Insofar as she does so, Beauvoir is also open to the criticism of determinism, as when she implies in the History chapters that domination by (male) farmers was necessary for economic 'progress', or more likely the criticism of voluntarism, as when she insists that women are responsible for striving to change the meaning of their own sexed identity. In *The Ethics of Ambiguity*, she had already noted the contradiction between Marxists' belief in the inevitability of socialist revolution and their urgent efforts to develop class consciousness.

And yet, as Bergson would have argued, both determinism and voluntarism presume that historical events follow one another in a linear way.[54] The causes we observe operating during a given historical period, as well as the effects whose causes interest us, are *selected* and put in spatial relation to one another from a vast welter of possible combinations and articulations of becomings and events. Indeed, only the most stable and repeatable causes and effects seem to show up as events *at all*, while becomings whose origins or results are unknown are like caterpillars we assume will persist and grow because we do not know that they were once eggs and will later be moths, or the solid form of a chemical whose liquid or gaseous form we have never encountered. Absent the right environmental or atmospheric conditions, an insect may never mature or a chemical vaporise. But once those conditions are met, a cascade of irreversible effects takes place; locusts decimate crops and profoundly alter a society's food supply; this changes regional import-export policies, or prompts peasants to leave the land.

The question of how to think about history from a Deleuzian standpoint is complex and several scholars have attempted to create a synthetic overview. Deleuze and Guattari contend that history is always written from the 'sedentary' point of view; in other words, the often backward-looking point of view from which beings are or have become stable; while 'nomadology' is written from the standpoint of an event unfolding in multiple directions (TP 23–4/34–6). Craig Lundy, however, questions the consistency of the dichotomy. He argues that to the two kinds of becomings found in most Deleuze texts – incorporeal and embodied, molecular and molar, aleatory and directional, we must interpolate another kind of becoming that links the two layers or series.[55] History is not merely historicism, for historicism presupposes that we are in agreement about the relevant features and speed of historical duration, an agreement that is always open to contestation. Despite their disparaging remarks about history, Deleuze and Guattari cite Braudel and Péguy approvingly because they conceive of history in terms of the *qualitative* experience of becoming characterising a given moment or event.

Other approaches to history via Deleuze focus less on identifying patterns of transformation that may involve non-linear effects and more on the problem of identifying *singular* points in those processes, patterns of functional homology between phenomena over time, or even clear-cut moments of causality. For example, Jay Lampert has tried to understand traditional historical causality using the models of temporal synthesis found in *Difference and Repetition* rather than those Husserlian or Hegelian models in which succession is the primary dimension.[56] For Lampert, the future is a function of *desire*.[57] One might investigate the ranking of events by intensity rather than temporal priority, or understand events in terms of functional relations that cut across geographical and temporal periods.

For Michel Serres, non-linear history means drawing the full implications of thinking time as a multiplicity. Like all events, sexist sense is a multiplicity.[58] It is a set of apparent regularities, causes and effects, just as Gene Holland describes the emergence of capitalism as an event with *multiple sources* – a *contingent* event, yet one that established lasting conditions under which exchanges and expropriation take place with remarkable regularity, so regular that they seem to be 'determined' and 'determining'.[59] It emerges from multiple causes in any given society and nothing guarantees that one society's sexist sense has the same scope, causes or effects (and therefore the same counter-actualising solutions) as the sexist sense of another society.

If sexist sense emerged from different conditions in different regions, the results were sufficiently similar to seem like – and to function as – a universal norm.[60] Just as Deleuze argues, following Bergson and Merleau-Ponty, that an organism can be stimulated to produce an eye in various ways from a set of common prior genetic conditions, systematic male domination can be produced in a society through different paths.[61] For Beauvoir, these were conditions of production during the Iron Age; today, they may be conditions of political splintering and small-arms proliferation. If sexism enables men – and their societies – to flourish in certain condition-bound ways, then it will become a universal currency, the way that various efforts to form computer links were eventually systematised in the formation of the World Wide Web. This would explain why some societies, as Peggy Reeves Sanday has explored, do manage to resist the social relations that Beauvoir thought were universal.[62] But nothing guarantees that the reasons a phenomenon came into existence will be the same reasons it remains in existence.

Perhaps appropriately, however, there are many ways to understand 'non-linearity'. Both Serres and Deleuze and Guattari are trying to think about history both at the *passive* level of the emergence, synthesis or stratification of events, and at the *active* level of historical writing, interpretation, and transmission or contestation of those events. If nature is not a closed system 'in itself', except insofar as conceptualised or given *sense* by humans, then picking any state of affairs to represent 'equilibrium' denies the role of chance and cumulative factors in bringing about events. We cannot assume that the beings or events of the future will resemble those we have become adept at identifying in the past. We cannot, therefore, assume that the *most important causal connections* between the past, present and future will ultimately be mapped using the causal relations we have observed linking beings and events in the past. This is particularly true for efforts to think about the history of philosophy: concepts, texts and strategies of resistance to one approach or another gather weight and sink to the riverbed like a backdrop for what comes later and for details playing across the surface; but if sufficient turbulence is introduced by a tide, for example, then Deleuze, for example, becomes the contemporary of Beauvoir and Lévinas.

From a perspective more influenced by hermeneutics, Victoria Browne describes at least four strategies through which historians can group events in order to produce written histories – histories that inevitably inform our experience of the present and our anticipation of the future.[63] She argues that feminist historians documenting women's global activism tacitly use 'time of the trace', 'narrative time', 'calendar time' and 'generational time' in order to situate themselves and their readers with respect to a historical world that does not *exist* except through multiple strategies. 'Time of the trace' orients historical research towards verifying or falsifying details in the archival record; 'narrative time' models history on the techniques for storytelling that humans use to make sense of their psychological lives; 'calendar time' shapes our vision of passing history according to the technologies by which we situate our activities in duration, and 'generational time' identifies events with respect to our past or anticipated interlocutors.[64] Generational time is particularly important for the history of philosophy; and one could see Deleuze's plane of immanence as a challenge to its self-evidence.

Together and individually, Browne's plural forms of historicality also challenge the very notion of a universal historical continuum on which the theorists of non-equilibrium rely (including, perhaps, Deleuze and Guattari's attempt to rehabilitate 'universal history'). Yet each form of historicality is 'non-linear' in its own way. Being aware of these strategies, employed around the world but particularly within the well-funded research and publishing apparatus of wealthy countries, makes it much more difficult to project the ontologies and chronologies of Western women's lives and movements for social justice onto feminist movements elsewhere in the world. Browne's goal is to cultivate awareness of the anachronism by which minority women's agitation is considered 'racial', not 'feminist', or ignored altogether during periods when white women retreated from the political arena. In another such anachronism, 'waves' of feminism are believed to follow one another in a sort of global *Aufhebung*, abolishing what went before while improving on it, when actual women inhabit a number of discursive and institutional spaces at once for long periods of their lives.

Beauvoir laid the ground for contemporary women's history by digging out the names of writers and agents, differentiating between the conditions of women belonging to different classes, if not races and nationalities. She also showed how men's seemingly endless ability to make history was propped up by the myth of women's *unhistoricality*. Before second-wave feminism, as Michelle Perrot has argued, the habits and extraordinary events of women's lives were simply not considered possible material for historical study;[65] the female record was what Browne would call a 'trace' demanding rectification. While being dismissive of what she finds in women's history and often, as her critics point out, comparing women's achievements negatively with men's, Beauvoir nevertheless does begin to identify long periods – and not only in Western societies – when women were defined by certain affects, certain abilities and experiences, and other moments of rapid change when being a woman came to mean something different, at least for rich women by comparison to poor women, or colonised women by comparison to those who were colonising, etc.[66]

Due to her association with Sartre, who resisted innovations in philosophy of history from the 1960s, the possibility of Beauvoir's contribution to historiography is overlooked by almost everyone (Michel Kail is one exception). Her phenomenological heritage and her ideas about 'committed literature', moreover, have made her seem like a logical partisan of the sort of female 'experience' critiqued by Joan Scott.[67] Scott questions the way that women from a given culture and historical moment, in legitimately claiming their political voice, threaten to eternalise their 'phenomenology' as if it were the only possible form of historical experience. By giving women a history, however, Beauvoir makes them aware of the way that identifications (with large 'molar' numbers) as well as subtle divergences and points of imperceptibility shape what it means to have a body, a 'situation' ambiguously natural and cultural but defined by neither. Such bodies become self-conscious in terms of their biological resemblances, but also in terms of their class, linguistic and national groupings, and finally in terms of regional variations, common memories of certain events and occupational or religious habits whose ultimate meanings are absolutely singular. She suggests that both molar and molecular becomings had different meanings for women in a given time and place than they did for the men around them. Implicitly, she asks how they could have counter-actualised that meaning, or become the cause of their own embodied situation.

To what non-linear processes does *The Second Sex* (and feminism in general) contribute? During the 1990s, the fear that many feminist gains would be overturned gave a new urgency to the question of how social processes emerging from multiple points could result in an irreversible change. It seems obvious that feminism is part of the process of *deterritorialisation* of formerly fixed, coded binaries organising people and goods, dividing populations by nation, sex, religion and productive role, described by Deleuze and Guattari in *Anti-Oedipus*. Variations on and within feminism(s) around the world take the form of efforts to reinscribe the flows of individualising women under this or that rubric: of 'neo-femininity', of community and nationality, of 'progress' (even if this means introduction to the world economy through sweatshops) and of religion. But the spread of technology that renders women's 'traditionally' subservient household labour obsolete, the transfer of production from the older industrialised countries to those countries where poverty makes women's factory labour socially and politically acceptable or even mandatory, and increased information about consumer opportunities make some aspects of feminism seem irreversible.[68]

Finally, one might ask about the role of chance or the 'indeterminate' remainder in historical understanding and events, the nonsense that seems to tie together a field of sense. Feminist phenomena (such as women's single motherhood or participation in migrant labour) are not only in a constant state of flux, both at the aggregate and individual levels; they are also responding to military and economic transformations whose contours are not easily defined.

In many cases, economic and political transformations in the direction of equality or at least contingent autonomy for individuals during the late twentieth century coincided with new reasons for stabilising sexual and racial divisions. As mentioned, Harriet Taylor Mill called for the emancipation of (white) women on the grounds that they would help to preserve class and race privilege, and the American war on Islamic terror has put women in combat and at the centre of foreign policy – albeit to preserve Western security. Igor Kopytoff notes that post-colonial societies in which women wield real political power tend to be those in which mothers, wives and sisters can take advantage of very clearly defined class privileges (and are also spared domestic labour because of their economic status). Individual freedom and equality are taken as political justifications for stability as well as change, since unregulated exchanges tend to reveal the inefficiency of many privileges and to eliminate public goods that cannot be easily 'exchanged'. The process of deterritorialisation once thought inevitable, called 'modernisation', is invoked as an excuse for stability ('our way of life') as well as excitement and desire, even when it introduces massive destabilisation in newly industrialising countries.

Many feminists hope that the inclusion of women's dignity and physical integrity in the growing body of international human rights law will be a lasting event that frames these other singular becomings.[69] Political bodies around the world have expressed scepticism when it comes to the human rights women demand, although they generally accept that male citizens should have religious, educational and political protections. On the other hand, there are women who express resistance to giving other women certain rights that would disrupt their own privilege and power. In a world where women have restricted opportunities to participate in economics and warfare, many derive power from their control over the labour and sexuality of other women, particularly young ones.

Heads of state and religious leaders have criticised the unwarranted universal imposition of norms they consider Western (usually ignoring local constituencies who believe they would be good non-Western norms as well). Sometimes they believe that these norms are simply efforts to destructure and restructure non-Western economies in accord with globalisation – especially since such legal institutions are still dominated by jurists from the older industrial societies with economic and strategic interests.[70] In other words, male or female, such countries see the universalism of human rights discourse, particularly for women, as the practical front of a legal and economic project that casts them as 'Other'.

For Deleuze, however, there can be no such universal as 'woman', although women and their situations may empirically have much in common. Thus there can be no morality founded on being a woman, or recommended for women. Nor can a political movement or legal action to defend women's singularity, freedom or transcendence begin by imposing a representation that obscures these differences. They cannot separate women from their contexts and activities and intimates, prescribing justice for the 'bare woman' rather than for the totality of her involvements. This is Deleuze's rationale for preferring 'jurisprudence' to projections of general global norms.[71] But his strongest reason for scepticism about the human rights movement is its inability to create the material institutions that would enable any universal norm to be effected.

> Human rights . . . can coexist on the market with many other axioms, notably those concerning the security of property, which are unaware of or suspend them even more than they contradict them . . . Who but the police and armed forces that coexist with democracies can control and manage poverty and the deterritorialization–reterritorialization of shanty towns? (WIP 107/103)

Abortion rights, sexual violence in wartime, and social dignity and economic support for the aged are examples of *problems* that give rise to institutions with their own site-specific rules of thumb. In 1949, Beauvoir could not have imagined the transition from clandestine abortionists – an institution supporting women in her own time, however poorly – to politically militant women's health collectives, much less the integration of women's full reproductive health, including abortion and contraception, into the medical establishment. And yet these nascent institutions gave rise to practices of collective decision-making and consultation with women patients about their needs and aspirations that were borrowed by other feminist institutions, including movements directly involved with the legal and legislative sphere. Activism for changes in the laws governing sexual violence, or in some cases the establishment of such laws in the first place, comparable to the conventions against torture or adding to them, did not take place on the basis of principles, even if the resulting laws have a universalist form. They took place on the basis of the evident needs of women who were being abused and the complexity of whose suffering required solutions at a 'higher' and more comprehensive level of management.

While Beauvoir believed that attitudes and conditions were improving for women in certain countries, she did not envision a political movement without some notion of woman as universal. *The Second Sex* took it for granted that women would not leave the homes where they supposedly identified with the men of their ethnic and economic strata. But obviously institutions are required to change, in the case of women's medical or educational needs, as well as employment policies that allowed women to be discriminated against in the workplace and laws restricting women's exercise of independence. The point would then be even sharper, however: such a politics could not be grounded on a universal, although it could result in near-universal or truly universal changes for women (and men, as a result). In practice, these sites of change cannot be deduced from a principle but are the singular beginnings from which any principles and institutions must emerge. While principles that are part of singular, even global *institutions* may be pragmatically necessary, principles that impose uniformity on women, even in their own defence, are either *part* of the problem or temporary components of the assemblages attempting to solve the problem.

From Deleuze's point of view, 'Woman' is a molar entity as well as the name of a tendency to change in every situation (becoming-woman), whether or not females are involved. As I have been discussing it, feminism means a movement on behalf of individuals constituted as female, ergo molar women. But it is also a movement that ought to liberate men's and women's tendencies to change or to become-imperceptible, even within and with respect to feminism.[72] This does not mean that legal and economic changes should be abandoned, militarism accepted, and so on – women and other sexed, desirous beings are not the *basis* for these freezes and changes but their *product*. The psychological and sexual variations among women, even the racial and religious variations, do not need to be standardised in order for women to create institutions that support their empirical diversity wherever they see needs. Put otherwise, Beauvoir's philosophy is not at all a matter of becoming-woman but of women's becoming *everything else* (TP 279–80/342–3). As Toril Moi suggests – instead of pervasive femininity, becoming-imperceptible despite one's female status at those moments when it doesn't and shouldn't matter.[73]

What can institutions do?

What if, one more time, we talk neither about morality and ethics, nor even politics, but justice? Is justice really at issue in *The Second Sex?* Is it one way of grasping the ambiguous continuum between ethics and politics? Often justice is thought in terms of recognition.

But if recognition is to be something other than facialisation; something other than supporting the freedom of others only insofar as they use it to become a being, to live up to a norm – then it would have to be a set of practices that always leaves room for one's own becoming-imperceptible and that of others.[74]

What would justice consist in? In 'An Eye for an Eye', Beauvoir acknowledged the limits on a society's ability to *compel* reciprocity from its members or to inculcate a feeling of empathy with those who suffer. What if one tried to use the courts to strengthen those who are weaker rather than enforce a common representation of some past event? First: if her right to individuation, to singularity, is to be upheld, justice must be done to a woman *as* an *assemblage*, not as a 'bare' individual, the biological or forensic object of reproductive medicine or criminology. Only as an assemblage – with her tools, her ideas, her followers and co-workers, her fields and savings accounts, can a woman *affect* her world as well as endure *being affected*. But second, justice must allow such a woman to appear and to act, at the symbolic level, as the *quasi-cause* of that which she has suffered involuntarily in the flesh and in psychology. This requires, first of all, that the event of suffering be delimited properly.[75]

Now, what *The Second Sex* showed above all is that women's histories, both personal and collective, had simply not been written, not been *turned into events*. How could justice be done? Neither the bodies with which women had been identified nor those from which they were actually composed – their Chronos – had been broken down in any serious way so that they could both *think* and *undergo* their own becomings – becoming secure, immanent or frustrated as well as changeable, transcendent and affirming. They were thrust outside of history by the fact that the kind of work they did was so difficult to translate into events, by contrast to the waging of wars and signing of charters. And much of that work – emotional, sexual, maternal – was viewed in the most self-serving way by the men who benefited from their enforced homogeneity. This, in a more concrete way, is what Deleuze and Guattari meant by the theft of girls' *becomings* as well as their *bodies* for a form of sense that has come to function both as *disruptive* and *generative* nonsense for many groups, not just women (TP 276/337–9).

Communities are like individuals in their pretensions to stable being over time. A different way of challenging the transformations associated with modernisation, which does not entail a glorification of past codes and forms of sense, is by shifting the locus of political legitimacy from individuals and communities to sub and supra-individual assemblages. This approach allows us to see that challenges to *individuation* and therefore transcendence do not always coincide with either modernisation or with the statist or war machinic aspects of that process. And they may be more visible when conceived as challenges to the individuation of *assemblages* than of legal or warrior subjects. Indeed, modernity and modernisation are ways of making sense of a historical phylum that may be even more complicated. Colonialism and neocolonialism, equaliberty, biopower, and capitalist deterritorialisation are events that traverse Beauvoir's work whether or not she knows it, involving time spans and geopolitical regions too vast to be encompassed in the time of a life – Beauvoir's life or the lives of her readers. As a historical phylum, feminist bodies and actions and their empirically, locally arising conflicts have been *read back into* Beauvoir's text, the way that solutions feed back on the Idea which was actualised in them.

Beauvoir's work has been carried on by others, but it would not have happened without this first liberatory division between *Chronos* and *Aion*, between the perpetual present of embodied suffering and the incorporeal becoming of events. Today, we might say that feminism itself was part of a larger, longer historical change touching all parts of the globe in which the forms of sexuality and labour radically changed. This shows how important institutions will be to any actualisation of the concepts produced in the course of this 'event-ive' *Second Sex*. It remains to be seen whether institutions are modelled, as for Hegel, on *universals* that identify salient similarities between participants – or whether they are singularities, like *concepts*, that introduce and sustain the differentiation of those they include. It also remains to be seen what these changes will mean and if they can persist if they are no longer exclusively identified as 'feminist'.

Notes

1. Schwarzer, *After The Second Sex*, 42.
2. Beauvoir, 'Moral Idealism and Political Realism' [1945].
3. In *Ethics of Ambiguity*, Beauvoir distinguishes between voting, governing, rivalling over power, and statesmanship or 'making history' (EA 139/200–1). However, she is primarily concerned to elicit

self-criticism in the latter and reduce the hold of 'seriousness' or 'adventurism' over their deeds. (EA 154/222) She also describes the 'political man' as concerned with history (by contrast to the professional politician) in 'Moral Idealism and Political Realism', 179, 187.
4. Arendt, *Human Condition*, 179–82.
5. Like 'Moral Idealism and Political Realism', this essay is found in Beauvoir, *Philosophical Writings*.
6. Beauvoir's and Sartre's post-war acclaim as cultural 'representatives' of the Resistance was eventually harshly criticised. Sartre was upset that Beauvoir signed a loyalty oath to the Vichy government in order to get a teaching job. Others have accused Sartre himself of taking advantage of job openings left by fleeing Jewish faculty. Beauvoir admitted that it took her longer than it should have to understand the danger faced by French Jews and to feel solidarity with fellow citizens; she was overwhelmed when Bourla, the lover of her friend Nathalie Sorokine (Lise in the memoirs), was killed by the Nazis during the final days of the Occupation. See Simons, 'Beauvoir and the Problem of Racism', and Galster, 'Simone de Beauvoir et Radio-Vichy'; on Bourla, see PL 457–8.
7. Benjamin, 'Critique of Violence'.
8. In *Spinoza: Practical Philosophy*, Deleuze seems to agree with Spinoza that ethics is about the cultivation of capacities to affect and be affected; whereas in *The Logic of Sense*, it is a matter of counter-actualising events. Neither book links ethics tightly to politics, although the reflections on desire and fascism in *Anti-Oedipus* and *A Thousand Plateaus* suggest, at the very least, that fascism is a failure of ethics as well as a self-destructive political form. For Beauvoir, on the other hand, the cultivation of affective capacities is not just a *goal* of political action but the *result* of specific institutional conditions.
9. Spinoza, *Ethics*, Part 2, Lemmas 4–7, pp. 74–5.
10. Hutchinson and Jok, 'Gendered Violence'.
11. Schwarzer, *After* The Second Sex, 62.
12. See Foucault, *The Birth of Biopolitics*, 4–9, 76–8.
13. In 'Many Politics', fascism is not associated with an extreme version of large-scale molar politics but with the breakdown or unexpected power of small pockets of identitarian passion that exist on 'molecular' lines of flight. Deleuze and Parnet, *Dialogues*, 138–9. One might hypothesise that right-wing parties alone cannot create fascism, although they might create tyranny: it is when they enter into combination with gangs and mafias (particularly those with a racial and sexual agenda) that these parties and the entire system can transform in terrifying ways (AO 257–8/306–7).
14. These essays are collected in Beauvoir, *Political Writings*. The third essay from *Privilèges* was 'Merleau-Ponty and Pseudo-Sartreanism'.

15. Theweleit, *Male Fantasies*.
16. On the other hand, in Algeria and many other former colonial countries, revolutions were led by a vanguard that was *far more* committed to women's political and economic equality than the colonial governments they were fighting against. See, for example, Fanon, 'Algeria Unveiled'. In many cases women's rights were among the advances the post-colonial governments – still led by men – sacrificed in order to salve the pride of ordinary (male) citizens whose hopes for general economic prosperity did not materialise. Le Sueur argues that the influence of Fanon and other French anti-colonial intellectuals on the European public image of revolutionary Algeria minimised the existence of internal conflicts between Algerian revolutionary factions, such as those between the secular/socialist FLN and the Muslim nationalist current of Messali Hadj (Le Sueur, *Uncivil War*, 12–13).
17. Boulbina, *L'Afrique et ses fantômes*, 42–3.
18. Beauvoir, 'Eye for an Eye', 253, 256–7.
19. The revolutionary FLN, like the French state, had a 'statist' side as well as a war machine; as in many wars of independence, women were enlisted as fighters and took on new roles of potential political importance, but the FLN also carried out violent reprisals against Algerians suspected of collaborating with the French. Murphy, 'Beauvoir and the Algerian War'. Meanwhile, the institutions of the colonial French state were shadowed by a 'war machine' in the form of the increasingly unmanageable and terroristic OAS, which vowed to preserve European supremacy in North Africa with or without the support of Paris. The Islamic *hijab* or 'veil' acutely symbolised this ambiguity of Algerian self-determination, for it signified both transformative resistance to the French denial of Arab singularity (particularly the singularity of male subjects) and the development or reinforcement of sexist gender relations within the state that they were building. See Fanon, 'Algeria Unveiled', and Golay, 'Féminisme et postcolonialisme'.
20. Murphy, 'Beauvoir and the Algerian War'.
21. Beauvoir's profound disappointment and outrage toward France during the Algerian War, reported in *Force of Circumstance*, was interpreted by the public as a sign of personal depression rather than political outrage.
22. Beauvoir, 'Preface to *Djamila Boupacha*'; Murphy, 'Beauvoir and the Algerian War'.
23. There is a vast literature on this topic. See Turshen and Twagiramariya, *What Women Do in Wartime*.
24. See, for example, Charlesworth, 'Human Rights as Men's Rights', 106–8; Sullivan, 'The Public/Private Distinction'.
25. Bumiller, *In an Abusive State*.

26. Schwarzer, *After The Second Sex*, 70–1.
27. White American feminist Drucilla Cornell has argued that such norms protect women's right to participate in shaping the societies that put forward claims about cultural independence (Cornell, *At the Heart of Freedom*). Similarly, Beauvoir expressed outrage at male Iranian activists in Paris who believed Iranian women were endangering their revolution against the Shah by protesting too vocally against religious restrictions on clothing (Simons, Benjamin and Beauvoir, 'Simone de Beauvoir: An Interview', 333). Nzegwu is, at the very least, adamant that men should not lay exclusive claim to the meaning of African traditions (Nzegwu, *Family Matters*).
28. This is seen most clearly and paradoxically in the demands for rights put forward by transgender men and women.
29. Mader, *Sleights of Reason*, 89–93.
30. Griffith, *In Her Own Right*, 124–5.
31. Balibar, '"Rights of Man" and "Rights of the Citizen": The Modern Dialectic of Equality and Freedom'.
32. Foucault, *History of Sexuality*, 39–40.
33. Balibar, 'Rights of Man', 54–7.
34. Balibar, 'Spinoza, The Anti-Orwell', 35.
35. Walzer, *Spheres of Justice*, 8–12.
36. Foucault, *History of Sexuality*, 142–3.
37. This discussion is primarily found in book 5 of the *Nicomachean Ethics*, where fairness is seen both as a part of justice and as a spirit animating and identifiable with justice as a whole. The discussion is divided between rectificatory justice (chapter 4) and distributive justice (chapter 3), which can either allocate goods relative to some property individuals have in different degrees or allocate them equally to all individuals qua individuals.
38. In particular, see the reference to suffragists and 'existentialist feminists' in Kristeva, 'Women's Time', 193–4; Irigaray, *Je, Tu, Nous*, 9–14; Cornell, *The Imaginary Domain*, 63–4.
39. The concept of 'dependency', frequently used in older democracies to delegitimate social programmes for the poor, has a fraught history in feminist scholarship. Not all cultures stigmatise dependency to the same degree as contemporary European and white majority societies. See Fraser and Gordon, 'A Genealogy of Dependency'; also Sennett, *Respect*.
40. See Schwarzer, *After The Second Sex*, 78–9, 113–18; Beauvoir, *All Said and Done*, 452.
41. Beauvoir, 'Must We Burn Sade?', in *Political Writings*, 45, 55.
42. Beauvoir, 'Must We Burn Sade?', in *Political Writings*, 45.
43. Beauvoir, 'Eye for an Eye', 248–50.

44. 'The individual who is inadvertently struck is not solely a body and he proves it; he defies the other with his voice, by a look; he hits him. The respect that he demands for himself, each person claims for his loved ones and finally for all men. The affirmation of the reciprocity of interhuman relations is the metaphysical basis of the idea of justice. It is what vengeance strives to reestablish in the face of the tyranny of a freedom that wants to be sovereign. But this enterprise runs up against an essential difficulty . . .' (Beauvoir, 'An Eye for an Eye', 249).
45. Beauvoir, 'Must We Burn Sade?', 62.
46. Mahmood, *The Politics of Piety*.
47. In recent years, a whole feminist literature has emerged encouraging women who accept corporate capitalism to demand equality with men in competitive institutions. Camille Paglia was an outspoken critic of American feminism who proposed to use the 'war of the sexes' to women's advantage, whom one cannot help but associate with Beauvoir's observation that the hetaera espouses a kind of Nietzscheanism. Coco Chanel, one of the most successful women of Beauvoir's own era, was a more ominous example of the combination of female ambition and economic/political opportunism; her name does not appear in *The Second Sex*, but her shadow hangs long over the novels in characters such as the designer and collaborator Lucie Belhomme (*The Mandarins*).
48. *The Ethics of Ambiguity* does not use the term 'complicity'; complicity seems to be a later version of 'seriousness'. In the earlier text, those who are oppressed by the seriousness or simple greed of others react to defend themselves automatically, and such action is moral even when it introduces obvious violence – though Beauvoir knows that no resistance or revolution is accomplished without a great deal of organisation, some of which is coercive even for the subjects of liberation. Those who are oppressed are provoked by need, by palpable unfreedom and do not need to be provoked by thought as well. Of course, *oppression* does not always lead to resistance and rebellion; it is more than *inequality*, and often it simply flattens the capacities of those it affects. Nor is oppression the only reason violence may be inevitable – there may be other clashes over priorities as groups seek to maintain the transcendence of their composite individuals.
49. On 'techniques of mutual betrayal', see Cutrofello, *Discipline and Critique*.
50. See, for example, Schwarzer, *After* The Second Sex, 78.
51. Arendt, *Between Past and Future*, 146–8.
52. 'He whose body is capable of the greatest amount of activity has a mind whose greatest part is eternal' (Spinoza, *Ethics*, Part 5,

Proposition 39, p. 222). 'Nobody as yet has determined . . . what the body can and cannot do, without being determined by mind' (Part 3, Proposition 2, Scholium, p. 106). 'We call *latitude* the affects of which it is capable at a given degree of power, or rather within the limits of that degree . . . We know nothing about a body until we know what it can do, in other words, what its affects are, how they can or cannot enter into composition with other affects, with the affects of another body' (TP 256–7/313–14).

53. In *We Have Never Been Modern*, Bruno Latour proposes that the geographical spread of technologies for investigating reality and testing theories can be very extensive without having to be 'universal' (117–20); technologies pertaining to various 'modes of existence' including natural science, religion, economic exchange and political persuasion are described in *An Inquiry Into Modes of Existence*; see, for example, pp. 285–8.
54. 'In short, in order to foresee the state of a determinate system at a determinate moment, it is absolutely necessary that something should persist as a constant quantity throughout a series of combinations, but it belongs to experience to decide as to the nature of this something' (TFW 151); meanwhile, 'we generally perceive our own self by refraction through space . . . and that our living and concrete self thus gets covered up with an outer crust of clean-cut psychic states' whose roots, however, do not relate to one another as a motives to their effects, but rather as the development of a singular movement (ibid., 167).
55. Lundy, *History and Becoming*.
56. Lampert, *Deleuze and Guattari's Philosophy of History*.
57. Lampert, *Deleuze and Guattari's Philosophy of History*, 60–4.
58. Herzogenrath, *Time and History*, 7.
59. Holland, 'Non-Linear Historical Materialism'.
60. Cynthia Enloe argues that societies are not 'naturally' patriarchal – or militarist – but can become so when the values of enough institutions dominated by men such as the military, banks and police can get women to agree that their values for success are the values that will rule an entire society (Enloe, *The Curious Feminist*, 4–7). She uses the same notion of 'tipping point' as Holland does. If political power only goes to those who have been approved by the military or worked with arms suppliers, then even the defence of women's rights will tend to benefit men more than it benefits women (ibid., 145–7). Thus Tony Jack has suggested that wartime rape, for example, may be a 'meme' that various fighting units adopt because they see that its tactical advantages outweigh, at least for now, the long-term drawbacks of social dysfunction resulting when women's lives are destroyed (personal communication).

61. Deleuze, *Coldness and Cruelty*, 46.
62. Sanday, 'Androcentric and Matrifocal Gender Representations'.
63. Browne, *Feminism, Time, and Non Linear History*.
64. On 'time of the trace', see Browne, *Feminism, Time, and Non Linear History*, 49–72; on 'narrative time', see ibid., 73–98; on 'calendar time', see ibid., 99–118; on 'generational time', see ibid., 119–41.
65. See, for instance, the preface by Georges Duby and Michelle Perrot to the five-volume *A History of Women*, 'Writing the History of Women'.
66. Interestingly, a quick comparison to a book like Scott's *Only Paradoxes to Offer* shows that *The Second Sex* says little about the legacy of many female figures in French history who might have been considered figureheads. Is that because Beauvoir wanted to detach herself from the conflicts among radical movements in which they were involved? Or is it because she wanted to focus on the myths and habits by which most women's individuation was blocked?
67. Scott, 'The Evidence of Experience'. Because the idea of 'experience' and the perspective of 'women's phenomenology' were politically important even to theorists who had little philosophical training, Scott's essay was very controversial. In fact, one can see how it continues the tension between a 'consciousness-centred' and an 'impersonal' approach to lived experience already described between Husserl and Sartre, for example.
68. See, for example, Ehrenreich and Hoschchild, *Global Woman*.
69. See Bergoffen, *Contesting the Politics of Genocidal Rape*.
70. See, for example, Philipose, 'Feminism, International Law, and the Spectacular Violence of the Other'. A similar concern is voiced with respect to queer rights by Puar, *Terrorist Assemblages*.
71. As he comments in *Abécédaire* with respect to care for the survivors of an earthquake in Armenia, 'What do we have here? This is an assemblage (*agencement*). . . . what can be done to suppress this enclave or to make it habitable? . . . This is a question of territory. It's not a question of human rights . . . all the abominations that humans endure are cases. It will be said that these cases may resemble one another, but these are situations of jurisprudence' (Deleuze, 'G comme Gauche', 4, my translation).
72. Deleuze and Guattari distinguish between becoming *impersonal* (with respect to subjectification), becoming *indiscernible* (with respect to signification) and becoming *imperceptible* (with respect to the inorganic world) (TP 279–82/342–6). Each involves a different layer of becomings that are denied or ignored for the sake of a stable, manageable and governable reality. However, most of their discussion focuses on *imperceptibility*, which is also the condition for provoking perception, and ultimately problematisation.

73. Moi, *What is a Woman?* 11–14, 201–4.
74. See the discussion of Drucilla Cornell's and Sara Murphy's ideas about multiculturalism and recognition in Grosz, 'A Politics of Imperceptibility' and Sharp, 'The Impersonal is Political'.
75. Julien Murphy shows, for example, that before they could conceptualise the wrong Boupacha suffered, the French public had to be educated by Beauvoir and Halimi on rape as well as on the importance of premarital virginity for an Algerian woman's lifelong well-being. The court officials stubbornly minimised her suffering because it was not as likely to be fatal as the sexual torture used by the French on male Vietcong. Debra Bergoffen contends that the ICTY decision was historic insofar as she believes it properly delimited the reasons why rape is a crime against humanity (Bergoffen, *Contesting the Politics of Genocidal Rape*).

Chapter 7

Conclusion

This book began with something like a gamble. What would happen if we read *The Second Sex* as an exercise in the creation of concepts, as Deleuze defined philosophy? In Beauvoir's Introduction, we found evidence that her thinking process was provoked by encounters with the various forms of nonsense that pockmarked 'sense' in a sexist culture. Part 2 of *The Second Sex* describes many of the habits inculcated in women that render them supports for men's sense but ultimately fail to give them a stable subject of self-recognition.

There already exists a tradition of reading *The Second Sex* as a critique of 'sense' or meaning in light of Beauvoir's involvement with phenomenology. How do we move from the critique of sense to the act of thinking? According to *Difference and Repetition*, thinking results when conflicting layers of habit are unable to generate a stable subject of recognition. An Idea whose object is ultimately a 'problem' takes the place of a 'fractured I'. But *Difference and Repetition* also describes thinking as the successive awakening of impersonal faculties. The dramatisation, actualisation or eventual implementation of the Idea changes the form of the psychological and phenomenological subject who first entered on this journey.

The 'Idea' of *Difference and Repetition* results in a reorganisation of the actual, both in thought and experience. The 'concepts' of *What is Philosophy?* are described as involving components with their own histories, conceptual personae, a pre-philosophical plane and relations of consistency with other domains of thought and life. To read *The Second Sex* along Deleuzian lines required an investigation of concepts Beauvoir drew from historical figures and philosophical contemporaries such as Hegel, Kierkegaard, Husserl, Sartre and Merleau-Ponty. As explored previously in Chapter 2, Beauvoir's text emerged from contact between her observations of sexism and her long-standing interest in human singularity, exemplified by Bergson and Leibniz. Tensions between thinkers such as Bergson and Sartre crystallise around concepts such as 'transcendence' that Beauvoir put to work on her own problem and that later feminists, in turn, found controversial. Beauvoir's attempt to preserve the freedom of singular individuals by referring its meaning to the freedom of all others in 'Pyrrhus and Cineas' and in *The Ethics of Ambiguity* gives us a broader picture of the kind of ethical and political vision underlying *The Second Sex*.

The situations that Beauvoir found thought-provoking in *The Second Sex* are drawn from a variety of personal, sociological and fictional sources. We must read the text in light of Beauvoir's novels to understand the relationships between characters that tend to produce or decompose sense in women's lives. But novels can also be the site for the exploration of problems proper to literature and other arts. Beauvoir's novels, like her autobiographies, help us to understand the 'multiplicity' of her own Idea. Looking at her corpus as a whole, it appears that Beauvoir did not anticipate that the problem of singularity and generality broached in *The Second Sex* with respect to women and in *The Coming of Age* with respect to the elderly could be entirely solved by political change, but that it would also require the cultural medium of literature.

'Ambiguity', 'reciprocity' and 'multiplicity' are concepts that help to flesh out this vision, while 'complicity' and 'oppression' are names for the obstacles that stand in the way of women's individuating freedom. *Mitsein* is a concept that looks in both directions, as it refers to the ambiguous zone of individual human implication in collective thoughts and habits. Drawing on Bergson and Leibniz, Beauvoir's efforts to define and solve the problem in political and literary terms have something in common with thinkers of the transindividual, such as Jean-Luc Nancy and Gilbert Simondon, who was roughly her contemporary. But Beauvoir's text was also claimed by a feminist political movement whose internal tensions were read back into and against *The Second Sex*. Today, we understand Beauvoir's sexual and intellectual relationships with men and with women differently than they were understood during the 1970s when lesbianism and bisexuality were mistrusted within many feminist circles while separatism was a common, if infrequently attempted, utopian idea.

Beauvoir's ambivalent relationship with philosophy as an academic discipline, her willingness to get along with men whose ideas she found stimulating, and her lack of familiarity with the gender traditions of other cultures posed problems for the reception of *The Second Sex* by feminists during the 1980s and 90s. I have argued that reading Beauvoir's text along Deleuzian lines allows us to reframe these problems in ways that are ultimately fruitful for the lives of contemporary feminists, including those practising academic philosophy. In particular, if feminists distinguish between common notions and universals when trying to identify political challenges and if they think about the subjects of sexist oppression and of feminist political action as *assemblages* rather than 'women' in an individual isolated sense, they may be better able to defend women's singularity.

Nevertheless, it is not to be expected that the solutions dramatised in *The Second Sex*, or in Beauvoir's corpus more generally, are without residual problems of their own. Beauvoir's *pre-philosophical plane* assumed egalitarianism and a form of socialism (as well as anti-colonialism) whose implementation would strengthen rather than damage the social bonds of older democracies. Moreover, she seems to have assumed that such structures would soon be implemented around the world, such that conflicts engendered by cultural difference or unequal exploitation by a global system of production would not overshadow women's common concerns. While sexual freedom has proven to be an incredibly successful vector for stimulating consumer desire, she did not imagine that many people, men or women, would turn down equality as sexual beings (especially if they could have the financial equality Beauvoir also sought) or would not consider sexual autonomy a primary expression of transcendence.

Such assumptions force us to ask what kind of event *The Second Sex* is, to what historical trajectory it contributes, and what philosophical trajectory it projects. How will the becomings whose freedom Beauvoir sought define themselves after a hundred years? As intentional consciousness? As desiring-machines? As neural networks? *The Second Sex* responds to a felt 'problem' or break in sense, and the Idea through which she encapsulates this problem is a multiplicity with many parts that do not always work when isolated from each other: transcendence, immanence, reciprocity, equality, the 'detotalised totality', gender, the social Other. Nonetheless, this Idea seems to have enabled Beauvoir to counter-actualise the incorporeal event of sexist sense, at least to a certain extent in her own life, and to hold out the promise of such counter-actualisation for millions of readers around the world – men as well as women.

Has the gamble been fruitful? The future, according to Deleuze, is the object of the dice throw, the multiplicity that rearranges the past in falling back on the plane. What connections might there be between Beauvoir's notion of the social Other and this *sense* of a future that would rearrange past forms of sense and habits? This future must be *created*, but creativity is not entirely under the control of the individual phenomenological subject. 'The new' is not an 'object' of consciousness that can be easily distinguished from reality and affirmed or negated. Deleuze's explorations of the conditions for creativity and newness are well known, but it has been remarked less often that a considerable portion of *The Second Sex*, particularly the chapter on 'The Independent Woman', deals with the effects of sexism on the quality of women's artistic production.

The question is this: if woman is the absolute Other to man under contemporary conditions of sexist sense, would the abolition of this inequity also abolish the category of the Other? What do we even mean by the Other? On the one hand, Beauvoir seems to think that Otherness is part of the human condition: 'The category of the Other is as original as consciousness itself' (SS 6/1:16). Like Sartre and Lévi-Strauss, she also seems to think that the identification of Otherness is intrinsic to the formation of human groups. This is what provokes her reflection on the master-slave dialectic in the Introduction to *The Second Sex*, where she comments that subject (Othered) populations generally rebel against their oppressors. Unlike these potentially reciprocal others, however, woman is the 'absolute' Other. In the world of greater reciprocity envisioned by Beauvoir, there would presumably be 'relative' others, as well as mutually acknowledged interdependence. Would there be any absolute Other? Is such an Other necessary for creativity?

For Husserl, the ordinary other person is a *part* of my consciousness, as well as a possible *object* of consciousness. Others (plural) are supports for the reality and stability of one's experiential contents. For Woman to be Other means that she possesses a consciousness analogous to that of men, but by her potential agreement or disagreement, she guarantees facets of reality that are intersubjectively and not just personally valid. Sartre and Merleau-Ponty note that the Other can be *felt* prior to being known. Sartre's Other makes his world more real by threatening to disrupt and 'steal' its meaning for his or her own project (BN 343). Merleau-Ponty, on the other hand, claims that the Other in a unified sense is merely a derivative category, for what we encounter or experience are multiple others, even if they can be grouped or homogenised.[1] We are never born into a world with only one Other; we either privilege one empirical other person or we construct a category following an experience of human plurality, both sensate and conscious. For others to become the Other, some institution like the sexual *Mitsein* must overshadow all encounters and cast them in the form of one-on-one relationships.

Now, it is well known that Lévinas thinks of the Other as the always-embodied structure preventing individuation from closing up entirely, thereby giving any indeterminacy in our boundaries moral significance by contrast to the undifferentiated threat of the *il y a*, or anonymous and impersonal being. It is also well known that the 'feminine' is one of Lévinas's names for this radical alterity, for Beauvoir criticised it as reviving a 'myth' about Woman (SS 6/1:15). Surely Beauvoir is right that women are similar to men in their reciprocal alterity. But one can argue that Beauvoir also thought women, too, need the resources of an Other-structure that would allow them to individuate from the phenomenal world and to oppose it (if only in imagination). However, this cannot be an Other-structure that divides human beings by gender.

In *Difference and Repetition*, the Other is not just a similar person in a single world, however interwoven with mine, but the expression of an Other world closing mine up and promising its completion (DR 259–60/333–5). The 'Other-structure' enables the cracked 'I' generating Ideas to coincide with the 'organised self' that results from an Idea's actualisation. The Other is a standpoint incorporating, enfolding or expressing possibilities that were never actualised in my own world (DR 260–1/333–5). In *Being and Nothingness*, for example, Sartre recounts being surprised by the Other's (dispassionate, curious or judgemental) gaze while peeping jealously through a keyhole. In an alternate illustration from *The Emotions*, cited by Deleuze, the face that suddenly appears in his window is frightened and reveals that the subject's own world is potentially frightening.[2]

In *The Logic of Sense*, the Other is a structure of the perceptual field (LS 305–7/354–7).[3] Thanks to this structure, the experience of sense, the principle of representation with which most Western philosophy deals, and the orientation of desire are possible. In other words, the I and the self are only *effects* of pre-personal singularities, but alterity allows them to be actualised and individuated – in relation to an Idea or a form of sense, as well as at the more radical level of an assemblage or singular becoming. However, this does not mean that the Deleuzian Other 'totalises', as Sartre or Beauvoir might object. The limit it imposes 'slows me down' without necessarily blocking my becomings.

The Logic of Sense further develops this understanding of the relation between personal and impersonal experience (LS 305–9/354–9). Deleuze reads Tournier's *Friday* as an exploration of what happens to the world when it *loses* the Other-structure that gave it coherence as a consciousness, as eventually happens to the marooned Robinson. Even though later an empirical 'other person' (Friday) is eventually added back to the island, it is too late, for Tournier's Robinson has become a wildly perceptive *thing among other things*, at least one of which is human.[4] The relationship between Robinson and Friday is more like Merleau-Ponty's description of self and other(s) as structures within the flesh of the world than it is like a Self or Cogito opposed to the Other and the World.

For Deleuze, unlike Lévinas or Sartre, the Other-structure therefore lends coherence to a phenomenological self that is doubly split. But in doing so, it testifies inadvertently to the existence of the pre-personal singularities that *need* to be rendered coherent (DR 259/332–3).[5] Moreover, the self for whom an Other exists is mortal, exhausting its differences the way Beauvoir spoke in her student notes about the exhaustion of Leibnizian possibles. But the singularities themselves are also 'deadly' in the sense that their individuation exceeds the sense and integrity of an organism's consciousness and life. Deleuze, like Beauvoir, is strongly influenced by Blanchot in his reflections on death (DR 259/333, LS 151–2/177–8, AO 330–1/394–6). At the moment of death, the I and the self are never actual; it is only 'one' who dies, a particular assemblage defined by its temporality (speeds and slownesses) with respect to other assemblages.

In her philosophical writings, Beauvoir almost always remains at the level of phenomenology. But in her memoirs and novels, she is uncannily aware of the conflict between the phenomenological self and the pre-personal singularities that underwrite the subject and its structure (including the Other). In *Prime of Life*, Beauvoir reports a series of dreams following the war in which one can see her attempting to formulate its events as 'counter-actualisable' (PL 472–8). In these dreams, she died and was killed in innumerable ways, but

> someone still remained to say 'I am dead.' . . . 'I am there.' Then I would awake, and the truth would catch me by the throat: when I am dead, that voice will speak no more. It sometimes seemed to me that if I succeeded in being *there* at the exact instant of my death, if I coincided with it, then I would compel it to *be*: this would be one way of preserving it. But no . . . I shall never apprehend death; all I will ever know is this illusive foretaste, mingled with the flavor of my living days. (PL 477)

Asleep, both series constituted by the fractured 'I' and its constitutive syntheses claim the subject's voice. 'So *that's* what it was!' 'I passed through death', Beauvoir writes, 'as Alice passed through the Looking Glass, and . . . Instead of dissolving into it, I absorbed it into myself' (ibid.). But once awake, the only alternative to selfhood she can imagine is an inanimate thing, an object for consciousness, a corpse.

How is death related to the possibility of creativity? In *The Second Sex*, Beauvoir protests that women are prevented or dissuaded from opposing the world in a way that enables them to disclose it in a global and therefore relatively radical way. They are prevented by lack of education and by the social customs that isolate affluent women in the home, leaving them lonely with too little stimulation to undertake serious intellectual or artistic work. And they are dissuaded by their own desire for companionship and by the emotional demands men and children place on them. Poorer women barely enter her analysis because most of their creativity is expended on survival, including the survival of their families. Beauvoir believes that solitude is required for creativity, but this solitude seems dangerously close to death, potentially deadly (or murderous), and a *failure* of individuation rather than one form of its *achievement*.

For comparison, René Descartes worked out the ideas that became his *Meditations* while on military campaign. It is unlikely that his female counterpart would have been permitted to travel alone even if she had received the appropriate education for a philosopher. Nancy Bauer notes the 'absence of opportunities for solitude can become positively menacing'.[6] Virginia Woolf, who insisted on the importance of 'a room of one's own', also speculated on the fate that might have befallen Shakespeare's sister.[7]

One wonders whether men are able to endure solitude, to tarry with the pre-personal, in part because they *do* have myths of Woman as Other on which to rely for imaginative validation. Here, Other means something so unlike a man that he has trouble being sure of her humanity, something on which he can rely to support his fears and fantasies while believing himself to be distinct and/or opposed to all other (similar) men – in other words, while believing he represents humanity as a whole. The Other is the form of what has been left implicit, undeveloped or contradictory in his world; which he may or may not choose to explicate for himself (DR 260/333). Many women, often identifying with men's wishful point of view, are led to be unsure of their own humanity at critical moments of stress or conflict. They struggle to find the true problems corresponding to their singularities amid the flotsam and jetsam of sexist sense.

'For the girl or the woman who has not completely abdicated, nature represents what woman represents for man: herself and her negation, a kingdom and a place of exile; she is all in the guise of the other' (SS 747/2:554). In nature, she can let go of selfhood without having to be an inanimate thing. And yet 'nature', in Beauvoir's opinion, did not seem to produce the same effect on women writers as the Other did on men; 'very rare are those [women] who approach nature in its inhuman freedom'.

> Art, literature, and philosophy are attempts to found the world anew on a human freedom: that of the creator; to foster such an aim, one must first unequivocally posit oneself as a freedom. The restrictions that education and custom impose on woman limit her grasp of the universe; when the struggle to claim a place in this world gets too rough, there can be no question of tearing oneself away from it; one must first emerge within it in sovereign solitude if one wants to try and grasp it anew; what woman primarily lacks is learning from the practice of abandonment and transcendence, in anguish and pride. (SS 748/2:555)

To paraphrase *Prime of Life*, if a writer is to *survive* the self bound up with a particular world, some voice must be able to say 'I am dead' even if this will never be *me*. As an intersubjective personality, 'I' am bound up with all the possible others of recognition and reciprocity. But as Beauvoir gradually seemed to decide in her essays about literature, there must be some One whose experiences are indefinitely shared.

Beauvoir's struggles to identify conditions for female creativity, to identify the Other's necessary or contingent role in that process, and to relate the Other to the death of a subject with no eternal soul as its double come together in a fictional scene depicting a girl's effort to be 'alone with the world'. At a certain moment in *She Came to Stay*, the character Françoise recalls coming home to an empty house as a child, seeing a coat on a chair, and wondering, essentially, if the coat would come to life if she said 'I' on its behalf. 'She opened her eyes again; she could see the jacket, it existed, yet it was not aware of it. There was something a little disturbing, a little frightening, about it all. What was the use of existing, if it wasn't aware of its own existence?'[8]

In her memory, however, wanting to say 'I' for the jacket changed nothing: 'the jacket stayed there, indifferent, a complete stranger, and she was still Françoise. Besides, if she were to become the jacket, then she, Françoise, wouldn't know anything.' The character fled, and Beauvoir (as author) presents this as a failure. Afterwards, Françoise 'would always feel she had been cheated out of one of the solemn moments of the world. Elsewhere something was in the process of existing without her being there, and it was that thing only which really mattered.'[9]

This memory surges up at a moment when Françoise knows Xavière and Pierre, with whose subjectivity she has completely identified until this point, are meeting elsewhere in Paris and she feels abandoned, excluded, no longer a subject, 'wandering about in some vague suburb'.[10] Holveck reads this moment of *She Came to Stay* as a turning point, when Françoise dimly realises that her own body has no more reality to her than a coat, as a result of her extreme effort to declare 'unreal' any part of her reality that Pierre (Françoise's other) cannot share.[11] The passage certainly begs for interpretation. Is it that Françoise cannot bear being excluded and identifies with the voicelessness of the jacket? Is the jacket's muteness a placeholder for the experience between Pierre and Xavière which has been concealed or withdrawn from her disclosure? Does Françoise have an inkling of the 'world without others' in which, as Deleuze describes, sense itself tumbles into oblivion? (LS 306/355–6). Or does Françoise recoil before the uncanny inkling that the jacket might express an impersonal aspect of herself that survives without being able to say 'I'?

I've been trying to understand this scene for years, in part because it seems so closely linked to Beauvoir's desire for the 'absolute' as a young philosopher and also to her dread of ageing and dying, of being a mere jacket whose inner differences no Leibnizian God would sustain. The jacket, she reports, could not 'murmur reassuringly: "here I am"', the way an immortal soul should have been able to (MDD 48–9). Murmur to whom: to itself, or to Beauvoir? Through the looking glass, as in Beauvoir's post-war dreams, would singularities extracted from the jacket and from her own being have been able to combine and formulate the thought 'here I am' – such that Françoise would have *survived* the crack in her 'I' that she felt able to prevent only through murder in adulthood?

Two unpublished chapters of the novel contain a different version of the story in which it seems clear that Beauvoir's intention was to portray an impersonal, unindividuated consciousness similar to the one that Holveck identifies with Françoise's awareness of the theatre in the opening chapter of the finished novel.[12] What makes this consciousness different from Sartre's is that it is not surprised and shamed by the Other's (dispassionate, curious or judgmental) gaze while peeping jealously through a keyhole. For the child described in these suppressed chapters feels unreal unless objects like the jacket *need* her to lend them reality through her disclosure, containing possibilities on which her further actualisation may depend.

It is not, as one might expect from Sartre, that the child Beauvoir describes wants to *be* stable and unambiguous like the object, rather than to *reveal* it. It is by revealing rather than being, even revealing the non-human world's *subjective potential*, that the small Françoise's desiring-machines produce a sense of completeness when alone, when 'no action was of any importance'. However, Françoise panicked because the jacket's imperviousness made her disclosure seem unnecessary, as if she herself were already dead.

The jacket scene may be autobiographical, since another version of the same story also appears in *Memoirs of a Dutiful Daughter*.

> I have related elsewhere how, at Meyrignac, I stupidly gazed at an old jacket thrown over the back of a chair. I tried to put myself as it were inside the jacket, and say, 'I am a tired old jacket.' It was

quite impossible, and I was stricken with panic. In the darkness of the past, in the stillness of inanimate beings I had dire forebodings of my own extinction; I conjured up delusive fallacies, and turned them into omens of the truth, and of my own death. (MDD 49)

The structure of the scene in Beauvoir's finished novel suggests that Françoise wants the jacket to serve as an Other capable of grounding her subjective structure with or without Pierre. Perhaps she wants to imagine herself as an Other capable of animating herself with speech again? Indeed, this interpretation holds up if we note a parallel between this thought experiment with the jacket and Françoise's childhood masturbation in the unpublished chapters.[13] Masturbation is certainly a very concrete effort to extinguish and reignite subjectivity via the flesh of the world. As an adult, Françoise's solution to her experience of ontological displacement is to wander through Paris with Gerbert. Françoise does not yet realise that this afternoon, spent with a new other, will lead her to develop a subjectivity not shared with Pierre (or Xavière) – indeed, to an affair with Gerbert. But the fact that Françoise has trouble drawing out Gerbert in conversation suggests a further parallel between the man and the jacket. Through the Other, to whom she lends subjectivity or from whom she *elicits* subjectivity, Françoise can be reborn at the centre of her own life. This Other secures her world rather than threatening it.

'In every psychic system', Deleuze writes, 'there is a swarm of possibilities around reality'. This clearly follows Husserl's idea that the intentional object is always surrounded by a cloud of potential variations as well as perceptual clues beneath the level of consciousness that orient the perceiver and thinker. However, probably following Leibniz, Deleuze believes 'our possibles are always Others' (DR 260/334) and the Other, as expressive/frightened, is the one for whom a certain sense *exists* to be expressed.[14] For the small Françoise's impersonal consciousness, the jacket was a possible Other. Even its closedness, as a 'refusal', held out a potential for participation in disclosure. In other words, the jacket should have functioned like nature in being an inhuman support for Françoise's becoming, or for the coalescing and dissolution of her singular machines, the way the myth of Woman functions for men. But the assemblage failed to form. Instead, the character initially identified with Beauvoir's friend Zaza (who mutated into Elizabeth in the finished novel) becomes the first being who *exists* without needing Françoise's disclosure and who also feels for herself, so intensely that Françoise is drawn into identifying completely with the ego she constructs for her friend by secretly reading her diaries (MDD 118–20).

Perhaps the jacket would have been a true Other if it had been a point of view enfolding the girl's unacknowledged singularity in the form of possibilities. Gerbert, quite literally, was a point of view from which what was merely possible for Françoise – having a personality and life of her own, a union between the cracked 'I' and the 'self' – was *actual*. This enabled him to draw out those capacities of hers, even though she thought she was drawing them out of him. What terrified Beauvoir and her character Françoise, like many people who fear losing touch with email or Facebook today, may have been the prospect of having the whole Other-structure collapse. Sociologist Rachel Simmons has written about the extreme terror that the feeling of abandonment can elicit in girls and women; an abandonment so radical that it cannot mean the loss of empirical others but the possibility of a world without Alterity or possibility, in which, as with a Dali painting, all of us are discarded coats and melting watches whom no *cogito* will reanimate.[15]

For Beauvoir, the fantasy of crime provided one way in which she could imagine creatively surviving the loss of all empirical others, if not a world without Alterity. While she was grateful to Sartre for allowing her to imagine someone else who might take responsibility for her existence, 'I felt that this was an immoral attitude . . . the only solution would have been to accomplish some deed for which I alone, and no one else, must bear the consequences' (PL 252). As for her character Françoise, Beauvoir states that she would rather have been a murderer than 'just a woman' (PL 474). It almost seems that only by conceiving writing as a crime, regardless of her feelings toward the empirical others with whom she had shared the trio, was she able to finish *She Came to Stay*: 'However attentive the encouragement and advice one receives, writing remains an act for which the responsibility cannot be shared with any other person' (PL 271).

This is the solitude Descartes believed he had achieved in his stove-heated room, the solitude for which Spinoza strived, so that he could start over again with one clear thought.[16] For Françoise, and maybe for Beauvoir herself, it's a frightening fantasy: indeed, she fears the loss of oxygen, of possibility, of winning truth in a world ruined by loneliness as if it were a desert island.[17] While truth might not be *possible* without others to bounce against, other freedoms whose disclosure supports her own, the myths and wishes of others also interferes with the necessary work of testing and clarification. Here finitude appears not in the form of limits on the solitary ego's powers but as the *impossibility* of escaping mixture, *Mitsein*, friendship. Even and maybe especially in the act of creation, humans are ambiguously both phenomenological subjects and impersonal becomings. Given this, it seems all the more important that Beauvoir chose to share authorship with Gisèle Halimi for the *Djamila Boupacha* book, in which she was fairly careful to *disclose* Boupacha's case and not to identify with her, in order to 'share the responsibility' as both she and Halimi were threatened by the OAS for their action.[18]

'The free woman is just being born', Beauvoir writes towards the end of *The Second Sex*. 'Her "worlds of ideas" are not necessarily different from men's, because she will free herself by assimilating them; to know how singular she will remain and how important these singularities will continue to be, one would have to make some foolhardy predictions' (SS 751/2:559). Is the Independent Woman the Other-structure making possible the 'world' of *The Second Sex*?

This chapter of *The Second Sex* is largely devoted to describing the *obstacles* to women's autonomy – economic, psychological and social. It gives all the reasons why they are not *possible* at Beauvoir's time of writing, in Beauvoir's actual world. For the Independent Woman, all would be actual that is merely *possible* for us, whether or not we have envisioned its possiblity. Moreover, the Independent Woman is not merely a relative other, like the men with whom Beauvoir hopes women will someday share the world (particularly heterosexual women), but an Other in whose shoes it is so difficult to stand, a being it is so difficult to *become* that she represents another world, albeit a better one. The Independent Woman could be the event, the becoming in which *this book* survived its author impersonally even though she was still alive. As a becoming, she is that '*in* the event' that allows us to go beyond the event. She suggests a model for counter-actualising the myriad events of 'everyday sexism'.[19]

This investigation of the Other *in Beauvoir's own problematic* also teaches us something about eventfulness, including the rate at which sexist sense can be challenged and reformulated productively. As mentioned earlier, in *The Logic of Sense* Deleuze distinguishes two ways of approaching time: from the point of view of constituted bodies and depths (*Chronos*), as well as from the point of view of their lability and tendency to reorganise and undergo transformations (*Aion*). We do not know what *bodies* we are composed of or mixed with, except in the confused and sometimes painful mode of affects. We do gain some clarity when we conceptualise and analyse the *event* or *situation* in which they are involved. Beauvoir says repeatedly that women's biological issues would be less troubling if they were not lived in a *situation* where they both cause and represent handicaps. For Deleuze, however, the only way to counteract a bad arrangement or situation of bodies is by conceptualising events. Tournier's Robinson eventually agrees to conceptualise his own relationship to the island, its flora and fauna, and the indigenous refugee Friday in a way that allows him to counter-actualise them joyfully.

In *Difference and Repetition*, Deleuze warns that the differentiation and explication of imperceptible, infra-individual differences into the extended physical world cannot be reversed, any more than Sartrean facticity can be 'undone' (DR 244/314). Thus,

> The ethics of intensive quantities has only two principles: affirm even the lowest, do not explicate (oneself) too much. We must be like the father who criticized the child for having uttered all the dirty words he knew – not only because it was wrong but because he had said everything at once, because he kept nothing in reserve, no remainder for the subtle, implicated matter of the eternal return.

In *A Thousand Plateaus*, the same basic principle animates Deleuze and Guattari's warning that deterritorialising or recomposing an assemblage too quickly will lead to fascism. If women's politics are 'real politics', as Beauvoir believed they are, then madness and fascism are no less dangers for molar women's movements than those founded on machismo. However, Deleuze's suggestion about the Other also serves as a caution against the militant attitude that would insist women tear themselves away from all the real-life phenomenal others, families and jobs with whom their lives are woven and against whose freedom they define their own freedom slowly over time. When Françoise believed her secrets were entirely known (even if mistakenly, and only to Xavière), and that she was hitherto an unspeakable creature, for whom loss could not be a liberation (as for other characters in Beauvoir's novels, such as Hélène and Marguerite), then she was impulsively driven to murder the other woman.

What might this mean in practice, for Beauvoir? Disclose the freedom of others, the least as equal to the greatest. But don't go so far as to lose one's consistency. For some women, 'femininity' is truly a part of their consistency; for many, however, 'femininity' is an obstacle to consistency. Wouldn't the Other be a feminist man? Unfortunately, although this has been the way many readers (and maybe Beauvoir herself) explained Sartre's presence in her life and thought, such a male Other would only reinforce the habit of organising female subjectivity around masculinity. Masculinity itself must someday be the name of a becoming or a range of becomings. If that has begun to happen, it is only due to women's effort to grasp themselves as something other than beings, as well as new experiments with habits of medicine and cultural visibility undertaken by transgender and intersex people.

In Beauvoir's novels, the Independent Woman is sometimes played by daughters: Anne's daughter Nadine in *The Mandarins*, Laurence's daughter Catherine in *Les Belles Images*. Of course these daughters struggle against all the obstacles Beauvoir describes in this chapter; the difficulty taking work seriously and reconciling an aggressive sexuality with the terms on which men are willing to love a woman (in Nadine's case); the racial and class ruses by which girls are distracted from learning about and formulating a real vocation for public affairs (in Catherine's case). Nevertheless, it is by imagining their daughters' future that the characters in these novels survive moments of global opposition to the world around them, usually forced on them unwillingly, although none of them has the creative breakthrough Beauvoir hopes future women will have.

Without being able to envision the Independent Woman, Françoise and her kin are threatened by the tired inanimate jacket. They are unable to survive their own dreams of death, to counter-actualise or respond creatively to solitude, even when it is available. They fall into the habits of near-psychotic love, narcissism or mysticism, even when they have means and education. The Independent Woman appears like a spectre on the street, a little like the figure turning back momentarily toward the era of representation in Foucault's reading of the painting *Las Meninas*. In *When Things of the Spirit Come First*, the character Marguerite, whose world has just fallen apart because of the bourgeois 'complicity' of the poet with whom she had hoped to share the underworld of Paris, passes a woman in boots with a flabby face and hand on her hip:

> I waited a moment to see if anyone would accost her; then I walked on, and all at once I caught myself smiling. This curiosity and this detachment were something new. A week earlier I should have seen this woman as the incarnation of all the temptations of despair and I should have hurried off, sad at heart, without noticing the color of her hair; I should have pictured her calling Denis from the depths of the night to offer him a hideous and miraculous escape. Something had changed in me.[20]

I imagine the Independent Woman as the joyful, or at least the curious, detached face in Deleuze's window.

Notes

1. Merleau-Ponty discusses this in the course of analysing *She Came to Stay* in 'Metaphysics and the Novel'.
2. The example of the keyhole is found at BN 347–52; for the face in the window, see Sartre, *The Emotions*, 82–5.
3. On the Other-structure, see Hughes, *Deleuze's Difference and Repetition*, 12–14; Bryant, *Difference and Givenness*, 254–62.
4. According to Peden, the world without Others of *Friday* (and by extension, Deleuze's philosophy) is suffocating, pure actuality with no possibility. Peden, *Spinoza Contra Phenomenology*, 203–4, 231–3. Jardine reads *Friday* as a tale in which the disappearance of the Other-structure is equivalent to the disappearance of women altogether from men's experience of one another and of self-transformation with the earth and things (Jardine, 'Woman in Limbo'). However, Peden acknowledges that Deleuze considers the Other-structure essential, at least for personal subjectivity, while presumably Jardine does not want women to be present as incarnations of the absolute Other.
5. Deleuze complains that Sartre could have used the Other as a *structure* rather than a content, so as to avoid subject-object binarism – he did see this – but then instead he made the Other into the one who casts me as a subject (LS 366, n. 12/360 n. 11).
6. Bauer, *Simone de Beauvoir, Philosophy, and Feminism*, 74.
7. Woolf, *A Room of One's Own*, 46.
8. Beauvoir, *She Came to Stay*, 114–15.
9. Beauvoir, *She Came to Stay*, 118.

10. Beauvoir, *She Came to Stay*, 114–15.
11. Holveck, *Lived Experience*, 80–1.
12. Holveck, *Lived Experience*, 78–9.
13. Beauvoir, 'Two Unpublished Chapters'.
14. 'From Leibniz, we had already learned that there are no points of view on things, but that things, beings, are themselves points of view.' (LS 173/203)
15. Simmons, *Odd Girl Out*, 32.
16. Bauer points out that some feminists were critical of *The Second Sex* because Beauvoir *did* begin in solitude. Bauer, *Simone de Beauvoir, Philosophy, and Feminism*, 49.
17. Peden, *Spinoza Contra Phenomenology*, 203–4.
18. Murphy, 'Beauvoir and the Algerian War', 275.
19. On 'everyday sexism', see Schwarzer, *After* The Second Sex, 63–4, 117.
20. Beauvoir, *When Things of the Spirit Come First*, 211.

Works Cited

Adkins, Brent, *Deleuze and Guattari's A Thousand Plateaus: A Critical Introduction and Guide* (Edinburgh: Edinburgh University Press, 2015).
Ahmed, Sara, *Queer Phenomenology: Orientations, Objects, Others* (Durham, NC: Duke University Press, 2006).
Alcoff, Linda Martìn, 'The Problem of Speaking for Others', *Cultural Critique* 20, 1991, pp. 5–32, <http://www.jstor.org/stable/1354221> (last accessed 17 April 2017).
Al-Hibri, Azizah and Margaret A. Simons (eds), *Hypatia Reborn: Essays in Feminist Philosophy* (Bloomington: Indiana University Press, 1990).
Allen, Jeffner, 'A Response to a Letter from Peg Simons, December 1993', in Margaret A. Simons (ed.), *Feminist Interpretations of Simone de Beauvoir* (University Park: Pennsylvania State University Press, 1995), pp. 113–35.
Altman, Meryl, 'Introduction' to Simone de Beauvoir, 'Notes for a Novel', in Margaret A. Simons and Marybeth Timmermann (eds), *'The Useless Mouths' and Other Literary Writings* (Chicago: University of Illinois Press, 2011), pp. 329–54.
Arendt, Hannah, *Between Past and Future: Eight Exercises in Political Thought* (New York: Penguin, 1977).
Arendt, Hannah, *The Human Condition* (Chicago: University of Chicago Press, 1958).
Aristotle, *The Basic Works of Aristotle*, ed. Richard McKeon (New York: Random House, 1941).
Aristotle, *Metaphysics*, in Richard McKeon (ed.), *The Basic Works of Aristotle*, pp. 681–926.
Aristotle, *Nicomachean Ethics*, in Richard McKeon (ed.), *The Basic Works of Aristotle*, pp. 927–1112.
Aristotle, *Of Generation and Corruption*, in Richard McKeon (ed.), *The Basic Works of Aristotle*, pp. 467–531.

Aristotle, *Politics*, in Richard McKeon (ed.), *The Basic Works of Aristotle*, pp. 1113–316.

Arnfred, Signe, 'Simone de Beauvoir in Africa': 'Woman = The Second Sex'? Issues of African Feminist Thought', *Jenda: A Journal of Culture and African Women Studies* 2(1), 2002, <http://www.jendajournal.com/vol2.1/arnfred.html> (last accessed 1 November 2013).

Arp, Kristana, *The Bonds of Freedom: Simone de Beauvoir's Existentialist Ethics* (Chicago: Open Court, 2001).

Asad, Talal, *Formations of the Secular: Christianity, Islam, Modernity* (Stanford: Stanford University Press, 2003).

Bahovec, Eva, 'Between Structuralism and Aleatory Materialism', in *The Blackwell Companion to Simone de Beauvoir*, ed. Laura Hengehold and Nancy Bauer (Oxford: Wiley/Blackwell 2017), pp. 249–59.

Bakare-Yusuf, Bibi, 'Yoruba's Don't Do Gender: A Critical Review of Oyeronke Oyewumi's *The Invention of Women: Making an African Sense of Western Gender Discourses*', in *African Gender Scholarship: Concepts, Methodologies and Paradigms* (Dakar: CODESRIA Gender Series 1, 2004), pp. 61–81.

Balibar, Étienne, '*Homo nationalis*: An Anthropological Sketch of the Nation-Form', in *We, The People of Europe? Reflections on Transnational Citizenship*, trans. James Swenson (Princeton: Princeton University Press, 2004) pp. 11–30.

Balibar, Étienne, '"Rights of Man" and "Rights of the Citizen": The Modern Dialectic of Equality and Freedom', in *Masses, Classes, Ideas: Studies on Politics and Philosophy Before and After Marx* (New York: Routledge, 1994), pp. 39–59.

Balibar, Étienne, *Spinoza: From Individuality to Transindividuality* (Delft: Eburon, 1997).

Balibar, Étienne, 'Spinoza, The Anti-Orwell: The Fear of the Masses', in *Masses, Classes, Ideas: Studies on Politics and Philosophy Before and After Marx* (New York: Routledge, 1994), pp. 3–37.

Bauer, Nancy, 'Beauvoir's Heideggerian Ontology', in Margaret A. Simons (ed.), *The Philosophy of Simone de Beauvoir: Critical Essays* (Bloomington: Indiana University Press, 2006), pp. 65–91.

Bauer, Nancy, *Simone de Beauvoir, Philosophy, and Feminism* (New York: Columbia University Press, 2001).

Beauvoir, Simone de [1946], *All Men Are Mortal: A Novel*, trans. Leonard M. Friedman (New York: W. W. Norton, 1955).

Beauvoir, Simone de [1972], *All Said and Done: 1962–1972*, trans. Patrick O'Brian, intro. Toril Moi (New York: Paragon House, 1993).

Beauvoir, Simone de [1947], *America Day By Day*, trans. Carol Cosman (Berkeley: University of California Press, 1999).

Beauvoir, Simone de, 'An Eye for an Eye (1946)', in *Philosophical Writings*, ed. Margaret A. Simons, with Marybeth Timmermann and Mary Beth Mader, pp. 245–60.

Beauvoir, Simone de [1966], *Les Belles Images*, trans. Patrick O'Brian (New York: Putnam, 1968).

Beauvoir, Simone de [1945], *The Blood of Others*, trans. Roger Senhouse and Yvonne Moyse (New York: Pantheon Books, 1983).

Beauvoir, Simone de, *The Coming of Age* [1970], trans. Patrick O'Brian (New York: Warner Paperback Library, 1973).

Beauvoir, Simone de, *Diary of a Philosophy Student: Vol. 1: 1926–27*, ed. Barbara Klaw, Sylvie Le Bon de Beauvoir, Margaret A. Simons, Marybeth Timmermann (Urbana and Chicago: University of Illinois Press, 2006).

Beauvoir, Simone de [1947], *The Ethics of Ambiguity*, trans. Bernard Frechtman (New York: Citadel Press, 1994). English translation of *Pour une morale de l'ambiguïté*, suivi de *Pyrrhus et Cinéas* (Paris: Gallimard, 1947), pp. 9–230 [EA].

Beauvoir, Simone de, *Force of Circumstance*, trans. Richard Howard (New York: G. P. Putnam's Sons, 1965). English translation of *La force des choses*, 2 vols (Paris: Gallimard, 1963) [FC].

Beauvoir, Simone de, *Letters to Sartre*, ed. and trans. Quentin Hoare (New York: Arcade Publishing, 1991).

Beauvoir, Simone de, 'Literature and Metaphysics (1946)', in *Philosophical Writings*, ed. Margaret A. Simons, with Marybeth Timmermann and Mary Beth Mader, pp. 269–77.

Beauvoir, Simone de [1954], *The Mandarins*, trans. Leonard Friedman (New York: W. W. Norton & Company, 1991).

Beauvoir, Simone de [1958], *Memoirs of a Dutiful Daughter*, trans. James Kirkup (New York: Harper & Row, 1959) [MDD].

Beauvoir, Simone de [1955], 'Merleau-Ponty and Pseudo-Sartreanism', in *Political Writings*, ed. Margaret A. Simons and Marybeth Timmermann, pp. 206–57.

Beauvoir, Simone de, 'Moral Idealism and Political Realism (1945)', in *Philosophical Writings*, ed. Margaret A. Simons, with Marybeth Timmermann and Mary Beth Mader, pp. 175–93.

Beauvoir, Simone de [1952], 'Must We Burn Sade?', in *Political Writings*, ed. Margaret A. Simons and Marybeth Timmermann, pp. 44–101.

Beauvoir, Simone de [1966], 'My Experience as a Writer', in *'The Useless Mouths' and Other Literary Writings*, ed. Margaret A. Simons and Marybeth Timmermann, pp. 282–301.

Beauvoir, Simone de, 'Notes for a Novel', in *'The Useless Mouths' and Other Literary Writings*, ed. Margaret A. Simons and Marybeth Timmermann, pp. 355–77.

Beauvoir, Simone de, *Philosophical Writings*, ed. Margaret A. Simons, with Marybeth Timmermann and Mary Beth Mader (Urbana and Chicago: University of Illinois Press, 2004).
Beauvoir, Simone de, *Political Writings*, ed. Margaret A. Simons and Marybeth Timmermann (Urbana, Chicago and Springfield: University of Illinois Press, 2012).
Beauvoir, Simone de [1962], 'Preface to *Djamila Boupacha*', in *Political Writings*, ed. Margaret A. Simons and Marybeth Timmermann, pp. 272–82.
Beauvoir, Simone de, *The Prime of Life: 1929–1944*, trans. Peter Green (New York: Paragon House, 1992). English translation of *La force de l'âge* (Paris: Gallimard, 1960) [PL].
Beauvoir, Simone de, *Privilèges* (Paris: Gallimard, 1955).
Beauvoir, Simone de, 'Pyrrhus and Cineas (1944)', in *Philosophical Writings*, ed. Margaret A. Simons, with Marybeth Timmermann and Mary Beth Mader, pp. 89–149. English translation of *Pour une morale de l'ambiguïté*, suivi de *Pyrrhus et Cinéas* (Paris: Gallimard, 1947), pp. 231–376 [PC].
Beauvoir, Simone de, 'A Review of *The Phenomenology of Perception* by Maurice Merleau-Ponty (1945)', in *Philosophical Writings*, ed. Margaret A. Simons, with Marybeth Timmermann and Mary Beth Mader, pp. 159–64.
Beauvoir, Simone de, 'Right-Wing Thought Today', in *Political Writings*, ed. Margaret A. Simons and Marybeth Timmermann, pp. 113–93.
Beauvoir, Simone de, *The Second Sex*, trans. Constance Borde and Sheila Malovany-Chevallier (New York: Vintage Books, 2011). English translation of *Le deuxième sexe*, 2 vols (Paris: Gallimard, 1949) [SS].
Beauvoir, Simone de [1943], *She Came to Stay*, trans. Yvonne Moyse and Roger Senhouse (Glasgow: Fontana Books, 1975).
Beauvoir, Simone de, 'Short Articles on Literature', in *'The Useless Mouths' and Other Literary Writings*, ed. Margaret A. Simons and Marybeth Timmermann, pp. 98–123.
Beauvoir, Simone de, 'Two Unpublished Chapters from *She Came to Stay* [1938]', in *Philosophical Writings*, ed. Margaret A. Simons, with Marybeth Timmermann and Mary Beth Mader, pp. 41–75.
Beauvoir, Simone de, *'The Useless Mouths' and Other Literary Writings*, ed. Margaret A. Simons and Marybeth Timmermann (Urbana, Chicago and Springfield: University of Illinois Press, 2011).
Beauvoir, Simone de, *Wartime Diary*, trans. and notes by Anne Deing Cordero, ed. Margaret A. Simons and Sylvie Le Bon de Beauvoir (Urbana and Chicago: University of Illinois Press, 2009).

Beauvoir, Simone de [1965], 'What Can Literature Do?', in *The Useless Mouths' and Other Literary Writings*, ed. Margaret A. Simons and Marybeth Timmermann, pp 197–209.

Beauvoir, Simone de [1979], *When Things of the Spirit Come First*, trans. Patrick O'Brian (New York: Pantheon Books, 1982).

Beauvoir, Simone de [1967], *The Woman Destroyed*, trans. Patrick O'Brian (New York: Pantheon, 1987).

Benjamin, Jessica, *The Bonds of Love: Psychoanalysis, Feminism, and the Problem of Domination* (New York: Pantheon, 1988).

Benjamin, Walter, 'Critique of Violence', in *Reflections: Essays, Aphorisms, Autobiographical Writings*, ed. Peter Demetz (New York: Harcourt Brace Jovanovich, 1978), pp. 277–300.

Bergoffen, Debra, *Contesting the Politics of Genocidal Rape: Affirming the Dignity of the Vulnerable Body* (New York: Routledge, 2012).

Bergoffen, Debra, *The Philosophy of Simone de Beauvoir: Gendered Phenomenologies, Erotic Generosities* (Albany: State University of New York Press, 1997).

Bergson, Henri, *Creative Evolution*, trans. Arthur Mitchell (New York: Random House, 1944).

Bergson, Henri, *Matter and Memory*, trans. N. M. Paul and W. S. Palmer (New York: Zone Books, 1991).

Bergson, Henri, *Time and Free Will: An Essay on the Immediate Data of Consciousness*, trans. F. L. Pogson, 1st edn (Mineola, NY: Dover Publications, 2001). [TFW]

Bergson, Henri, *Two Sources of Morality and Religion*, trans. R. Ashley Audra, Cloudesley Brereton, and W. Horsfall Carter (New York: Henry Holt and Co., 1935).

Björk, Ulrika, 'Simone de Beauvoir and Life', in Lester Embree and Thomas Nenon (eds), *Husserl's Ideen, Contributions to Phenomenology* 66, 2013, Dordrecht: Springer Science+Business Media, pp. 351–64. DOI 10.1007/978-94-007-5213-9_21

Blumenberg, Hans, *Paradigms for a Metaphorology*, trans. Robert Savage (Ithaca: Cornell University Press, 2010).

Boulbina, Seloua Luste, *L'Afrique et ses fantômes: Écrire l'après* (Paris: Présence Africaine, 2015).

Braidotti, Rosi, *Nomadic Subjects: Embodiment and Sexual Difference in Contemporary Feminist Theory* (New York: Columbia University Press, 1994).

Braidotti, Rosi, *Patterns of Dissonance: A Study of Woman in Contemporary Philosophy*, trans. Elizabeth Guild (London: Polity Press, 1991).

Braidotti, Rosi, *Transpositions* (Cambridge; Malden, MA: Polity Press, 2006).

Brison, Susan J., 'Beauvoir and Feminism: Interview and Reflections', in Claudia Card (ed.), *The Cambridge Companion to Simone de Beauvoir* (Cambridge: Cambridge University Press, 2003), pp. 189–207.
Browne, Victoria, *Feminism, Time, and Nonlinear History* (New York: Palgrave/Macmillan, 2014).
Bryant, Levi R., *Difference and Givenness: Deleuze's Transcendental Empiricism and the Ontology of Immanence* (Evanston: Northwestern University Press, 2008).
Buchanan, Ian, and Claire Colebrook (eds), *Deleuze and Feminist Theory* (Edinburgh: Edinburgh University Press, 2000).
Bumiller, Kristin, *In an Abusive State: How Neoliberalism Appropriated the Feminist Movement Against Sexual Violence* (Durham, NC: Duke University Press, 2008).
Butler, Judith, *Undoing Gender* (New York and London: Routledge, 2004).
Card, Claudia (ed.), *The Cambridge Companion to Simone de Beauvoir* (Cambridge: Cambridge University Press, 2003).
Chanter, Tina, *Ethics of Eros: Irigaray's Rewriting of the Philosophers* (New York and London: Routledge, 1995).
Charlesworth, Hilary, 'Human Rights as Men's Rights', in *Women's Rights, Human Rights: International Feminist Perspectives*, ed. Julie Peters and Andrea Wolper (New York: Routledge, 1995), pp. 103–13.
Chiwengo, Ngwarsungo, 'Otherness and Female Identities: Simone de Beauvoir's *The Second Sex*', *Bulletin de la Société Americaine de Philosophie de Langue Française* 13(1), 2003, pp. 167–76.
Chodorow, Nancy, *The Reproduction of Mothering: Psychoanalysis and the Sociology of Gender* (Berkeley: University of California Press, 1978).
Cohen-Solal, Annie, *Sartre: A Life* (New York: Pantheon, 1987).
Collins, Patricia Hill, *Black Feminist Thought: Knowledge, Consciousness, and the Politics of Empowerment*, 2nd edn rev. (New York and London: Routledge Classics, 2009).
Coorebyter, Vincent de, *Sartre face à la phénoménologie: Autour de l'intentionnalité et de 'La Transcendance de l'égo'* (Brussels: Éditions Ousia, 2000).
Cornell, Drucilla, *At the Heart of Freedom: Feminism, Sex and Equality* (Princeton: Princeton University Press, 1998).
Cornell, Drucilla, *The Imaginary Domain: Abortion, Pornography, and Sexual Harrassment* (New York: Routledge, 1995).
Cutrofello, Andrew, *Discipline and Critique: Kant, Poststructuralism, and the Problem of Resistance* (Albany: State University of New York Press, 1994).

Daigle, Christine, 'The Second Sex as Appeal: The Ethical Dimension of Ambiguity', PhiloSOPHIA 4(2), 2014, pp. 197–220. Project MUSE, <https://muse.jhu.edu/article/565883> (last accessed 17 April 2017).

Daigle, Christine and Jacob Golomb (eds), *Beauvoir and Sartre: The Riddle of Influence* (Bloomington: Indiana University Press, 2009).

Davis, Angela, 'Reflections on the Black Woman's Role in the Community of Slaves', in Beverly Guy-Sheftall (ed.), *Words of Fire: An Anthology of African-American Feminist Thought* (New York: The New Press, 1995), pp. 200–18.

Deleuze, Gilles, *Bergsonism*, trans. Hugh Tomlinson and Barbara Habberjam (New York: Zone Books, 1991).

Deleuze, Gilles, 'Bergson's Conception of Difference', trans. Melissa McMahon, in John Mullarkey (ed.), *The New Bergson* (Manchester: Manchester University Press, 1999), pp. 42–65.

Deleuze, Gilles, *Cinema 2: The Time-Image*, trans. Hugh Tomlinson and Robert Galeta (Minneapolis: University of Minnesota Press, 1997).

Deleuze, Gilles [1945], 'Description of Woman: For a Philosophy of the Sexed Other', trans. Keith W. Faulkner, *Angelaki* 7(3), 2002, pp. 17–24.

Deleuze, Gilles, *Difference and Repetition*, trans. Paul Patton (New York: Columbia University Press, 1994). English translation of *Différence et répétition* (Paris: Presses Universitaires de France, 1968) [DR].

Deleuze, Gilles, *The Fold: Leibniz and the Baroque*, trans. Tom Conley (Minneapolis: University of Minnesota Press, 1993).

Deleuze, Gilles, 'G Comme Gauche', *L'Abécédaire de Gilles Deleuze*, with Claire Parnet, produced by Pierre-André Boutang, Video Éditions Montparnasse, 1996 [1988], <www.lipsheim.org/forum/agora/view-lipsheimorg_ schizoforum-1184944189-300-349.html> (last accessed 27 April 2013).

Deleuze, Gilles, *The Logic of Sense*, trans. Mark Lester with Charles Stivale, ed. Constantin V. Boundas (New York: Columbia University Press, 1990). English translation of *Logique du sens* (Paris: Éditions de Minuit, 1969) [LS].

Deleuze, Gilles, *Masochism: Coldness and Cruelty, with Venus in Furs* by Leopold von Sacher-Masoch, trans. Jean McNeil (New York: Zone Books, 1989).

Deleuze, Gilles, *Negotiations: 1972–1990*, trans. Martin Joughin (New York: Columbia University Press, 1990).

Deleuze, Gilles, *Nietzsche and Philosophy*, trans. Hugh Tomlinson (New York: Columbia University Press, 1983).

Deleuze, Gilles, *Proust and Signs: The Complete Text*, trans. Richard Howard, Theory Out of Bounds, Vol. 17 (Minneapolis: University of Minnesota Press, 2000).
Deleuze, Gilles, *Pure Immanence: Essays on a Life*, trans. Anne Boyman (New York: Zone Books, 2001).
Deleuze, Gilles, *Spinoza: Practical Philosophy*, trans. Robert Hurley (San Francisco: City Lights, 1988).
Deleuze, Gilles and Félix Guattari, *Anti-Oedipus: Capitalism and Schizophrenia*, Vol. 1, trans. Robert Hurley, Mark Seem, and Helen R. Lane (New York: Viking Press, 1977). English translation of *L'Anti-Œdipe* (Paris: Éditions de Minuit, 1972) [AO].
Deleuze, Gilles and Félix Guattari, *A Thousand Plateaus: Capitalism and Schizophrenia*, trans. Brian Massumi (Minneapolis: University of Minnesota, 1987). English translation of *Mille Plateaux: Capitalisme et Schizophrénie* (Paris: Éditions de Minuit, 1980) [TP].
Deleuze, Gilles and Félix Guattari, *What is Philosophy?*, trans. Hugh Tomlinson and Graham Burchell (New York: Columbia University Press, 1994). English translation of *Qu'est-ce que la philosophie?* (Paris: Éditions de Minuit, 1991) [WIP].
Deleuze, Gilles and Claire Parnet, *Dialogues*, trans. Hugh Tomlinson and Barbara Habberjam (New York: Columbia University Press, 1987).
Delphy, Christine, 'The Invention of French Feminism: An Essential Move', *Yale French Studies*, Another Look, Another Woman: Retranslations of French Feminism 87, 1995, pp. 190–221, <http://www.jstor.org/stable/2930332> (last accessed 10 April 2008).
Deutscher, Penelope, *The Philosophy of Simone de Beauvoir: Ambiguity, Conversion, Resistance* (Cambridge: Cambridge University Press, 2008).
Diprose, Rosalyn, *The Bodies of Women: Ethics, Embodiment, and Sexual Difference* (London and New York: Routledge, 1994).
Direk, Zeynep, 'Immanence and Abjection in Simone de Beauvoir', *The Southern Journal of Philosophy* 49(1), 2011, pp. 49–72.
Duby, Georges, and Michelle Perrot, 'Writing the History of Women', in Georges Duby and Michelle Perrot (eds), *A History of Women, Vol 1: From Ancient Goddesses to Christian Saints*, English edn ed. Pauline Schmitt Pantel (Cambridge, MA: Harvard University Press, 1992), pp. ix–xxi.
Duchen, Claire, *Feminism in France From May '68 to Mitterand* (London and New York: Routledge & Kegan Paul, 1986).
Duras, Marguerite, *The Malady of Death*, trans. Barbara Bray (New York: Grove Weidenfeld, 1986).

Ehrenreich, Barbara, and Arlie Russell Hochschild, *Global Woman: Nannies, Maids, and Sex Workers in the New Economy* (New York: Henry Holt and Co., 2002).

Enloe, Cynthia, *The Curious Feminist: Searching for Women in a New Age of Empire* (Berkeley: University of California Press, 2004).

Faludi, Susan, *Stiffed: The Betrayal of the American Man* (New York: William Morrow and Company, 1999).

Fanon, Frantz, 'Algeria Unveiled', in Carl Oglesby (ed.), *The New Left Reader* (New York: Grove Press, 1969), pp. 161–85.

Fanon, Frantz, *Black Skin, White Masks*, trans. Charles Lam Markmann (New York: Grove Press, 1967).

Foucault, Michel, *The Birth of Biopolitics: Lectures at the Collège de France 1978–1979*, ed. Michel Senellart, trans. Graham Burchell (New York: Palgrave MacMillan, 2008).

Foucault, Michel, *The History of Sexuality Vol. 1: An Introduction*, trans. Robert Hurley (New York: Vintage Books, 1978).

Foucault, Michel, 'Polemics, Politics, and Problematizations', in *Ethics: Subjectivity and Truth, Essential Works of Foucault, 1954–1984*, ed. Paul Rabinow, trans. Robert Hurley and others (New York: The New Press, 1994), pp. 111–19.

Foucault, Michel, 'Truth and Power', in *Power: Essential Works of Foucault, 1954–1984*, ed. James Faubion, trans. Robert Hurley and others (New York: The New Press, 1994), pp. 111–33.

Foucault, Michel and Gilles Deleuze, 'Intellectuals and Power', in *Language, Countermemory, Practice: Selected Essays and Interviews*, ed. Donald F. Bouchard, trans. Donald F. Bouchard and Sherry Simon (Ithaca: Cornell University Press, 1977), pp. 205–17.

Franz, Carol E., and Kathleen M. White, 'Individuation and Attachment in Personality Development: Extending Erikson's Theory', in *Journal of Personality* 53(2), 1985, pp. 224–56.

Fraser, Mariam, *Identity without Selfhood: Simone de Beauvoir and Bisexuality* (Cambridge: Cambridge University Press, 1999).

Fraser, Nancy, and Linda Gordon, 'A Genealogy of Dependency: Tracing a Keyword of the U.S. Welfare State', in *Signs* 19(2), 1994, pp. 309–36, <http://www.jstor.org/stable/3174801> (last accessed 19 April 2011).

Fricker, Miranda, 'Life-story in Beauvoir's Memoirs', in Claudia Card (ed.), *The Cambridge Companion to Simone de Beauvoir*, pp. 208–27.

Fullbrook, Kate, and Edward Fullbrook, *Simone de Beauvoir and Jean-Paul Sartre: The Remaking of a Twentieth-Century Legend* (New York: BasicBooks, 1994).

Galster, Ingrid, *'Le Deuxième Sexe' de Simone de Beauvoir, Textes réunis et presentés* (Paris: Presses de l'Université de Paris-Sorbonne, 2004).
Galster, Ingrid, 'Simone de Beauvoir et Radio-Vichy: A propos de quelques scenarios retrouvés', *Aufsätze | Romanische Forschungen* 108, 1996, pp. 112–32, <http://www.jstor.org/stable/27940753> (last accessed 2 February 2015).
Gardner, Sebastian, *Sartre's Being and Nothingness: A Reader's Guide* (London: Continuum, 2009).
Gatens, Moira, 'Beauvoir and Biology: A Second Look', in Claudia Card (ed.), *The Cambridge Companion to Simone de Beauvoir*, pp. 266–85.
Gines, Kathryn T., 'Comparative and Competing Frameworks of Oppression in Simone de Beauvoir's *The Second Sex*', *Graduate Faculty Philosophy Journal* 35(1–2), 2014, pp. 251–73.
Gines, Kathryn T., 'Sartre, Beauvoir, and the Race/Gender Analogy: A Case for Black Feminist Philosophy', in *Convergences: Black Feminism and Continental Philosophy*, ed. Maria del Guadelupe Davidson, Kathryn T. Gines and Donna-Dale Marcano (Albany: State University of New York Press, 2010), pp. 35–51.
Golay, Annabelle, 'Féminisme et postcolonialisme: Beauvoir, Fanon et la guerre d'Algérie', in *International Journal of Francophone Studies* 10(3), 2007, pp. 407–24.
Green, Ronald M., and Mary Jean Green, 'Simone de Beauvoir: A Founding Feminist's Appreciation of Kierkegaard', in Jon Stewart (ed.), *Kierkegaard and Existentialism (Kierkegaard Research: Sources, Reception, and Resources vol. 9)* (Farnham: Ashgate, 2011), pp. 1–19.
Griffith, Elizabeth, *In Her Own Right: The Life of Elizabeth Cady Stanton* (New York: Oxford University Press, 1985).
Grosz, Elizabeth, 'A Thousand Tiny Sexes: Feminism and Rhizomatics', in Constantin V. Boundas and Dorothea Olkowski (eds), *Gilles Deleuze and the Theater of Philosophy* (New York and London: Routledge, 1994), pp. 187–210.
Grosz, Elizabeth, 'A Politics of Imperceptibility: A Response to "Antiracism, multiculturalism and the ethics of identification"', *Philosophy and Social Criticism* 28(4), 2002, pp. 463–72.
Grosz, Elizabeth, *Volatile Bodies: Toward a Corporeal Feminism* (Bloomington: Indiana University Press, 1994).
Halley, Janet, *Split Decisions: How and Why to Take a Break from Feminism* (Princeton: Princeton University Press, 2006).
Hansberry, Lorraine, 'Simone de Beauvoir and *The Second Sex*: An American Commentary', in Beverly Guy-Sheftall (ed.), *Words of Fire: An Anthology of African-American Feminist Thought* (New York: The New Press, 1995), pp. 128–42.

Hartsock, Nancy, 'Foucault on Power: A Theory for Women?', in Linda J. Nicholson (ed.), *Feminism/Postmodernism* (New York: Routledge, 1990), pp. 157–75.

Hartsock, Nancy, *Money, Sex, and Power: Toward a Feminist Historical Materialism* (Boston: Northeastern University Press, 1985).

Hegel, G. W. F., *Phenomenology of Spirit*, trans. A. V. Miller (Oxford: Oxford University Press, 1977).

Heidegger, Martin, *Being and Time*, trans. John Macquarrie and Edward Robinson (New York and San Francisco: Harper & Row, 1962).

Heinämaa, Sara, 'The Background of Simone de Beauvoir's Metaphysical Novel: Kierkegaard and Husserl', in Floora Ruokonen and Laura Werner (eds), *Acta Philosophica Fennica*, 79: 'Visions of Value and Truth: Understanding Philosophy and Literature', Helsinki, 2006, pp. 175–90.

Heinämaa, Sara (2003), 'The Body as Instrument and as Expression', in Claudia Card (ed.), *The Cambridge Companion to Simone de Beauvoir*, pp. 66–86.

Heinämaa, Sara, *Toward a Phenomenology of Sexual Difference: Husserl, Merleau-Ponty, Beauvoir* (Lanham, MD: Rowman & Littlefield, 2003).

Hengehold, Laura, 'When Safety Becomes a Duty: Gender, Loneliness, and Citizenship for Urban Women', *WSQ: Women's Studies Quarterly* 39(1/2), 2011, pp. 48–69.

Herzogenrath, Bernd (ed.), 'Introduction' to *Time and History in Deleuze and Serres* (London: Bloomsbury, 2012).

Holland, Alison, *Excess and Transgression in Simone de Beauvoir's Fiction: The Discourse of Madness* (Farnham and Burlington, VT: Ashgate, 2009).

Holland, Eugene, 'Non-Linear Historical Materialism, Or, What is Revolutionary in Deleuze and Guattari's Philosophy of History?', in Bernd Herzogenrath (ed.), *Time and History in Deleuze and Serres* (London: Bloomsbury, 2012), pp. 17–30.

Hollywood, Amy, '"Mysticism is tempting": Simone de Beauvoir on Mysticism, Metaphysics, and Sexual Difference', in *Sensible Ecstasy: Mysticism, Sexual Difference, and the Demands of History* (Chicago: University of Chicago Press, 2002), pp. 120–45.

Holveck, Eleanore, *Simone de Beauvoir's Philosophy of Lived Experience: Literature and Metaphysics* (Lanham, MD: Rowman and Littlefield, 2002).

Honneth, Axel, 'Between Justice and Affection: The Family as a Field of Moral Disputes', in Beate Rössler (ed.), *Privacies: Philosophical Evaluations* (Stanford: Stanford University Press, 2004), pp. 142–62.

hooks, bell, 'True Philosophers: Beauvoir and bell', in Shannon M. Mussett and William S. Wilkerson (eds), *Beauvoir and Western Thought from Plato to Butler*, pp. 227–36.
Hughes, Joe, *Deleuze's Difference and Repetition: A Reader's Guide* (London and New York: Continuum, 2009).
Hurtado, Aida, *The Color of Privilege: Three Blasphemies on Race and Feminism* (Ann Arbor: University of Michigan Press, 1996).
Husserl, Edmund, *Cartesian Meditations: An Introduction to Phenomenology*, trans. Dorion Cairns (Dordrecht: Martinus Nijhoff, 1960).
Husserl, Edmund, *The Crisis of European Sciences and Transcendental Phenomenology: An Introduction to Phenomenological Philosophy*, trans. David Carr (Evanston: Northwestern University Press, 1970).
Husserl, Edmund, *Ideas Pertaining to a Pure Phenomenology and to a Phenomenological Philosophy: First Book: General Introduction to a Pure Phenomenology*, trans. F. Kersten (Dordrecht: Kluwer, 1982).
Husserl, Edmund, *Ideas Pertaining to a Pure Phenomenology and to a Phenomenological Philosophy, Second Book: Studies in the Phenomenology of Constitution*, trans. Richard Rojcewicz and André Schuwer (Dordrecht: Kluwer, 1989).
Husserl, Edmund, *On the Phenomenology of the Consciousness of Internal Time (1893–1917)*, trans. John Barnett Brough (Dordrecht: Kluwer, 1991).
Husserl, Edmund, 'On Static and Genetic Phenomenological Method', in *Analyses Concerning Passive and Active Synthesis: Lectures on Transcendental Logic*, trans. Anthony J. Steinbock (Dordrecht: Kluwer Academic Publishers, 2001), pp. 624–48.
Hutchings, Kimberly, *Hegel and Feminist Philosophy* (Cambridge: Polity Press, 2003).
Hutchinson, Sharon Elaine, and Jok Madut Jok, 'Gendered Violence and the Militarisation of Ethnicity: A Case Study from South Sudan', in Richard Werbner (ed.), *Postcolonial Subjectivities in Africa* (London: Zed Books, 2002), pp. 84–107.
Irigaray, Luce, *Je, Tu, Nous: Toward a Culture of Difference*, trans. Alison Martin (New York and London: Routledge, 1993).
Irigaray, Luce, *Speculum of the Other Woman*, trans. Gillian C. Gill (Ithaca: Cornell University Press, 1985).
Jagger, Alison M., and William L. McBride, '"Reproduction" as Male Ideology', in Azizah Al-Hibri and Margaret A. Simons (eds), *Hypatia Reborn: Essays in Feminist Philosophy*, pp. 249–69.
Jardine, Alice, 'Woman in Limbo: Deleuze and his Br(others)', *SubStance* 13 (3/4), issue 44/45, 1984, pp. 46–60, <http://www.jstor.org/stable/3684774> (last accessed 8 January 2015).

Kail, Michel, *Simone de Beauvoir Philosophe* (Paris: Presses Universitaires de France, 2006).

Kant, Immanuel, *Critique of Pure Reason*, trans. Werner S. Pluhar (Indianapolis: Hackett, 1996).

Kierkegaard, Søren, *Two Ages: The Age of Revolution and the Present Age: A Literary Review*, ed. and trans. Howard V. Hong and Edna H. Hong (Princeton: Princeton University Press, 1978).

Klossowski, Pierre, 'The Philosopher-Villain', in *Sade My Neighbor*, trans. Alphonso Lingis (Evanston: Northwestern University Press, 1991) pp. 11–42.

Kojève, Alexandre, *Introduction to the Reading of Hegel*, assembled Raymond Queneau, ed. Allen Bloom, trans. James H. Nichols, Jr (Ithaca: Cornell University Press, 1980).

Kopytoff, Igor, 'Women's Roles and Existential Identities', in Peggy Reeves Sanday and Ruth Gallagher Goodenough (eds), *Beyond the Second Sex: New Directions in the Anthropology of Gender* (Philadelphia: University of Pennsylvania Press, 1990), pp. 77–98.

Kristeva, Julia, 'Women's Time', in *The Kristeva Reader*, ed. Toril Moi (New York: Columbia University Press, 1986), pp. 187–213.

Kruks, Sonia, *Retrieving Experience: Subjectivity and Recognition in Feminist Politics* (Ithaca: Cornell University Press, 2001).

Kruks, Sonia, 'Simone de Beauvoir: Teaching Sartre About Freedom', in Margaret A. Simons (ed.), *Feminist Interpretations of Simone de Beauvoir*, pp. 79–95.

Lacan, Jacques, 'The Mirror Stage as Formative of the *I* Function as Revealed in Psychoanalytic Experience', in *Écrits*, trans. Bruce Fink (New York: W. W. Norton, 2007), pp. 75–81.

Lakoff, George, *Moral Politics: How Liberals and Conservatives Think*, 2nd edn (Chicago: University of Chicago Press, 2002).

Lampert, Jay, *Deleuze and Guattari's Philosophy of History* (London and New York: Continuum, 2006).

Landes, Joan, *Women and the Public Sphere in the Age of the French Revolution* (Ithaca: Cornell University Press, 1988).

Langer, Monika, 'Beauvoir and Merleau-Ponty on Ambiguity', in Claudia Card (ed.), *Cambridge Companion to Simone de Beauvoir*, pp. 87–106.

Latour, Bruno, *An Inquiry Into Modes of Existence: An Anthropology of the Moderns*, trans. Catherine Porter (Cambridge, MA: Harvard University Press, 2013).

Latour, Bruno, *We Have Never Been Modern*, trans. Catherine Porter (Cambridge, MA: Harvard University Press, 1993).

Lawlor, Leonard, 'The End of Phenomenology: Expressionism in Deleuze and Merleau-Ponty', *Continental Philosophy Review* 31, 1988, pp. 15–34.

Lawlor, Leonard, *Thinking Through French Philosophy: The Being of the Question* (Bloomington: Indiana University Press, 2003).
Le Dœuff, Michèle, *Hipparchia's Choice: An Essay Concerning Women, Philosophy, etc.*, trans. Trista Selous (Oxford: Blackwell, 1991).
Le Dœuff, Michèle, *The Philosophical Imaginary*, trans. Colin Gordon (London: Athlone, 1989).
Lefebvre, Alexandre, *The Image of Law: Deleuze, Bergson, Spinoza* (Stanford: Stanford University Press, 2008).
Lee, Kyoo, '(Un)naming the Third Sex After Beauvoir: Toward a Third-Dimensional Feminism', in Henriette Gunkel, Chrysanthi Nigianni, and Fanny Söderbäck (eds), *Undutiful Daughters: New Directions in Feminist Thought and Practice* (New York: Palgrave Macmillan, 2012), pp. 195–207.
Leibniz, G. W., and Samuel Clarke, *Correspondence*, ed. Roger Ariew (Indianapolis: Hackett, 2000).
Leibniz, G. W., *Discourse on Metaphysics, Correspondence with Arnauld, Monadology*, trans. George Montgomery (La Salle: Open Court, 1997).
Leibniz, G. W., *New Essays on Human Understanding*, ed. and trans. Peter Remnant and Jonathan Bennett (Cambridge: Cambridge University Press, 1996).
Léon, Céline T., 'Beauvoir's Woman: Eunuch or Male?', in Margaret A. Simons (ed.), *Feminist Interpretations of Simone de Beauvoir*, pp. 137–59.
Le Sueur, James D., *Uncivil War: Intellectuals and Identity Politics During the Decolonization of Algeria*, 2nd edn (Lincoln: University of Nebraska Press, 2005).
Lloyd, Genevieve, *The Man of Reason: 'Male' and 'Female' in Western Philosophy* (Minneapolis: University of Minnesota Press, 1984).
Lorraine, Tamsin, *Deleuze and Guattari's Immanent Ethics: Theory, Subjectivity, and Duration* (Albany: State University of New York Press, 2011).
Lundgren-Gothlin, Eva, *Sex and Existence: Simone de Beauvoir's* The Second Sex, trans. Linda Schenck (Hanover, NH: Wesleyan University Press/University Press of New England, 1996).
Lundgren-Gothlin, Eva, 'Reading Simone de Beauvoir with Martin Heidegger', in Claudia Card (ed.), *The Cambridge Companion to Simone de Beauvoir*, pp. 45–65.
Lundgren-Gothlin, Eva, 'Simone de Beauvoir's Notions of Appeal, Desire and Ambiguity and their Relationship to Jean-Paul Sartre's Notions of Appeal and Desire', *Hypatia* 14(4), 1999, pp. 83–95.
Lundy, Craig, *History and Becoming: Deleuze's Philosophy of Creativity* (Edinburgh: Edinburgh University Press, 2012).

McCall, Dorothy Kaufmann, 'Simone de Beauvoir, "The Second Sex", and Jean-Paul Sartre', *Signs* 5(2), 1979, pp. 209–23, <http://www.jstor.org/stable/3173557> (last accessed 25 January 2017).

McClintock, Anne, *Imperial Leather: Race, Gender and Sexuality in the Colonial Contest* (New York and London: Routledge, 1995).

Mader, Mary Beth, *Sleights of Reason: Norm, Bisexuality, Development* (Albany: State University of New York Press, 2011).

Mahmood, Saba, *Politics of Piety: The Islamic Revival and the Feminist Subject* (Princeton: Princeton University Press, 2005).

Marks, Elaine, *Simone de Beauvoir: Encounters With Death* (New Brunswick, NJ: Rutgers University Press, 1973).

Mehta, Uday Singh, *Liberalism and Empire: A Study in Nineteenth-Century British Liberal Thought* (Chicago: University of Chicago Press, 1999).

Merleau-Ponty, Maurice, 'Metaphysics and the Novel', in *Sense and Non-Sense*, trans. Hubert L. Dreyfus and Patricia Allen Dreyfus (Evanston: Northwestern University Press, 1964), pp. 26–40.

Merleau-Ponty, Maurice [1945], *Phenomenology of Perception*, trans. Colin Smith (London: Routledge and Kegan Paul, 1962).

Mill, John Stuart, *Three Essays: On Liberty, Representative Government, The Subjection of Women* (Oxford: Oxford University Press, 1975).

Miller, Elaine P., 'Saving Time: Temporality, Recurrence, and Transcendence in Beauvoir's Nietzschean Cycles', in Shannon M. Mussett and William Wilkerson (eds), *Beauvoir and Western Thought from Plato to Butler*, pp. 103–23.

Moi, Toril, *Simone de Beauvoir: The Making of an Intellectual Woman* (Oxford and Cambridge, MA: Blackwell, 1994).

Moi, Toril, *What is a Woman? And Other Essays* (Oxford: Oxford University Press, 1999).

Morgan, Ruth, and Graeme Reid, '"I've got two men and one woman": Ancestors, Sexuality and Identity among Same-sex Identified Women Traditional Healers in South Africa', in *Culture, Health and Sexuality*, 5(5), 2003, pp. 375–91, <http://jstor.org/stable/4005344> (last accessed 10 June 2008).

Murphy, Ann V., 'Ambiguity and Precarious Life: Tracing Beauvoir's Legacy in the Work of Judith Butler', in Shannon M. Mussett and William Wilkerson (eds), *Beauvoir and Western Thought from Plato to Butler*, pp. 211–26.

Murphy, Julien, 'Beauvoir and the Algerian War: Toward a Postcolonial Ethics', in Margaret A. Simons (ed.), *Feminist Interpretations of Simone de Beauvoir*, pp. 263–97.

Mussett, Shannon M. and William Wilkerson (eds), *Beauvoir and Western Thought from Plato to Butler* (Albany: State University of New York Press, 2012).
Nancy, Jean-Luc, *The Inoperative Community*, ed. Peter Connor, trans. Peter Connor, Lisa Garbus, Michael Holland and Simona Sawhney, Theory and History of Literature, Vol. 76 (Minneapolis: University of Minnesota Press, 1991) [IC].
Natanson, Maurice, *Anonymity: A Study in the Philosophy of Alfred Schutz* (Bloomington: Indiana University Press, 1986).
Nzegwu, Nkiru Uwechia, *Family Matters: Feminist Concepts in African Philosophy of Culture* (Albany: State University of New York Press, 2006) [FM].
O'Donnell, Aislinn, 'Beyond Sexuality: Of Love, Failure, and Revolutions', in Frida Beckman (ed.), *Deleuze and Sex* (Edinburgh: Edinburgh University Press, 2011), pp. 217–37.
Okely, Judith, *Simone de Beauvoir* (London: Virago Press Limited, 1986).
Olkowski, Dorothea, *Gilles Deleuze and the Ruin of Representation* (Berkeley: University of California Press, 1999).
Ortega, Mariana, 'Phenomenological Encuentros: Existential Phenomenology and Latin American and U.S. Latina Feminism', *Radical Philosophy Review* 9(1), 2006, pp. 45–64.
Oyěwùmí, Oyèrónké, *The Invention of Women: Making an African Sense of Western Gender Discourses* (Minneapolis: University of Minnesota Press, 1997).
Parker, Emily Anne, 'Singularity in Beauvoir's *The Ethics of Ambiguity*', *Southern Journal of Philosophy*, 53(1), 2015, pp. 1–16.
Peden, Knox, *Spinoza Contra Phenomenology: French Rationalism from Cavaillès to Deleuze* (Stanford: Stanford University Press, 2014).
Philipose, Elizabeth, 'Feminism, International Law, and the Spectacular Violence of the 'Other': Decolonizing the Laws of War', in Renée J. Heberle and Victoria Grace (eds), *Theorizing Sexual Violence* (New York: Routledge, 2009), pp. 176–204.
Pilardi, Jo-Ann, 'Feminists Read *The Second Sex*', in Margaret A. Simons (ed.), *Feminist Interpretations of Simone de Beauvoir*, pp. 29–43.
Pilardi, Jo-Ann, *Simone de Beauvoir Writing the Self: Philosophy Becomes Autobiography* (Westport, CT: Greenwood Press, 1999).
Puar, Jasbir K., *Terrorist Assemblages: Homonationalism in Queer Times* (Durham, NC: Duke University Press, 2007).
Rivas, Lynn May, 'Invisible Labors: Caring for the Independent Person', in Barbara Ehrenreich and Arlie Russell Hochschild (eds), *Global Woman: Nannies, Maids, and Sex Workers in the New Economy* (New York: Henry Holt and Company, 2002), pp. 70–84.

Salamon, Gayle, 'Musings: Justification and Queer Method, or Leaving Philosophy', *Hypatia* 24(1), 2009, pp. 225–30.

Sanday, Peggy Reeves, 'Androcentric and Matrifocal Gender Representations in Minangkabau Ideology', in Peggy Reeves Sanday and Ruth Gallagher Goodenough (eds), *Beyond the Second Sex: New Directions in the Anthropology of Gender* (Philadelphia: University of Pennsylvania Press, 1990), pp. 141–68.

Sartre, Jean-Paul [1943], *Being and Nothingness: A Phenomenological Essay on Ontology*, trans. Hazel E. Barnes (New York: Washington Square Press, 1956) [BN].

Sartre, Jean-Paul, *The Emotions: Outline of a Theory*, trans. Bernard Frechtman (New York: Philosophical Library, 1948).

Sartre, Jean-Paul, *Imagination: A Psychological Critique*, trans. Forrest Williams (Ann Arbor: University of Michigan Press, 1972).

Sartre, Jean-Paul, *Saint Genet: Actor and Martyr*, trans. Bernard Frechtman (New York: Pantheon Books, 1963).

Sartre, Jean-Paul [1936–7], *The Transcendence of the Ego: An Existentialist Theory of Consciousness*, trans. Forrest Williams and Robert Kirkpatrick (New York: Hill and Wang, 2001) [TE].

Scarth, Fredrika, *The Other Within: Ethics, Politics, and the Body in Simone de Beauvoir* (Lanham, MD: Rowman & Littlefield, 2004).

Schwarzer, Alice (ed.), *After* The Second Sex: *Conversations With Simone de Beauvoir*, trans. Marianne Howarth (New York: Pantheon, 1984).

Scott, Joan Wallach, 'The Evidence of Experience', *Critical Inquiry* 17(4), 1991, pp. 773–97, <http://jstor.org/stable/1343743> (last accessed 28 October 2011).

Scott, Joan Wallach, *Only Paradoxes to Offer: French Feminists and the Rights of Man* (Cambridge, MA: Harvard University Press, 1996).

Secomb, Linnell, 'Beauvoir's Minoritarian Philosophy', *Hypatia* 14(4), 1999, pp. 96–113.

Seigfried, Charlene Haddock, '*Second Sex:* Second Thoughts', in Azizah Al-Hibri and Margaret A. Simons (eds), *Hypatia Reborn: Essays in Feminist Philosophy*, pp. 305–22.

Sennett, Richard, *Respect: In a World of Inequality* (New York: W. W. Norton, 2003).

Sharp, Hasana. 'The Impersonal is Political: Spinoza and a Feminist Politics of Imperceptibility', *Hypatia* 24(4), 2009, pp. 84–103.

Simmons, Rachel, *Odd Girl Out: The Hidden Culture of Aggression in Girls*, 2nd edn (Boston; New York: Mariner Books/Houghton Mifflin Harcourt, 2011).

Simondon, Gilbert, *L'individuation psychique et collective, à la lumiére des notions de Forme, Information, Potentiel et Métastabilité* (Paris: Éditions Aubier, 1989) [IPC].
Simons, Margaret A., 'Beauvoir and Bergson: A Question of Influence', in Shannon M. Mussett and William Wilkerson (eds), *Beauvoir and Western Thought from Plato to Butler*, pp. 153–70.
Simons, Margaret A., 'Beauvoir and the Problem of Racism', in Julie K. Ward and Tommy L. Lott (eds), *Philosophers on Race: Critical Essays* (London; Blackwell, 2002), pp. 260–84.
Simons, Margaret A., 'Beauvoir and Sartre: The Question of Influence (1981)', in *Beauvoir and* The Second Sex, pp. 41–54.
Simons, Margaret A., *Beauvoir and* The Second Sex: *Feminism, Race, and the Origins of Existentialism* (Lanham, MD: Rowman & Littlefield, 1999).
Simons, Margaret A., 'Beauvoir's Early Philosophy: The 1927 Diary (1998)', in *Beauvoir and* The Second Sex, pp. 185–243.
Simons, Margaret A., 'Bergson's Influence on Beauvoir's Philosophical Methodology', in Claudia Card (ed.), *The Cambridge Companion to Simone de Beauvoir*, pp. 107–28.
Simons, Margaret A (ed.), *Feminist Interpretations of Simone de Beauvoir* (University Park: Pennsylvania State University Press, 1995).
Simons, Margaret A. (ed.), *The Philosophy of Simone de Beauvoir: Critical Essays* (Bloomington: Indiana University Press, 2006).
Simons, Margaret A., 'The Silencing of Simone de Beauvoir: Guess What's Missing from *The Second Sex* (1983)', in *Beauvoir and* The Second Sex, pp. 61–72.
Simons, Margaret A., Jessica Benjamin and Simone de Beauvoir, 'Simone de Beauvoir: An Interview', *Feminist Studies* 5(2), 1979, pp. 330–45, <http://www.jstor.org/stable/3177599> (last accessed 6 July 2013).
Smith, Daniel W., 'Analytics: On the Becoming of Concepts', in *Essays on Deleuze*, pp. 122–45.
Smith, Daniel W., 'Dialectics: Deleuze, Kant, and the Theory of Immanent Ideas', in *Essays on Deleuze*, pp. 106–21.
Smith, Daniel W., *Essays on Deleuze* (Edinburgh: Edinburgh University Press, 2012).
Smith, Daniel W., 'The Idea of the Open: Bergson's Theses on Movement', in *Essays on Deleuze*, pp. 256–67.
Spelman, Elizabeth V., *Inessential Woman: Problems of Exclusion in Feminist Thought* (Boston: Beacon Press, 1988).
Spinoza, Baruch, *The Ethics and Selected Letters*, trans. Samuel Shirley, ed. Seymour Feldman (Indianapolis: Hackett, 1982).

Spinoza, Baruch, 'Treatise on the Emendation of the Intellect', in *Spinoza: Complete Works*, trans. Samuel Shirley, ed. Michael L. Morgan (Indianapolis: Hackett, 2002), pp. 3–30.

Spivak, Gayatri Chakravorty, 'Can the Subaltern Speak?', in Cary Nelson and Lawrence Grossberg (eds), *Marxism and the Interpretation of Culture* (Urbana and Chicago: University of Illinois Press, 1987), pp. 271–313.

Stavro, Elaine, 'The Use and Abuse of Simone de Beauvoir: Re-Evaluating the French Poststructuralist Critique', in *European Journal of Women's Studies* 6, 1999, pp. 263–80, <http://ejw.sagepub.com/cgi/content/abstract/6/3/263> (last accessed 4 October 2008).

Sullivan, Donna, 'The Public/Private Distinction in International Human Rights Law', in *Women's Rights, Human Rights: International Feminist Perspectives*, ed. Julie Peters and Andrea Wolper (New York: Routledge, 1995), pp. 126–34.

Táíwò, Olúfẹ́mi, *How Colonialism Preempted Modernity in Africa* (Bloomington: Indiana University Press, 2010).

Theweleit, Klaus, *Male Fantasies Vol. 1: Women, Floods, Bodies, History*, trans. Stephen Conway, Erica Carter and Chris Turner. *Theory and History of Literature*, Vol. 22 (Minneapolis: University of Minnesota Press, 1987).

Tidd, Ursula, *Simone de Beauvoir, Gender, and Testimony* (Cambridge: Cambridge University Press, 1999).

Tournier, Michel, *Friday, or The Other Island*, trans. Norman Denny (London, Penguin, 1984).

Turshen, Meredeth and Clotilde Twagiramariya, *What Women Do in Wartime: Gender and Conflict in Africa* (London: Zed Press, 1998).

Van Breda, H. L., 'Merleau-Ponty and the Husserl Archives at Louvain', in Hugh J. Silverman and James Barry, Jr. (eds), *Maurice Merleau-Ponty, Texts and Dialogues: On Philosophy, Politics, and Culture* (Atlantic Highlands, NJ: Humanities Press International, Inc., 1992), pp. 150–61.

Van Leeuwen, Anne, 'Beauvoir, Irigaray, and the Possibility of Feminist Phenomenology', in *Journal of Speculative Philosophy* 26(2), 2012, pp. 474–84.

Veltman, Andrea, 'The Sisyphean Torture of Housework: Simone de Beauvoir and Inequitable Divisions of Domestic Work in Marriage', *Hypatia* 19(3), 2004, pp. 121–43.

Veltman, Andrea, 'Transcendence and Immanence in the Ethics of Simone de Beauvoir', in Margaret A Simons (ed.), *The Philosophy of Simone de Beauvoir: Critical Essays*, pp. 113–31.

Virno, Paolo, *Grammar of the Multitude*, trans. Isabella Bertoletti, James Cascaito and Andrea Casson (New York: Semiotext(e), 2004).

Walzer, Michael, *Spheres of Justice: A Defense of Pluralism and Equality* (New York: Basic Books, 1983).

Ward, Julie K., 'Beauvoir's Two Senses of "Body" in *The Second Sex*', in Margaret A. Simons (ed.), *Feminist Interpretations of Simone de Beauvoir*, pp. 223–42.

Wasser, Audrey, 'What is a Literary Problem? Proust, Beckett, Deleuze', *The Art of the Concept*, Frakcija 64/65, 2012, pp. 114–21.

Weiss, Gail, 'Ambiguity, Absurdity, and Reversibility: Responses to Indeterminacy', *Journal of the British Society for Phenomenology*, 26(1), 1995, pp. 43–51.

Weiss, Gail, 'Beauvoir and Merleau-Ponty: Philosophers of Ambiguity', in *Beauvoir and Western Thought from Plato to Butler*, ed. Shannon M. Mussett and William S. Wilkerson, pp. 171–89.

Wekker, Gloria, 'What's Identity Got to Do With It?: Rethinking Identity in Light of the *Mati* Work in Suriname', in Evelyn Blackwood and Saskia E. Wieringa (eds), *Female Desires: Same-sex Relations and Transgender Practices Across Cultures* (New York: Columbia University Press, 1999), pp. 119–38.

Welton, Donn, *The Other Husserl: The Horizons of Transcendental Phenomenology* (Bloomington: Indiana University Press, 2000).

Winkler, Rafael, 'Husserl and Bergson on Time and Consciousness', in Anna-Teresa Tymieniecka (ed.), *Logos of Phenomenology and Phenomenology of the Logos* Book Three, Analecta Husserliana XC (Dordrecht: Springer, 2006), pp. 93–115.

Woolf, Virginia, *A Room of One's Own* (New York: Martino Fine Books [Harcourt], 2012).

Young, Iris Marion, 'Pregnant Embodiment: Subjectivity and Alienation', in *Throwing Like a Girl and Other Essays in Feminist Philosophy and Social Theory* (Bloomington: Indiana University Press, 1990), pp. 160–74.

Young-Bruehl, Elisabeth, *The Anatomy of Prejudices* (Cambridge, MA: Harvard University Press, 1998).

Zahavi, Dan, *Husserl's Phenomenology* (Stanford: Stanford University Press, 2003).

Zahavi, Dan, 'Merleau-Ponty on Husserl: A Reappraisal', Ted Toadvine and Lester Embree (eds), *Merleau-Ponty's Reading of Husserl* (Dordrecht: Kluwer Academic Publishers, 2002), pp. 3–29.

Zakin, Emily, 'Beauvoir's Unsettling of the Universal', in Lori Jo Marso and Patricia Moynagh (eds), *Simone de Beauvoir's Political Thinking* (Urbana and Chicago: University of Illinois Press, 2006), pp. 31–53.

Zakin, Emily, 'The Drama of Independence: Narcissism, Childhood, and the Family Complexes', in *The Blackwell Companion to Simone de Beauvoir*, ed. Laura Hengehold and Nancy Bauer (Oxford: Wiley-Blackwell, 2017), pp. 99–100.

Zerilli, Linda M. G., 'A Process Without a Subject: Simone de Beauvoir and Julia Kristeva on Maternity', *Signs* 18(1), 1992, pp. 111–35, <http://www.jstor.org/stable/3174729> (last accessed 30 January 2009).

Index

abortion, 74, 76, 77, 165, 188
affects, 105–7, 116, 138, 140, 190,
    192n8, 195–6n52, 212
  and care labour, 78, 80, 83–4, 86, 144
  political, 118–20, 153
  and Spinoza, 19n7
African-Americans, 85, 179
Age of Discretion (Beauvoir novella), 81
Algerian War, 169, 193n16, 193n19,
    198n75
All Men are Mortal (Beauvoir novel), 49,
    80, 105, 106, 110
ambiguity, 10, 21–2n23, 36, 41–2, 67–9,
    103–9, 112–14, 148–9, 180
  and binary sexual difference, 138,
    142–3
  in literature, 107–10, 120, 133
  and politics, 163, 164, 167–8
  in sexual relationships, 82, 137–40
anthropology, 147, 153
anti-colonialism, 150, 168, 193n16, 201
Anti-Oedipus (Deleuze and Guattari), 4,
    64, 97, 117, 142, 145, 171, 186
appeal, 93n48, 102
Arendt, Hannah, 97, 150, 164, 179
Aristotle, 95, 97, 123n1, 175; *see also*
    hylomorphism
assemblage, 138, 140, 154, 166, 189–91,
    201, 204–5, 209
  maternity as, 160
  Mitsein as, 59, 96, 141
  right to form, 116, 143
  sexual self as, 142–4
  woman as, 149–50, 152, 188, 190, 201
authorship, shared, 122, 211

bad faith, 36, 41, 60, 67, 68, 86, 139
  and immanence, 52n41, 52–3n42
Balibar, Étienne, 115, 173, 174
Bataille, Georges, 109, 110, 119, 120
Bauer, Nancy, 3, 9, 25, 68, 107, 206

Beauvoir, Simone de
  alleged masculinism, 135–6, 138,
    140–1, 146–7, 176–8
  biography vs thought, 17, 40, 45–7,
    133–4
  conceptual personae, 33–4, 42–4
  as ethicist, 96–105, 106–12, 113–15,
    116, 117–20, 139–41
  on Hegel, 58, 74–5, 77, 81–2, 98, 99,
    105–6
  on immanence, 66–8, 81–2
  on individuation, 55n65, 59–62, 99,
    101–2, 113–15, 116, 137
  novels, 69, 76–7, 80, 81, 87–8, 105–6,
    110–11, 134–5, 207–10, 212–14
  as phenomenologist, 3, 5, 6, 11–12, 14,
    22n29
  as philosopher, 2–4, 28–31, 32–4, 45–7
  political vision, 163–7, 168–70, 171–5,
    180, 139–90
  student diaries, 12–13, 40
  on transcendence, 34–9, 47–8, 53n54,
    68, 80, 154
  on women's situation, 70–80, 82–3,
    83–6, 140
  writings on literature, 119, 122, 130–1,
    133–4, 176–7
becoming(s), 1–2, 197n72
  becoming-woman, 16, 43, 144–8, 190
  in Deleuze's texts, 4, 8
  and ethics, 68, 174, 180
  and events, 32, 181–2, 185, 190
  and individuating repetition, 13, 175–6
  men's, 213
  and stratification, 30, 39, 40, 46, 73,
    95, 145, 172
  women's, 75–6, 78, 146
Being and Nothingness (Sartre), 35, 36,
  47, 54n55, 60, 62, 67, 68, 93n41,
  100, 101, 112, 125–6n39; *see also*
  Sartre, Jean-Paul

Benjamin, Walter, 165
Bergoffen, Debra, 13, 52n39, 55n68, 109, 114, 150, 198n75
Bergson, Henri, 3, 12, 27, 49n8, 60, 87, 99, 100, 106, 131, 137, 181
   Creative Evolution, 66, 73
   and Deleuze, 22n31, 39, 59, 90–1n19
   on ethics, 102
   on freedom, 39, 47, 81, 87, 94, 108, 181
   and mysticism, 84–5, 93n48
   on qualitative multiplicity, 44, 81, 93n41, 100–1, 137
   on recognition, 109, 126n45, 126n47
   and Sartre, 9n14, 54n55, 59–60, 93n41, 99, 100–1
   on temporality, 23n36, 90–1n19, 101, 137
   on true and superficial self, 27, 37–9, 81
biography
   as interpretive key, 46, 133–5
   vs a life, 32, 46, 47, 119, 131, 135, 154
biology, as fact and social meaning, 33, 42, 58, 72–6, 114, 136, 212
biopower, 174–5
bisexuality, Beauvoir's, 92n23, 142, 143
Blanchot, Maurice, 113, 156n14, 204
Blood of Others (Beauvoir novel), 68, 80, 76, 77, 87, 110, 135, 165
body, human
   biological and historical, 33, 41, 58, 72–5, 141
   boundaries, 54n61, 72–3
   female, 28, 31, 166, 185
   in Spinoza, 19–20n7, 50n18, 195–6n52
Boupacha, Djamila, 169, 198n75, 211
Browne, Victoria, 184–5
Brunschvicg, Léon, 45, 56n74, 93n47
Butler, Judith, 94n56, 122, 125n38

capitalism, 64, 92n36, 116, 142, 158n35, 180, 181, 183, 186, 195n47; see also work/labour
Catholicism, 45
causality, historical, 182, 183, 184, 186
choice, 23n40, 37–40, 47, 108, 115, 164
Chronos and Aion, 16, 51n25, 182, 183, 190, 191, 212
colonialism, 29, 44, 125n30, 137, 141, 146, 147, 153, 168, 170, 173, 181, 191, 193n19
   and sexual violence, 141–2, 179

Coming of Age, The (Beauvoir), 13, 14, 200
common sense *see* sense: common and good
communication, 102, 108, 109, 110, 120, 121
community, 95, 115–18, 120
complicity, 66, 67, 71–2, 83, 176, 177, 178, 195
concept
   consistency of, 48
   creation of, 3–4, 14, 26, 33, 46, 49n8, 63–4, 199
   definition, in Deleuze, 33–4, 42–5, 200
   history of, 33, 65
   vs Ideas, 26, 49–50n9
   as multiplicity, 33, 43, 45, 52n32, 59, 200, 201
   and personae, 33–4, 40, 43–4
   and plane of immanence, 34
consciousness
   class, 171, 181
   and freedom, 36–7, 99, 100, 101
   genesis of, 32, 63–5, 204
   Hegelian, 74, 77, 96
   impersonal, 11, 59–62, 89n6, 103, 208–9
   individuation of, 60–2, 81, 89n6, 99, 100, 106
   in phenomenology, 4–11, 20n13, 32, 35, 55, 93, 202
   in Sartre's critique of Bergson, 67, 106, 107, 125–6n39
   and sense, 60
continuity, 30, 46, 99–101, 103
   historical, 183, 186
contradiction, 37, 150, 180
   and difference, 75, 77
conversion, 33, 36, 40, 48, 123
Cornell, Drucilla, 41, 55n62, 194n27
counter-actualisation, 16–17, 31, 32, 40, 47, 121, 135, 166, 186, 211
   failure of, 83, 87–8, 213
   and Stoics, 16–17, 96, 111
creativity, 41, 77, 81, 88, 132, 144, 202, 205, 211
   women's, 206, 207
   see also concept: creation of
critique, 14–15, 26, 24n43, 143, 199

death, 84, 110, 117–19, 134, 135, 204, 205, 207, 209, 213
   and Hegel, 74, 81

Deleuze, Gilles, 3, 4, 6, 7, 8, 11, 13, 14, 15, 16, 17, 18, 22n31, 30, 31, 39, 40, 43, 46, 48, 59, 75, 86, 88, 121, 122, 149, 180, 187, 199
and Bergson, 39, 22n31, 90–1n19
critique of Hegel, 96–7
on difference and repetition, 175, 177–8
on explication of Idea, 154–5, 211–12
and Guattari, 4, 8, 15, 18, 43, 46, 64, 95, 116, 117, 167, 183, 184, 186, 190
on human rights, 189
on Other-structure, 203–4, 209
on philosophy as critique of representation, 26–7, 64–5, 131
on philosophy of history, 182, 183–4
on problems, 131–3
on reciprocity and love, 143–5
on state and war machine, 167–72
on synthesis and concept formation, 32–3, 63–4, 59, 81
Democratic Republic of the Congo, 170
dependence, 72, 86, 176, 194n39
male, 177
see also interdependence; woman: independent
Descartes, René, 206, 210
desiring-machines, 19, 64
deterritorialisation, 46, 109, 145, 186, 187, 191, 212
Deutscher, Penelope, 33, 103, 123, 130, 133, 139, 148, 149
devotion, 55, 101, 103, 108, 110
difference(s)
among women, 178, 179, 181, 188, 189
and contradiction, 47, 75, 77, 96–7, 180, 201
and equality, 174–80, 201
inner, 12, 38, 39, 41, 87
productive, 27, 175–6, 179
sexual, 18, 55n62, 72, 111, 149, 171, 174, 179, 190
Difference and Repetition (Deleuze), 7, 26–7, 30, 32, 40, 59, 64, 86, 97–8, 131, 143–4, 154–5, 199, 203, 212
differentiation, 39, 42, 48, 61, 72, 89n4
and differenciation, 51
and struggle, 74–5
disclosure, 103, 105, 113, 120n29, 149, 164, 208, 209
conditions for, 164, 171
and recognition, 109–10, 117, 211

domination, male, 29, 30, 44, 181
as institution, 166, 167, 168, 169
see also woman: subordination of
dramatisation/actualisation, 10, 27, 33–4, 40, 44, 49n9, 212; see also faculties (in dynamic genesis)
duration, 2, 16, 38–9, 46, 54n55, 90–1n19, 93n41, 101, 102, 106, 112, 124n21

egalitarianism, 16, 45, 162, 163, 172–80, 187, 193n16; see also equaliberty
epoché, phenomenological, 5, 8
equaliberty, 173–5, 179
equality, 16, 18, 136, 147, 162, 174–80, 195n47, 201
and difference(s), 174–80, 201
see also equaliberty
ethics, 18, 36, 40, 52n31, 96, 104–8, 109, 111, 113–15, 117, 120
and the appeal, 15, 102
and politics, 163, 164, 165, 171, 189, 192n8
see also morality, existentialist; oppression
Ethics of Ambiguity, The (Beauvoir), 12, 13, 32, 36, 44, 53n54, 104, 106, 107, 108–9, 120, 165, 166, 168, 169, 170, 171, 173, 178, 180–1
concept of ambiguity in, 103, 163, 164
on conversion, 40, 61, 109
on existentialist morality, 32, 52n31
on freedom of others, 15, 114, 171, 180, 200
Hegel and recognition in, 96, 98, 105
history in, 110, 181
on oppression, 13, 44
seriousness in, 67, 195n48
Stoicism in, 95, 111
event, 87, 147
counter-actualisation of, 47, 83, 121, 205, 211, 212
feminism as, 3–4, 140, 149, 185, 190, 211
historical, 11, 30, 181–4, 190, 191, 201
incorporeal, 31, 32
linear or nonlinear, 11, 17, 30, 181–4
in Stoics, 7–8, 16, 17, 21n16, 51n25, 111, 191
existentialism
in *Being and Nothingness*, 35–6
in *The Ethics of Ambiguity*, 36, 115
as socio-historical phenomenon, 129, 143
see also morality, existentialist

expression, 91, 106, 144, 147–8, 155, 203, 209
'Eye for an Eye, An' (Beauvoir essay), 165, 169, 178, 190

faciality, 142, 172, 190
faculties (in dynamic genesis), 32, 63–4, 131, 199
Fanon, Frantz, 20, 148, 193n16
fantasy, 140, 152
fascism, 118, 148, 167–8, 192n13, 212
femininity, 28–30, 110, 140–1
  as being and becoming, 168, 178
  as ideal, 177
  'pervasive', 25, 189
  as set of habits, 32, 65, 88, 135–6, 213
feminism(s) 98, 149, 173, 176, 191
  and capitalist deterritorialisation, 181, 186
  history of, 184–6, 201
  and human rights, 170–1, 187–8
  as liberationist movement, 150, 154, 171, 173, 186, 189
  as molar politics, 15, 144–5, 162–3, 171, 172, 212
  place of *The Second Sex*, 17–18, 129, 151, 176
finitude, 84, 118, 131, 180, 211
Fitzgerald, F. Scott, 88
Foucault, Michel, 92n25, 97, 117, 130, 167, 174, 213
Fraser, Mariam, 142–3, 154
freedom, 35, 73, 96, 99, 104, 100, 111, 163, 179, 180
  in Bergson and Leibniz, 39, 40, 47
  vs choice, 38–40, 47, 108, 115
  and counter-actualisation, 87
  and ethics, 113
  of others, 104, 105, 211
  see also equaliberty

gender, 8, 25, 53, 66, 163
  as stratification/segmentation, 9, 43, 145–8, 167, 184
genesis, dynamic and static, 15, 27, 31n15, 24n43, 63, 102, 131
globalisation, 187
Grosz, Elizabeth, 145, 160n67
Guattari, Félix *see* Deleuze, Gilles: and Guattari

habit(s), 27, 64, 65–6, 70, 83
  of being-with, 14–15, 58, 125, 127, 138
  in Deleuze, 7, 8, 26–8, 32, 81, 131
  of femininity and masculinity, 62–5, 70, 72–3, 80, 83, 84, 88, 94n56, 167, 185, 213
  of love and mysticism, 83–6
  of maternity and motherhood, 72, 75–7
  political, 168, 170
Halimi, Gisèle, 169, 211
Hegel, G. W. F., 46, 58, 99, 150
  in Beauvoir, 3, 6, 14, 23n39, 28–9, 31, 58, 74, 77
  on becoming and being, 31, 99
  Deleuze's critique of, 13, 98
  on politics, 18, 125n24, 191
  and recognition, 74, 77, 81–2, 96, 98, 102, 109–10, 139
  on standpoint of history as a whole, 105, 107–8, 182
  on transcendence, 34, 37, 176
Heidegger, Martin, 46, 65, 103, 117–18, 119, 120, 124n16
  on disclosure, 103, 117, 164
  on finitude and death, 84, 127–8, 180
  Mitsein, 15, 30, 58, 89n1, 91n21, 95, 117–18
hetaera, 63, 80, 83, 116, 195n47
hierarchy, 16, 29, 162, 178, 179
history, 11, 17–18, 29, 30, 98, 110, 201
  of the concept, 11, 33, 42
  of feminism, 17, 184–5, 191
  linear, 162, 163, 181
  and multiplicity, 105, 184
  and nature, 10, 29, 58, 183, 185
  nonlinear, 2, 17, 122, 182–3, 184–5
  of philosophy, 2, 18, 43, 180, 183–4
  totalising, 99, 106, 108
  of women, 70, 129, 140, 184, 185, 190
  see also event
Holveck, Eleanore, 5–6, 13, 56n74, 90n12, 140, 207–8
Husserl, Edmund, 4–8, 10, 11–12, 20n13, 20n14, 21n15, 22n29, 27, 30, 209
  and intersubjectivity, 14, 23n41, 24n42, 60, 65, 202
  on the Other, 34–5, 37, 102, 202, 124n22
  on temporality, 23n36, 124n21
hylomorphism, 23n36, 46, 51n24, 95, 175

'I', fractured, 27, 63, 82, 84, 117, 199, 203, 205, 210
Idea
  Beauvoir's, 15n49, 171–2, 200

as becoming, 15, 16
vs concept, 26, 49–50n9, 54n59, 59
gender as, 66
as multiplicity, 59, 149
immanence, 14, 37, 58–9, 66–71, 75–9, 103
  and bad faith, 52n41
  in love and mysticism, 84–5
  men's, 140, 142
  and oppression, 142
  plane of, 14, 15, 32, 48, 96
  vs transcendence, 35–7, 53n42, 76–80, 108, 138
imperceptible, becoming, 145, 172, 189, 190, 148
incorporeal, 21n16, 51n25, 202
indiscernibles, in Leibniz, 12, 38
individualisation, 41–3, 48, 81–2, 112, 113–16, 126–7n52, 138, 178
individuation, 143, 175
  in Bergson, 39
  biological, 73–4
  blocked, 54n59, 58–9, 68–9, 153, 179
  and combination with others, 84, 85, 94–6, 126–7n52, 144, 191
  of consciousness, 60, 61, 62, 89n6
  as differentiation, 48, 61, 86, 89n6, 139, 144
  in Husserl, 20n14, 60
  and individualisation, 41, 42, 112, 113–15
  in literature, 119–20
  and maternity, 72, 73, 74, 75, 76, 79
  and multiplicity, 138, 143, 203, 204, 180
  as problem, 132, 134
  in psychoanalysis and psychology, 40–1, 54n61
  and rights, 180, 190, 191
  in Simondon, 111–16, 126–7n52
  and singularity, 13
  as transcendence, 42, 76, 82, 174
  and transindividuality, 113–15, 119, 174
  and work/labour, 78–82
inequality, 16, 141, 147, 162–3, 174–80, 195n48, 201
  productive, 27, 178, 180
influence, 4, 33–4, 46, 86, 134, 154
institutions, 12–13, 32, 44, 136, 146, 147, 163, 166–70, 177, 178, 180, 191
  feminist, 170, 173, 188, 189

  legal, 85, 159n45, 165, 169, 170, 187
  as singularities, 166, 189
intentionality, 4, 7–9, 35–6, 102, 125n29, 133
  in *The Ethics of Ambiguity*, 36, 67, 113
  Sartrean, 54n55, 60–1, 67, 112–13
  see also disclosure; phenomenology; Sartre, Jean-Paul
interdependence, 155, 202
intersectionality, 148, 149, 171
intersubjectivity, 104, 109
  in Hegel, 14, 37, 98
  in Husserl, 11–12, 14, 20n14, 23n41, 24n42, 37, 60–1, 89n6, 100–2
  transcendental, 60–1, 203
isolation, women's social, 78, 79, 82, 205, 210; *see also* solitude, women's

jurisprudence, 188, 197n71
justice, 16, 139, 165, 169, 170, 189, 190

Kail, Michel, 29, 137n53, 185
Kant, Immanuel, 12, 27, 68, 107, 163
  Deleuze's reading of, 63, 64
Kierkegaard, Søren, 13, 33–4, 68, 96, 98
  Beauvoir's engagement with, 23n39
  and repetition, 23n40
kinship, 145–9
Kojève, Alexandre, 29, 74

labour, care, 75–6, 78, 80, 83–4, 92n34, 135–7, 150
Lacan, Jacques, 90n9, 61
Lampert, Jay, 182
law, 107, 118
  positive, 67, 77, 139–40, 147, 163–70, 178, 187–9
Le Doeuff, Michèle, 68, 81, 123
learning, 48, 57n84, 86
Lee, Kyoo, 149
Leibniz, G. W., 12, 44, 47, 87, 121–2
  in Beauvoir's student diaries, 37–8
  Deleuze's engagement with, 22n31, 39, 41–2, 209
  on freedom, 39, 94n54
  and intersubjectivity, 105–8
Les Belles Images (Beauvoir novel), 43, 69, 135, 213
lesbians, 70–1
Lévinas, Emmanuel, 143, 202, 203, 204
Lévi-Strauss, Claude, 28, 37, 202
liberalism, 18, 40–1, 107, 116, 173–5
liberation movements, 107, 108, 150, 168

life, a, 17, 40, 46–8, 54n48, 54n58, 135, 154
  vs biography, 40, 46, 47, 135, 154
  as singularity, 40, 47, 48, 54n58
literature, 12, 108, 110, 119, 120, 121, 131, 200
  Beauvoir's, 43, 48, 49, 69, 76–7, 80–1, 83, 87–8, 105–6, 110, 135, 200, 213–14
  and communication, 108–10, 118–22
  and philosophy, 12, 130–4
  and sexist sense, 130, 132–4
  see also philosophy: of literature, Beauvoir's; problem: literary
Logic of Sense, The (Deleuze), 7, 32, 86, 88, 147–8, 204
Lorraine, Tamsin, 52n36, 172
loss, 45, 48–9, 70, 82, 87, 88, 106, 212
love
  as affect, 83–4, 86, 87, 140, 144
  and individuation, 84–6, 98, 143
  and mysticism, 84–6
  and reciprocity, 70–1, 109, 110
  and temporality, 84, 140
Lundy, Craig, 182

madness, 82, 86, 87
majoritarian and minoritian, 145, 146
Mandarins, The (Beauvoir novel), 49, 69, 80, 83, 87, 135, 213
Marx, Karl, 107, 123
Marxism, 173, 180, 181
Marxist-Leninism, 13, 150
masculinism, 145, 176–8
  Beauvoir's supposed, 78, 135–7, 141, 143, 176, 178, 187–8
  and domination, 151, 166, 170, 175, 187
  in philosophy and literature, 130, 132–4
  universalism of, 146–8, 181–3
  see also oppression; sexist sense
masculinity, 5, 92n36, 41, 136, 140, 141–2, 145
  as being and becoming, 9, 48, 147–8, 178, 213
  constituting habits, 62, 88
  and femininity, 28, 73–4, 83, 88, 135–8, 141–2, 147–8, 168
masochism, 139, 159n45
master/slave dialectic, 58, 74, 77, 81, 82, 202
maternity, 72–9, 136, 160n70, 166, 167
memoirs, Beauvoir's, 12, 44, 48, 61, 122, 130, 134, 205, 208

memory (second passive synthesis), 27, 63–4
Merleau-Ponty, Maurice, 11–12, 20n14, 21n18, 55n65, 60, 203
  on ambiguity, 22–3, 41–2, 103
  and Sartre, 55n65, 121, 124
  understanding of the body, 20n13, 33
metaphors, 44, 153
metastability, 112–13, 115
Mill, Harriet Taylor, 173, 196
Mill, John Stuart, 41
Mitsein, 15, 30, 62, 66, 87, 95–7, 112, 144, 150
  as concept and assemblage, 59, 66, 117–19, 122, 200
  and motherhood, 75
  and sexual difference, 15, 30, 58–9, 111, 203
modernisation, 9, 18, 172, 173, 187, 190, 191
Moi, Toril, 2, 3, 25, 68, 133, 134, 152, 189
molar and molecular, 15, 21n17, 145–6, 171–2, 185–6
morality, existentialist, 14, 24, 32, 34, 42, 45, 49, 66
motherhood, 72–9, 82; *see also* maternity
movements, political, 3, 4, 154, 162, 168, 180, 184, 188, 212
multiplicity
  and ambiguity, 103, 138
  of assemblage, 10, 138, 149, 166
  of concept, 33, 45, 52n32, 59, 200, 201
  continuous/qualitative, 18, 44, 66, 90–1n9, 100–3, 107, 112, 117, 137, 138
  of event, 147, 148, 182, 202
  'interpenetrative', 54n55, 93n41, 103
  sexual or maternal self as, 142–3, 160n70
  and singularity, 97–8, 137, 138, 145, 152
multitude, 115, 116
mysticism, 84–7, 93n47, 93n48
myth, 30, 31, 118–20, 133, 203, 206, 209

Nancy, Jean-Luc, 118–20
narcissism, 80, 82–3, 84, 85, 87, 110
narrative, 11, 17, 30, 31, 163, 184
nationalism, 115
nature, 82, 98, 121, 139, 172, 183, 206, 209
  as essence, 30, 59, 63, 123n1
  and history, 10, 29, 58, 183, 185

neo-liberalism, 116, 175; *see also* capitalism
Nietzsche, 4, 18, 31, 111
nomadology, 182
nominalism, 28, 151
nonsense, 8, 9, 10, 84, 88, 123, 131, 186, 190, 209
Nzegwu, Nkiru, 136, 146–8

Occupation, German, 77, 165, 192n6
Old Age (Beauvoir) *see The Coming of Age*
oppression, 13, 44, 66, 85, 104, 106, 111, 125n30, 142, 151–3, 165–9, 171, 180, 195n48, 201
Other, 9, 14, 43, 101, 113, 117, 155
  absolute, 6, 7, 30, 147, 202
  and creativity, 144, 202, 205–7
  in Leibniz, 12, 37–8, 42, 209
  look of, 80–2
  'mirage' of, 52–3n41, 61, 62, 155
  in phenomenology, 35, 37, 101–2, 160, 165
  in *The Second Sex*, 6, 7, 13, 28–9, 30, 33, 37, 38, 202–3, 211
  as singularity, 42, 110, 211
Other-structure in Deleuze, 143, 144, 154, 203, 204, 209, 210, 212, 214n5
others, world without, 204, 207–10, 214n4

personae, conceptual, 33–4, 42–4, 132, 134
phenomenology, 3, 5, 14, 20n13, 30, 33, 97, 204
  Beauvoir's engagement with, 22n12, 60–1, 103, 205
  genetic, 7, 11, 20n14
  and pre-personal singularities, 204, 205, 208
  and the sciences, 5, 6, 7
  transcendence in, 34–7
  see also Heidegger, Martin; Husserl, Edmund; Merleau-Ponty, Maurice; Sartre, Jean-Paul
philosophy, 1–2, 9, 40, 130, 131
  as creation of concepts, 3–4, 26, 32–3, 46, 199
  as discipline, 130, 136, 201
  distinct from biography, 17, 32, 40, 46
  feminist, 4, 18–19
  as formulation of problems, 15, 97, 117
  independent of individual thinkers, 4, 14, 18, 46, 54, 117
  of literature, Beauvoir's, 107, 108, 109, 118, 119, 120, 121, 130, 131
  ordinary language, 3, 25, 49n3, 133
phylum, 46, 191
plane, pre-philosophical, 44, 201
plane of immanence *see* immanence: plane of
politics
  and community, 105
  and equaliberty, 174–5, 189–90
  and ethics, 163, 164, 165, 171, 189, 192n8
  feminism as, 155, 171, 212
  and singularity, 152, 165
power, 29, 67, 84, 97, 117, 146–7, 167, 171, 187
  of differences, 96, 178, 179
  see also biopower
pregnancy, 53, 72–5, 160n70
problem, 47, 117
  false, 25, 132
  of feminism, 142, 151
  and institutions, 180, 188–9
  literary, 132–4, 152
  as multiplicity, 45, 149
problem/Idea nexus, 27, 28, 49n9, 50n10, 51n30, 82, 97, 131, 132, 161n78
problem/solutions nexus, 27, 28, 162, 191, 201
problematisation, 10, 15, 65–6, 115, 117, 122, 127n65
psychoanalysis, 41, 54n61, 73, 134, 136
'Pyrrhus and Cineas' (Beauvoir essay), 15, 32, 98–102, 103, 104, 109

quality, 4–5, 12, 48, 81, 101–2, 104, 106–8, 112, 121, 150
quantity, extensive and intensive, 90–1n19

race, 79, 148–9, 172
  analogised to sex in *The Second Sex*, 148, 173
racism, 67, 132, 142, 148, 153, 158n41, 179, 186
reciprocity
  and equaliberty, 173–4
  failures of, 28–9, 83, 87, 177
  as ideal, 15, 96, 132, 134, 136, 139–41, 143, 150, 163, 172, 202
  in sexual relationships, 71, 79, 139, 140, 141
  and singularity, 177–8
  and thinking, 144

recognition
  in Beauvoir's philosophy, 98, 102, 105–6, 109–11, 114, 120
  and Bergson, 126n45
  as moral ideal, 84, 96
  and prepersonal singularities, 131, 144, 163, 172–4
  reciprocal, 139–40, 149
  self-recognition, failure of, 40, 72, 73–4, 81, 86, 117, 199
  struggle for, 74, 77, 84
  see also synthesis, passive
reduction, phenomenological, 5–6, 23n41
religion, 84–6
repetition, 6–7, 16–18, 26, 30, 40, 64, 76, 98, 181
  and conversion, 33
  and event, 17, 51n28, 135
  and Kierkegaard, 23n40, 33
  and singularity, 13, 47, 53n43, 97–8, 109
  and work, 78
representation, 13, 16, 26–7, 65, 179
  critique of, 15, 26, 97
  genesis of, 63
  and recognition, 97
  of women, 14, 154, 187–8
rights, 145
  human rights, 170–1, 187–8, 207n71
  women's, 163, 168, 196n60
risk, 106, 109

Sade, Marquis de, 114, 139–40, 177, 178
Sartre, Jean-Paul, 41, 42, 81
  on bad faith, 67–8, 86
  and Beauvoir's status as philosopher, 130, 133–4
  critique of Bergson, 54n55, 93n41, 100, 101
  detotalised totality, 106–7, 121, 125–6n39
  on freedom, 44, 87
  idea of the Other, 101, 144, 202–3, 208
  impersonal consciousness, 59–63, 89n5
  and Merleau-Ponty, 121, 124n20, 203
  metastability, 112, 113, 115
  phenomenology, 11–12, 14, 22n29, 35–7, 39, 89n4, 93n41
Scott, Joan, 185, 197n66, 197n67
Second Sex, The (Beauvoir), 1, 3, 8–10, 13–15, 25–6, 28–34, 45, 48, 58, 65–88, 96–8, 111, 116, 118, 129–30, 132–4, 136–42, 143–4, 151, 162–6, 171, 172–4, 176–7, 180–1, 185–6, 188–90, 199–203, 205–7, 211–12
  critiques of, 45, 88, 133–4, 135–6, 141, 146–7, 150, 153, 181
  as event, 181, 186, 190, 191, 201
  and feminist politics, 17–18, 129, 151, 176
  as phenomenology, 5–6, 8, 10–12, 18
  problem of, 9, 26, 28, 95, 149, 151, 200
  translations of, 155–6n5
self, true and false, 27, 40, 81–2
sense, 6–8, 16, 29–30, 58, 175, 209
  blocking concepts, 54n59, 60
  breakdown of, 86–8, 148, 208–10
  common and good, 26, 28, 29, 48, 177
  and habits, 58, 64, 71–2, 88, 117
  in Husserl, 7, 10, 20n13, 21n16, 21n18
  multiple, 146, 182–3
  and sexual violence, 141
  see also sexist sense
separation, 73, 79, 83–4, 86, 101–2, 108, 114, 119, 120, 130–1, 134
seriousness, 67–8, 76, 83, 103, 108, 195n48
Serres, Michel, 182, 183
sexist sense, 9, 10, 14–15, 31, 36, 43–8, 71, 95–6, 137, 141–2, 149, 154, 168, 182–3, 190, 193n16, 199, 200
  critique of, 26, 199, 200
  as event, 137, 166, 182, 196, 202
  in literature, 132–3
  produced by habits, 54n59, 58, 117
sexual difference
  as becoming and being, 72, 75, 76
  as meaning and biological fact, 6, 28, 73
  and *Mitsein*, 111
  political visions for, 18, 55, 163, 174, 176
  see also body, human; gender
She Came to Stay (Beauvoir novel), 43, 62, 69, 80, 87, 207–10
  unpublished chapters, 62, 208
Simondon, Gilbert, 15, 39, 41, 98, 112–15, 119, 131
  and ethics, 114–15
Simons, Margaret, 12, 43, 45, 155–6n5, 93n47
singularity, 49, 119, 175
  and ethics, 79, 97–8, 111, 114, 113–15, 177–8
  in fiction, 121, 131, 134

and freedom, 8–9, 12–13, 36
Idea as, 26, 27
and institutions, 166, 191
of a life, 48, 54n58
pre-personal, 32, 40, 144, 159, 171, 204–5, 208
and universals, 60, 83, 97, 105, 107, 150, 151–2
situation, 99, 101–4, 106–8, 110, 112, 126n40, 131, 165, 180, 189
literary, 120, 121, 133, 152
woman as, 9, 10, 13, 28, 150–2, 185–7, 212
slavery
in Hegel, 74, 81–2
historical, 29, 74, 76, 137, 146, 153, 173, 179
socialism, 173, 180, 201
solitude, women's, 82, 117, 132, 205, 206, 210, 213; *see also* isolation, women's social
South Sudan, 166
sovereignty, 82, 114, 115, 195n44, 206
Spinoza, 19–20n7, 121, 122, 151, 160–1n77, 174, 179, 192n8, 195–6n52, 210
state, 105, 116, 165–70, 193n19
Stoicism, 7–8, 16, 17, 95–6, 111
stratification, 9, 10, 15, 21n17, 31, 40, 51n24, 145, 183
and gender, 43
stupidity, 65, 144, 149, 177
synthesis, passive, 7, 21n15, 27, 31, 47, 51n24, 60, 63
in *Anti-Oedipus*, 64, 117
third synthesis of recognition, 62–3, 64, 71, 72, 81, 86, 117
see also memory

temporality
of authorship and readership, 121, 122
in Bergson, 23n36, 90–1n19, 98–9, 100
of disclosure, 101–3, 105
in dynamic genesis, 27, 29, 49, 63
in Husserl, 23n36, 124n21, 124n22
of love, 83–4, 140
multiple, 115, 184
two series, 16, 63, 190–1
see also duration; event
thinking, 26–7, 32, 40, 49n8, 97, 121–2, 131, 144, 199
and living, 40, 59
refusal of, 177–8

thought, image of, 13, 26, 47, 64, 65
Thousand Plateaus, A (Deleuze and Guattari), 8, 46, 51n24, 142, 144–5, 149, 165–6, 171, 212
totality, detotalised, 34, 107–8, 113, 121, 126n40, 125–6n39
Tournier, Michel, 204, 212
transcendence, 40, 46, 47, 61
and counter-actualisation, 40, 111
and freedom, 9, 28, 35–7, 39, 47, 66, 70, 73, 87, 138, 174, 200
in Hegel, 34, 37, 53n54, 176
vs immanence, 36, 67, 76, 79, 80
in phenomenology, 34–7
in *The Second Sex*, 39, 42
vicarious, 83, 87, 137, 140
Transcendence of the Ego (Sartre), 11, 89n4, 89n5, 93n14, 100
transcendental ego, 11, 60, 61, 89n4
transindividuality, 15, 112, 115–16, 119, 121, 174, 200

universalism, 4, 6–7, 68, 96, 99, 119, 130–1, 146, 149–53, 177, 179, 183
of historical perspective, 106, 184
of norms, 187–9
universals, 4, 13, 20n13, 35, 45, 68–9, 71, 75, 83, 95, 107, 150, 151–2, 161n78, 166, 183, 187, 191, 201
univocity of being, 175
utilitarianism, 13, 106, 175

Van Leeuwen, Anne, 3, 10, 21–2n23
variation, continuous, 103, 185–6, 189, 209
violence, 164, 166, 167, 169, 170, 178
human possibility/necessity, 125n38, 163, 165
sexual, 88, 140–2, 152, 170, 188, 198n75
women's lack of access to, 67
Virno, Paolo, 92n36, 115, 117
visibility, 53n43, 172, 213
vulnerability, 80, 117, 125n38, 138

war machine and state, 167–70, 193n19
Wasser, Audrey, 132
What is Philosophy? (Deleuze and Guattari), 26, 32–3, 117, 156n14, 199–200

When Things of the Spirit Come First (Beauvoir novel), 43, 48, 56n74, 69, 213–14
Wittgenstein, Ludwig, 3, 30
Woman Destroyed, The (Beauvoir novella), 69, 87, 135
woman/women, 9, 10, 14, 18, 36, 48, 63, 65, 67, 68, 69, 70, 74, 150, 212
   as assemblages, 150, 152, 188, 190
   colonised, 44
   of different cultures, 150–3, 178–9, 181, 186–7, 188–9
   independent, 202, 211, 213
   molar and molecular, 15–16, 144–9, 171, 189
   as stratum, 8, 9, 31–2
   subordination of, 9–10, 29, 30, 44
   thought nonmetaphysically, 25–6

work/labour, 70, 79, 92n36, 117, 152, 153, 190, 213
   conditions of, 179, 180, 189
   creative/philosophical, 40, 80–2, 134, 205
   domestic/housework, 77, 78, 79, 93n45, 186–7
   emotional/care/sex, 69, 74, 78, 140, 151
   and individuation, 78, 79, 80, 81, 82
   and masculinity, 137, 141, 152
   and motherhood, 74, 77, 78
   productive, paid, or public, 37, 53n43, 74, 77–82, 83–5
   and repetition, 78
   on the self, 33, 122
   sexist limitations on, 136–7, 147
   transcendence and immanence of, 37, 79, 80

EU representative:
Easy Access System Europe
Mustamäe tee 50, 10621 Tallinn, Estonia
Gpsr.requests@easproject.com

www.ingramcontent.com/pod-product-compliance
Lightning Source LLC
Chambersburg PA
CBHW050850230426
43667CB00012B/2233